"[Pipher] wrote [*Another Country*] to help Boomers like herself better understand their parents and grandparents and to glimpse what might await them in their own old age."  —*Chicago Tribune*

"The author of *Reviving Ophelia* unflinchingly takes us into the heart of this largely uncharted territory."  —*Rocky Mountain News*

"[The] combination of cultural and psychological factors is this excellent book's greatest strength. . . . She is especially acute at spotting pressure points where culture, both past and present, collides cruelly with individual emotional needs."  —*The Washington Post*

"A field guide to old age, combining personal stories with social theory."  —*The Boston Globe*

"Dr. Pipher sees aging from a broader perspective. [She] emphasizes the need for the elderly to become elders—people who can help us find a deep structure for our communities—[and] she makes a persuasive case for roots."  —*The Christian Science Monitor*

(*continued on next page . . .*)

*(continued on next page . . . )*

# Another

RIVERHEAD BOOKS
*New York*

# Country

### Navigating the Emotional Terrain of Our Elders

## MARY PIPHER, PH.D.

Riverhead Books
Published by The Berkley Publishing Group
A division of Penguin Putnam Inc.
375 Hudson Street
New York, New York 10014

Permissions appear on pages 327–28.

Copyright © 1999 by Mary Pipher, Ph.D.
Book design and title page photograph by Deborah Kerner
Cover design © 1999 by Royce M. Becker

First Riverhead hardcover edition: March 1999
First Riverhead trade paperback edition: March 2000
Riverhead trade paperback ISBN: 1-57322-784-6

The Library of Congress has catalogued the Riverhead hardcover edition as follows:

Pipher, Mary Bray.
Another country: navigating the emotional terrain of our elders / by Mary Pipher.
p. cm.
ISBN 1-57322-129-5
1. Aging parents—United States—Psychology. 2. Aging parents—United States—Family relationships. 3. Aging parents—Care—United States. 4. Adult children—United States—Family relationships. 5. Loss (Psychology) in old age—United States. I. Title.
HQ1063.6.P57 1999
306.874—dc21    98-31877 CIP

PRINTED IN THE UNITED STATES OF AMERICA

10   9   8

*To Jim*

*We loved the earth*
*but could not stay.*

— LOREN EISELEY

# Author's Note

Some of the place names, mainly of the rest homes and hospitals, have been changed in the book. Some of the people I interviewed wanted their names used, and others did not. A few requested that identifying details be changed. I have respected their wishes. All clients are composite characters, to protect confidentiality.

# *Acknowledgments*

TO MY READERS—Pam Barger, Henrietta Isbell, Margaret Nemoede-Harris, Jamie Pipher, Jim Pipher, Sara Pipher, Marge Saiser, Karen Shoemaker, Theo Sonderegger, and Jan Zegers.

TO ALL THOSE WHO HELPED WITH THIS BOOK—the Brays, the Piphers and the Pages, my friends who told me their stories, and my clients, and specifically Randy Barger, Rowena Boykin, John and Beatty Brasch, Leola Bullock, Joette Byrd, Jim Campbell, Jim Cole, Laura Cravens Wertz, John and Sylvia Darling, Rose Dame and Gertrude Fisher, Laura Freeman, Sarah Gordon, Dr. George and Chiyo Hachiya, Sherri and George Hanigan, Tom and Twyla Hansen, Herb and Sue Howe, Max Isbell, Jane Jarvis, Jerry Johnston, Ted Jorgensen, Karen Larsen, Pat Leach, Scott Long, Agnes and Clair Loutzenheiser, Carol McShane, Pat Mielnick, Nancy Nemmick, Randall Nemoede-Harris, Lucy Nevels, Bonnie Newell, Elaine Peters, Jim and Susie Peterson, Reynold and Jill Peterson, Bernard and Phyllis Pipher, Zeke Pipher, Natalie Porter, Betty Robinson, Linda Roos, Crystal Sato, Carl Schreiner, Rich Simon, Joe Starita, Jan and Neal Stenberg, Grace and Otis Teague, Janet Trout, and Kathryn Watterson.

ALSO TO Susan Petersen, Wendy Carlton, Mih-Ho Cha, Marilyn Ducksworth, Cathy Fox, Joanne Wycoff, Rachel Tarlow-Gul, and my beloveds, Susan Lee Cohen and Jane Isay.

# *Contents*

# Lake Louise

In May Jim and I hiked the Moraine Trail in Banff National Park. We walked through a river valley surrounded by snow-covered peaks and up switchbacks to the frozen shores of Lake Annette. We ate our Powerbars and apples and watched the clouds collide with the mountains. When we threw rocks into the lake, the ice broke easily and the water splashed turquoise.

Walking back down, we saw a black bear, mountain goats, and wapiti. We watched the miraculous water ouzels, plain brown birds that dive into icy streams to fish and reemerge later to sing on river rocks. We worried about the grizzlies, especially Grizzly Number Ten, nicknamed "The Volks-wagen" by the rangers. However, today we were spared.

In the evening, with our muscles sore and our minds calm, we dined at Lake Louise Lodge, the site of a halcyon event in the life of Jim's family. Forty years earlier, Jim, his sister, and his parents had crossed the country, camping in national parks and eating in good restaurants. On a July day on the lawn at Lake Louise, they had tea and crumpets. The story of that day was part of Pipher family history, told and retold until even I, who wasn't there, could envision every detail clearly. It was a Camelot story about elegance, natural beauty, and good luck.

From the Edelweiss room, we watched the lake at sunset. Two days before, Lake Louise had been frozen, but tonight she was free-flowing and, depending on the sun, gleaming one of the many colors between royal blue and jade green. By looking at the sky and in the mirror of the lake, we could see Victoria Glacier, the ice fields of Mount McLeod, and the Canadian Rockies shrouded in pink clouds.

The room was dark and opulent, with oak furniture, ornate silver, and heavy gold and white china. Our waiter was dignified and deferential. I ordered squash soup and trout, Jim ordered the lamb. We were the youngest guests; most of the others were in their seventies, mainly because, as Jim pointed out, younger people couldn't afford this place. One woman with beautiful clothes and a regal bearing reminded me of my mother-in-law, Phyllis. One man in a green suit coat smelled of my father-in-law's pipe tobacco.

We talked about Jim's original trip, his mother's love of elegance, and his father Bernie's belligerence regarding dress codes. Jim spoke of the color of the water that day, decades ago, when the sun shone brightly at high noon. Looking at the lake, I envisioned Jim as a boy running along its green shores and his dad in Bermuda shorts and Gold Toe black socks. I could see Jim's sister Pam in pedal pushers and a pageboy walking hand in hand with Phyllis in her soft summer dress.

We were having a wonderful pilgrimage to this sacred site, but I thought about my parents-in-law who weren't having such a good summer this year. They were in Nebraska with Phyllis too ill to travel and neither of them able to hike mountain trails. They were unlikely ever to see Lake Louise or a water ouzel again. I pictured my own parents, who never in their lives had a day like this one, a day in the wilderness, walking and laughing, followed by a gourmet meal and a quiet peace. My mother would have loved this meal, but she had died five years ago. My father could have caught trout in the Bow River, but he'd been dead for twenty-four years. The sun turned the green of the water blue.

As I get older, when I dine at places like this, I feel like more and more people are with me at the table. When I have a moment this grand, I share it with my parents; Jim's parents; Aunt Betty, who never spent more than four dollars on a meal in her life; and my Colorado grandmother, who had a hard life as a ranch woman and died without ever seeing the Canadian Rockies.

In the Edelweiss Room, I looked closely for these people I had loved. We didn't have enough chairs at the table for all the ghosts. There was Jim as a scrawny ten-year-old, and Phyllis as a svelte, young wife. There was my dad in his Army uniform, and my mom with her doctor's bag, professional suit, and high heels. My own faraway children were there as well. First they were children throwing stones in the water, and then they were adults, as they are now, toasting our meal and telling us their good fortunes. Together we walked the trail to Lake Moraine to watch the ouzels dive.

Jim and I ordered dessert and coffee. Now the lake was the color of steel and the mountains loomed as dark as thunderheads. I thought of Michael Ventura's line: "Time doesn't kid around." Time was our adversary, our worthy opponent, to whom we would always lose. Grizzly Number Ten would find us all in the end.

Some of us sit on the shores of Lake Louise, and others wait in doctor's offices for reports that will only cause more pain. Still others, yet unborn, will sit here a hundred years from today, drinking tea and eating crumpets in the sun. As an old man I once saw in a cemetery said, "They come and they go."

But time is our friend as well as our enemy. In that great sea of memory, time collapses and we all are together in that place where time doesn't exist. We can be quiet and see our worlds collide. The old become young again; the children grow up and have new children. The dead return to hike and fish. Our grandchildren go crawling onto the laps of our great-grandparents. We all are at the table. We can see everything. We can talk to one another. The lake is calm.

# Introduction

*I wake up in another country, there is no more north or south.*
*Asleep we pass through one another like blowing snow,*
*all of us, all.*

—LINDA HOGAN,
"Our Houses"

I HAVE ALWAYS LOVED OLDER PEOPLE. MY HAPPIEST MEMO-
RIES from childhood involve my grandmothers and my mother's father.
My father's father spent most of his life in a mental hospital, but the other
three grandparents held my world in place. I think of Glessie May, my
father's mother, a sturdy, dark-haired woman who made her living selling
Avon in Christian County, Missouri. When we planted corn in her garden,
my job was to bury a little bluegill beside each seed for fertilizer. Together
we hiked through woods looking for poke, wild berries, or mushrooms.
Glessie never had indoor plumbing, but when our family came to visit, she

fixed fried chicken, gravy, fresh biscuits, and pie—and that was for break-fast. When we left, she'd hug me to her ample chest and beg my father to move us back to the Ozarks where we belonged.

My grandfather Page was a stout, bald rancher who dressed in overalls and a felt hat. Every morning after breakfast he'd walk to the post office and then to the pool hall for a glass of root beer and a game of checkers. Twice a day he would lie with his head hanging over the bed, and my grandmother would squirt Murine into his eyes. Before meals he said grace, and after meals he buried the leftovers in the garden. After his nap, we'd ride out in his pickup to feed the cattle. He'd tell me stories—about his animals, all of whom had names and personalities, and about storms and other disasters in Kit Carson County, Colorado.

Summer evenings he'd build a fire in his cement barbecue grill and we'd roast wieners and marshmallows. We'd feel the earth cool down and watch the fireflies light up the night. (I later bought a disastrous house because it had a grill that reminded me of those evenings.) After dinner in the winter, Grandfather would pull out the card table and we'd play dominoes, rook, cribbage, or hearts. We'd finish the evening with pie and cookies; the children drank milk and the adults drank cups of thick black coffee.

My grandmother Page *needed* to be outdoors. She walked at dusk so that she could see the sunset. Whenever her workload slackened, she read for hours at a time. When we visited her house, she made stewed beef, chicken with homemade noodles, rolls, and creamed peas with potatoes. We washed dishes together. Later we would sit under the ash trees, listen to the birds, and watch the gray squirrels.

While my own family was disorganized and loud, my grandparents' home was calm and quiet. There was order and ritual. There were fresh gingersnaps in the cookie jar, and stacks of *Reader's Digest*s. There were lessons as well. Grandmother said, "Before you worry about the mote in your neighbor's eye, worry about the log in your own." She quoted that best of all rules, "Do unto others as you would have them do unto you," and its corollary, "Judge not that you be not judged."

My grandfather told my grandmother that he loved her so frequently that people kidded him about it. He was accused of being uxorious and henpecked, even though my grandmother never "pecked." But I think that he was just wise: to not have loved Agnes Page inordinately would have been pure foolishness.

I lost my last grandparent when I was in college almost thirty years ago. I still fall asleep with pictures of all of them in my head. They are calming pictures that help me let go of the day. Glessie was earthy and outspoken; the Page grandparents were well-educated and a little Puritanical. I know they all had faults. However, in all my time with my grandparents, none of them ever said a cross or ungenerous word to me.

Mrs. Van Cleave, a white-haired immigrant in her seventies, taught me pottery making. After school I'd stop by her house. I was a big-boned, gawky adolescent who lived in a state of continual amazement at the cruelty and stupidity of many of the kids at school. Each afternoon around three, I'd reach Mrs. Van Cleave's house, shell-shocked and so rattled that I could barely speak.

She'd greet me with hot tea in a china cup and thin lemon cookies on a hand-painted plate. We'd walk to the quiet back room that was her pottery workshop. Side by side, we'd knead clay, glaze pots, and paint figurines. We rarely spoke, but in her studio smelling of banana oil, clay, and turpentine, I could forgive. My body went slack with relief.

As I write this book, I am fifty, a baby boomer born just after World War II. If life can be divided into seasons, each approximately twenty years long and beginning with spring, I'm in the mid-autumn of my life. My next season will be winter. If my parents were alive, I'd be caring for them. Twenty years from now, most probably, my children will be caring for me.

Wallace Stegner wrote, "After sixty you are aware how vulnerable everything is, including yourself." Though I haven't yet reached that age, I feel intimations of that time. I deal with anxiety-provoking situations by gathering information, by anticipating problems and thinking them through. Partly I explore the issues of aging to calm myself down. I want to be prepared. Like the gray squirrels of eastern Colorado, I want to store up supplies for winter.

For *Another Country*, I interviewed and saw in therapy mostly Caucasian and African-American Midwesterners in their seventies, eighties, and nineties. Most were middle-class rural people, although some were from cities or were immigrants. Some were indigent, and a few were rich. I know that there are hundred-year-old joggers, figure skaters, and other miraculous elders. I have tremendous respect for such people, but I chose not to focus on them. Rather, I selected ordinary people who were coping with the standard amounts of loss and disability. I felt they were the ones who had lessons to teach me. I cannot claim to represent all the voices of the old in America. But I do hope that I articulate many of the issues that all the elders face.

What every person I interviewed had in common was a life that spanned the century. They were around when Henry Ford designed the first assembly lines, when sliced bread was invented, and when the first movie theaters opened. They were alive when the *Titanic* sank and the Lindbergh baby was kidnapped. They were the last generation in this country to be raised in a communal culture and to grow up on pre-Freudian terrain.

I wanted to learn about our community-based country that has almost vanished, and also to understand the country of old age, which most of us one day will inhabit. Old people know about loss, ill health, and diminishment. They cope with experiences that would take down a younger person. There is an old joke that goes: "But other than that, Mrs. Lincoln, how did you like the play?" We can ask of all our elders, "But other than the facts that your friends and family are dying and you are ill, how are you doing?"

I cannot imagine maintaining good mental health under the conditions that most old people eventually experience—under conditions Aunt Betty alluded to when she wrote, "Most of the people I know are gone now." The old face physical problems, the loss of friends and family, and their own impending deaths. Many of them do so with courage and dignity, even humor. I wanted to learn how they do it.

Many of my friends and clients have sick and aging parents. They worry about their parents' doctors, their driving, their finances, and their houses. Some have put their parents in rest homes or hired live-in help. Others are worried because no one is caring for their aging relatives. Every time the phone rings, they fear catastrophe.

Adults have always worried about aging parents, but our current situation is unique. Never before have so many people lived so far away from the old people they love. And never have old people lived to be so old. Recently I called one of my aunts, who was in a hospital and scheduled for morning surgery. It took more than an hour to get through—lots of people love my aunt, who was on the phone with her children, her siblings, and her favorite nieces around the country. When I finally spoke to her she was upset about a laxative she'd been given. It was too strong, and she hadn't been able to get herself out of bed and to the bathroom. She was stressed by her "accident" and fearful of the surgery.

From a thousand miles away, I told her I loved her. My aunt croaked out an "I love you, too," but she was distracted by her current worries. After the call, I thought realistically about her situation. She had a daughter nearby who would be by her side when she could get off work and who would do a heroic job supervising my aunt's situation. After the surgery, my aunt would have a roomful of flowers and balloons, but right this minute she didn't have anyone to get her to the bathroom. That's what she really needed, someone who was there "this minute."

Many old people are living in a world designed for young people. They can't drive, walk through shopping malls or airports, or deal with rushed doctors in managed care systems. Many can't handle stairs, small-print books, or menus in darkened restaurants. They have access to expensive and sophisticated medical care that prolongs their lives, but many must sacrifice their savings to afford it. Some must choose between medications and food. Modern technological advances, such as dialysis and organ replacement surgeries, keep people alive but create chronic problems of their own. Some people live to be more than a hundred, but they often outlive their support systems, neighborhoods, and bank accounts.

I hear stories from clients and friends about their struggles to make good decisions about aging relatives. Almost everyone wants to do the right thing, but adult children have busy, complicated lives that often include full-time jobs, long commutes, and family responsibilities. They may be a thousand miles away from the people who need their time and attention, and they may not have the financial resources to care for their loved ones.

As I write, I think of Heather, who called last night to talk about her dilemma. Just out of graduate school, Heather was lucky enough to get a tenure-track position at a large university on the East Coast. Unfortunately it's a continent away from her mother, who is dying from cancer. She mentioned her concerns to the department chair, who said, "You aren't going to be a baby about this, are you?" Heather was debating giving up this job. "It makes me nervous and sad. My career is going so great. But I can't abandon my mother. Do you know of any work in Nevada?"

I think of my friend Betsy, a working mother with two small children who has spent the winter caring for her faraway parents. In the fall she had to fire an incompetent doctor in the middle of a medical emergency. She wasn't sure at the time whether her action was heroic or lethal. Several times this winter, her parents were in hospitals in different towns, and Betsy set up phones so that her parents could at least talk to each other. When her father died, she took her mother out of a rehabilitation center and drove her across our snowy state to the funeral. "I haven't read a newspaper, seen a movie, or even had my hair cut in six months," Betsy told me. She was considering going on Prozac.

I think of my friend Marilyn, whose parents live in a retirement community in Arkansas. Once a month she makes the ten-hour drive to be with them. Her father is institutionalized with Alzheimer's and no longer recognizes her. Marilyn still writes him two letters a week, which her mother reads to him. Marilyn told me, "I go for Mom. She takes care of Dad, and I take care of her."

My client Carla's mother had a heart attack in her Arizona condo. Carla took time off work and flew down to be with her during the surgery. She stayed on for the opportunistic infection and later the pneumonia. It was a difficult month. Her mother had recently married a man who drove a Lincoln Continental, gambled, and liked rare steaks and bourbon. He made fun of Carla's vegetarianism, her casual clothes, and even her Honda. The two of them stood across the room from each other in the ICU, trying, but barely able, to maintain the illusion of civility. They hardly knew each other, and yet they had to make life-and-death decisions together about a person they both loved.

I recently met a woman whose parents, when they retired, had moved to Palm Beach to play golf. This woman and her family were a thousand miles away, and her children grew up hardly knowing their grandparents. Then last year her mother died and her father insisted on moving back to be near his daughter. "He wants us to treat him like the prodigal son," she said. "But my kids don't know him. He's depressed and ill, and all of a sudden I am his daughter again. I'll try to help him and I want my children to know him, but I resent that he had nothing for us during his healthy years."

From both generations I hear stories of conflict, frustration, guilt, and anger. While the old often feel abandoned and misunderstood, their younger relatives often feel unappreciated, stressed, and guilty. Hurt feelings often come from taking personally problems that are cultural or developmental. As a nation, we are not organized in a way that makes aging easy.

Right now we are in a crisis. We lack the housing arrangements, social structures, traditions, and wisdom to make the last years of life manageable. No one wants to die surrounded by hired help. No one wants their parents to be anxious about money and in pain their last years. Yet these things happen all the time. There is an enormous gap between what we believe is right and what is practical.

When logistics can be worked out so that families are together, there are still conflicts caused by the personalities involved and by different ways of interpreting the world. The generations have very different mental landscapes, and that interferes with communication and compassion. A father is upset that his daughter wants to bring up the past and "open old wounds." She wants to process events; he wants to "let sleeping dogs lie." A son wants to know his mother's medical condition, and she "doesn't want him to worry." He says, "My main worry is that I don't know what is going on."

My goal is to map out the terra incognita between old people and their children, to help each generation understand the other. The last years of a relationship are important ones. Sadness and conflict are inevitable, but much pain can be avoided with better information, empathy, and planning.

My mother was hospitalized for eleven of the last twelve months of her life. She had diabetes, along with its cruel problems—peritonitis, heart and liver failure, vomiting, chills, and legs that cramped and jerked from potassium deficiency. She was bedridden, bloated, and brain damaged. She had skin cancer and osteoporosis. She broke her arm when she fell out of bed, and her vertebrae when she tried to lift a small suitcase.

Sometimes she hallucinated. One night she delivered babies all night long and admonished the nurses, "Don't drop that child. Wash the floor, wash the floor." Another night she called out for a large pot, onions, and tomatoes, and she cooked spaghetti for a big crowd. Other days she saw dollar bills on the ceiling or held conversations with her long-dead parents and husband.

She had months of ups and downs, and then just downs and downs. In all those horrid months, when she never felt the breeze on her face, saw the sun, had a good meal, or slept without pain, she never complained. She appreciated a glass of ice, a back rub, or a story. She smiled when she recognized the faces of friends.

I was the oldest daughter, three hours away, but I had two teenagers, a book to write, and a full-time job. For months I drove to her hospital every other weekend, then every weekend. I took the calls from relatives and doctors and tried to handle her money, her medical care, and her house.

That year, no matter where I was, I felt guilty. If I was with my mother, I wasn't caring for my own kids or my clients. If I was working, I was ignoring my family. When I was with my children, I thought of my mother alone in a faraway hospital. I got depressed and crabby. My husband and I fought more and my children didn't get the supervision and nurturing they needed. I got a speeding ticket.

My mother never expected to die, and her affairs were not in order. Her money and her legal papers were a mess. She'd insist on leaving the hospital, go home alone, then be readmitted in crisis. She wouldn't move closer to her children, yet she hated being alone. Her unrealistic plans and her disorganization made my life complicated and stressful.

I alternated between guilt and anger. I'd be furious about a decision she made, and resolve to confront her. Then I'd find her vomiting or too weak to lift her head from her pillow, and I'd back down. I'd feel like a horrible daughter and try to be more nurturing. Then I'd hear about another bad decision.

My mother's last year was a worst-case scenario. She was nauseated and in pain, then she died alone. By the time she died, I felt a weird combination of being stressed to my limits and ashamed I hadn't done more. Mother and I had some good talks, but many things didn't happen the way I wished that they had. I had spent a year tired, anxious, and sad. Then I lost my mother.

That whole year I felt isolated and alienated. While my friends were taking ski trips and going to parties and movies, I was worried that I couldn't get to the grocery store, help my kids with their studies, or schedule an anxious client. At social gatherings I wasn't much fun. All my stories were sad ones. When I talked about the complexity of Mother's situation, it overwhelmed me and bored others. I wondered if I would ever be happy again.

One reason I am writing this book is to help others in my situation feel less alone. I want to increase our information about and interest in the plight of older people and their families. I want to explore social and psychological arrangements that allow the old and young to be connected to each other. Together we can create a culture in which it's easier to do the right thing.

Those last years can be difficult, but also redemptive. As we care for our parents, we teach our children to care for us. As we see our parents age, we learn to age with courage and dignity. If the years are handled well, the old and young can help each other grow.

This book has some very sad stories and, especially in the middle, plenty of bad news. But I hope I have captured the humor and resilience of this older generation as well as the sorrow and hardships. I hope I've shown their tendency to laugh and joke, to tough it out, and to put on their best clothes and go dancing. By the end, I hope the reader sees the possibilities for joy and wisdom that come from connecting to our parents' generation.

I encourage adults to seek out their older relatives and get reacquainted. We live in a fragmented culture, and many of us have lost contact with extended family. Indeed there is little in our culture that encourages these contacts. If you say you are going to a family reunion or having relatives visit for a week, people are likely to feel sorry for you. Extended families are often viewed as boring and bothersome, as thieves of our valuable time.

My five aunts were important to me in childhood. My Missouri aunts, Grace and Henrietta, took me fishing and helped me catch crawdads in Ozark creeks. My aunt Agnes from Colorado cooked Sunday dinners for twenty of us. My aunt Margaret talked about books and plays, and Aunt Betty helped me find huckleberries for pies. During my middle years, with work and children, I had been too busy for them, and while I was away, they all became old.

For this book I interviewed them about their lives now and when they were young. These visits were among the best experiences of my life. I learned about my family and myself. I had very different talks with them from the ones I have with my peers. I gained some perspective on the century and the life cycle. I absorbed valuable information about how to age and how to approach death. Alex Haley said, "The death of an old person is like the burning of a library." Visiting my aunts allowed me to read some of the books before they burned.

I also spent a great deal of time in rest homes and assisted-living facilities. For the most part, I found caring, if overworked, staffs and well-intentioned administrative personnel. And I found some residents who liked their rest homes. There was more interaction between the homes and the outside world than I imagined. I saw children stopping by, school groups coming to sing or read with their buddies, and friends and relatives who were loyal and devoted visitors. However, there weren't enough connections between the old and the young. Many residents went months or even years without hearing the laughter of children or holding a baby.

Many people in rest homes or even in their own homes or apartments had almost no contact with anyone but other old people and/or their caregivers. Meanwhile, all over America we have young children hungry for "lap time" and older children who need skills, nurturing, and moral instruction from their elders. We have street gangs of ten-year-olds, and old-age ghettos in which our elders are more and more cut off from the real world. Children play with cyberpets while old women stare out their windows at empty streets. Grandparents feel lonely and useless while a thousand miles away their grandchildren are not getting the love and attention they desperately need. There is a lot wrong with this picture.

Each generation has its own gifts to share with all other generations. I hope this book inspires people to work on new ways to connect the generations. I hope adults will call, write, and visit their own aunts and great-aunts. I want grandchildren and grandparents to spend summers together and maybe even figure out ways to live near each other. I hope my writing inspires people to plan family reunions and intergenerational bonding events. I want community activities organized not by age but by formed families so that people of all ages can work together. I want schools to be facilities where people of all ages work and play. In short, I hope we all can become one country.

*Part One*

# Landscape
# of Age

# CHAPTER 1

# *Another Country*

*The trouble is, old age is not interesting until one gets there.
It's a foreign country with an unknown language to the
young and even to the middle-aged.*

—MAY SARTON,
*As We Are Now*

THE METAPHOR OF AGING AND DEATH AS VISITING ANOTHER
country is at least 1,500 years old. Thomas Cahill quotes St. Patrick in his
book *How the Irish Saved Civilization*: "In the end, your hungers are
rewarded: you are going home. Look, your ship is ready." Old age, especially in the last hard years, is really a search for a place in the universe, both
figuratively and literally. The old look for their existential place. They ask,
"How did my life matter?" "Was my time well spent?" "What did I mean
to others?" "What can I look back on with pride?" "Did I love the right

people?" And they search for a home and a village where they will be comfortable, useful, and loved.

This search for place becomes the central issue during people's final years. Family members want to help, but we live in a culture in which this journey into another country is hard for everyone. We are scattered across the continent living hurried, scheduled lives. We have few road maps to help us navigate the new lands. Aging in America is harder than it needs to be.

As we approach the millennium, we are entering a new territory, with very different family structures, work options, kinds of old age, and choices about living situations and health care. Earlier in the century, Robert Frost wrote, "Home is the place where, when you have to go there, they have to take you in." That has been less true in the last half of our century.

Families are struggling with all the common problems of aging relatives plus the new dilemmas of the nineties. There aren't many rituals to guide us. Asian, Native American, and African-American cultures have rich traditions of caring for the aged, but nobody is prepared for managed care or housing units that require $200,000 deposits. In short, we are not ready for today.

We've experienced enormous demographic changes across this century. In 1900, the life expectancy at birth was forty-nine; today it is seventy-six. Today one family in four is caring for an older relative. As James Atlas wrote in "The Sandwich Generation" in *The New Yorker*, soon, for the first time in history, many middle-aged people will have more parents alive than they have children. He bemoaned the distance between modern parents and children: "Geographic freedom means we are dispersed." He wrote of the hassles of caring for children and parents at the same time: "All of a sudden you must rescue the people you thought were superhuman. To see your parents as vulnerable is hard. At the same time you feel sorry for yourself. It's tough on your own kids. You want to spend time with them but there are only so many hours in the day."

We are in a new world with no real prototypes for dealing with all these aging people. Medicine has both helped and complicated our situation. Many people live longer and healthier lives. But unhealthy people live longer, too. We have thousands of citizens who lie comatose in long-term health-care facilities. Bodies last longer than brains, support systems, or savings accounts. We don't have the resources, the rituals, or the institutions to make our old feel like elders.

There is an urgency to understand and accommodate an aging culture because most of us baby boomers have aged relatives. We are the pig in the python, the big demographic bulge that has moved across the last half of our century. What happens to us happens to millions of people at once. Right now our parents are becoming old people.

Of course, everything we do to help the old surely will help us all later on. Soon our country will be avalanched by old people, and those people will be us. In a few decades, our solutions to the dilemmas of caring for our elders will be applied to our own lives. The kindness, the indifference, the ignorance, and the wisdom will be passed on. The more we love and respect our elders, the more we teach our children to love and respect us. The more we think through problems today, the more organizational and cultural structures will be in place to handle our generation's needs.

Right now we don't even know how to talk about our problems. We have no language for nurturing interdependency. The traditional ways of caring for our parents don't work, and new ways haven't been invented. Decisions about living arrangements, money, and health are complicated, and much of the information that would help is not available. We don't really know how long we or our parents will be healthy, what will happen to the economy, or how much medical care will cost.

Our general confusion is compounded by a new kind of ignorance. Until late in this century, we humans spent time with people of all generations, but today we aren't likely to have much contact with old people until we are relatively old ourselves. We baby boomers live in what Robert Bly calls "sibling societies," and we are educated away from relationships with our elders. We are not taught how interesting they are. We don't know their needs, and they don't know ours.

Many old people live in segregated communities. Some choose to live separately from the young—they don't like their noise and bother—but most just slowly become more isolated. For example, I know an Italian immigrant who moved into an assisted-living unit for health reasons. He deeply misses his old neighborhood, his friends of a lifetime, his grandchildren, the cafe on the corner that served real Italian pizza, and his boccie-ball-playing buddies.

We group people by age. We put our three-year-olds together, our thirteen-year-olds together, and our eighty-year-olds together. Children and teenagers can go months at a time with no contact with the old. Adolescent peer culture is especially noxious, but so are the cultures of isolated day-care centers or senior citizens' homes.

A great deal of the social sickness in America comes from this age segregation. If ten fourteen-year-olds are grouped together, they will fight with one another. They will form a "lord of the flies" culture with its competitiveness, social anxiety, and meanness. But if ten people aged two to eighty are grouped together, they will fall into a natural age hierarchy that nurtures and teaches all of them. Because each person has a niche, competition will subside. Each person will have something unique to contribute. Values will deepen, and experience will grow richer. For our own mental and societal health, we need to reconnect the age groups.

My client Irena just returned from visiting her parents in a Southwestern retirement community. She talked about how depressing it was, rows of identical suburban houses baking in the 110-degree weather. There was no one on the streets. Pollution and heat kept everyone trapped in air-conditioned houses, "waiting to die," as Irena put it. "My parents' lives have become their medical conditions," she told me. "It was the worst week of my life."

The two biggest changes over the course of this century have been our move from a pre-psychology to a post-psychology culture and our move from a communal to an individualistic culture. Most older people grew up surrounded by family. They shared bedrooms with half a dozen siblings and had grandparents or great-aunts in their homes or living nearby. They knew their neighbors, and their fun was other people. They tend to be gregarious and communal and turn toward others for support and entertainment.

There are very real cultural differences between generations that create what I call time-zone problems. Generations have different attitudes about everything from authority to expressing feelings to R-rated movies. The generations have different attitudes even toward attitudes. My generation is more comfortable being sacrilegious, skeptical, and ironic.

Our parents' generation was pre-irony. Of course, some people were ironic, but most were not. Irony implies a distance between one's words and one's world, a cool remove that is a late-century phenomenon. One theory is that irony became widespread in this country during World War I, when soldiers realized the gap between their own experiences and civilian perceptions. Freud also helped create the culture of irony. He gave my generation the notion that underneath one idea is another, that behind our surface behavior is a different motive. Advertising also layers meaning in a way that teaches ironic thinking. There is an apparent message, and a subliminal message about something very different. By now we all learn to think ironically. But many people older than a certain age grew up believing that the surface is all there is.

The old, like the young, come in all varieties. However, differences aside, there are some things we can say about the old as a group. The old are segregated by interests, by history, by physical health, by attitudes about mental health, and by shared trauma. They have in common three sets of experiences—they have participated in the events of the twentieth century, they have passed through the same developmental hurdles, and they now live in the landscape of old age.

They have lived before television, cars, electricity, *Playboy*, and the Green Revolution. Older African-Americans had parents who remembered slavery. Older Native Americans had relatives who fought in the Indian wars of the last century. Rural old men know how to mend harnesses, butcher hogs, build fences, cut hay, slice the testicles off a bull, and fix an engine. Older women can bake, quilt, make soap, sew trousers, and doctor sick animals. Many of the old know how to play instruments, sketch portraits, and recite poetry.

Older people have passed through seven of Erik Erikson's eight stages of development. Middle age is in the distant past. Most of the old have been parents and grandparents. They have lost parents, siblings, and friends. They have seen vigorous bodies grow frail, and active minds grow forgetful.

In his book *The Summing Up*, Somerset Maugham noted that with old age, one is free of certain passions. Most people become less sexual, less competitive, and less envious. Most people have figured out that life is tough for everyone. They tend to be kinder and more compassionate than they were as young people. Many are like Gladys, described below—as sweet as honey over sugar. Generally, the old like verbal and physical affection and, unlike the young, are under no illusion that they do not need love.

## GLADYS   *(age 90)*
*"TV is my best friend."*

GLADYS WAS REFERRED to my office by her family physician after she talked to him about what she called her "weird eye problem." When she was alone, she hallucinated bugs, squirrels, and rotting food. The people on TV talked to her and sometimes even stepped out of the screen into her living room. Gladys knew these experiences weren't normal, but she thought her eyes were playing tricks on her.

Gladys's son, Roger, drove her to my office. Gladys dressed carefully in a mauve suit, a pink silk blouse, and a cluster of pink costume jewelry. She had sparkly blue eyes and soft, powdered skin etched with delicate lines. I invited Roger to come into the session, but he politely declined by saying he wanted his mother to have her privacy. As I escorted Gladys into my office, Roger pulled a James Lee Burke paperback out of his pocket.

I asked Gladys if she knew why she was here. She answered, "Aren't you a nerve doctor?"

"I'm a psychologist," I said. Gladys shook her head in confusion, and I added, "We listen to people's problems and help find ways to solve them."

"Well, that sounds lovely," she said amiably. I offered her some tea and asked about her situation. She explained that her husband had died when she was in her sixties and that Roger was her only child. "I wish we'd had some daughters," she said sadly.

When Gladys retired from the hospital where she cooked, Roger and his wife, Nell, had invited her to move to Nebraska. On their acreage, Roger and Nell had fixed her up a trailer with central air and a big-screen TV. Until Nell died, Gladys had been happy there. However, when she mentioned Nell, the sparkle left her eyes and her shoulders drooped. She told me that Nell had been a wonderful wife to Roger and a great daughter-in-law to her. They had canned peaches and chowchow, made slaw and homemade ketchup, and gone "garage saling" on weekends. Gladys boasted, "Nell could refinish furniture, sew a dress in a morning, and fix the plumbing in the afternoon. When she was around, something was always going on."

However, Nell had died of breast cancer two years earlier. As she spoke of Nell's death, Gladys got a hanky out of her purse and wiped her eyes. Since Nell died, Gladys had been lonely. Roger was busy with his work for the railroad and sometimes gone for days at a time. When he was home, Roger liked to putter around in his shop and garden. He made Gladys nice furniture, but he rarely ate with her. He believed in minding his own business. He was a big kidder, but, as Gladys said, "if he doesn't feel like answering me, he doesn't answer."

Gladys also missed her granddaughter, Molly, who lived in Los Angeles with her husband and baby. Gladys was far from her friends in South Dakota, most of whom could no longer write her. She rarely left her trailer.

Her town had no public transportation, and she didn't ask her son for rides. She hated to bother Roger, who "works so hard and deserves a little peace and quiet when he's at home."

Gladys told me how Nell had come over first thing every morning for coffee. She said, "We'd gab all morning long. I'd help her shell peas or cut corn. We'd think up mischief if there wasn't work to do. Now days pass slowly, and at night I am tired. But I wonder why. I haven't gone anywhere or seen anyone. What have I done to tire myself out?"

To pass the time, she watched television. She said, without a trace of sarcasm, "TV is my best friend. I get sixty channels."

While we talked about TV, Gladys brought up her "eye problem." She knew that she saw things that weren't really there and that her problems went away when she was busy. "Like today," she said as she took my hand in hers, "when I see people, my eyes don't act up."

I was grateful that her doctor had sent her to me instead of giving her tranquilizers or antipsychotic medications. I had a hunch we could treat this eye problem. We scheduled another appointment, and I walked her back to Roger. He stood up immediately and gallantly helped Gladys with her coat.

After Gladys left, I thought about how she insisted on nothing. She was grateful for a ride from Roger and forty-five minutes of my time. Like so many older people, she would rather go mad quietly than be a bother. I thought about Roger, a good son who had been concerned about his mother's physical comfort but less aware of her other needs and unsure how to help without interfering. Plus, Roger had needs of his own. As a grieving man with a job that required constant travel, he might well be lonely and depressed himself.

Gladys reminded me of another client who, when speaking of her loneliness, had said, "For the elderly there is no village." That was the essence of Gladys's problem. Her heart was strong, and her memory was good. If Roger could help her develop a community, Gladys could have a mostly "good time" her last years. I was sure that with more activity, Gladys would stop seeing things that weren't there. At the next session I wanted to work with Roger and Gladys together.

## Session Two

This time Roger agreed to come into my office with his mother. He looked uneasy but determined to do the right thing for Gladys. Gladys patted his arm and said that after our visit, Roger had volunteered to take her to church and Sunday school. Roger shrugged and said, "Mom perked up after seeing you. I figured she needed to get out more."

I asked how he thought his mother was doing in general. Roger answered, "She's been lonely since Nell died." His words caught in his throat. "We both have. Maybe I should take her more places. But when I get home from work, I just want to stay put."

Gladys quickly reassured Roger that he did all he could, and he didn't disagree. She explained to me that Roger had work piled up when he got back from his train trips. She told me again how much effort Roger put into making her trailer comfortable.

In this difficult situation—a widowed middle-aged man and his slightly unstable mother—I observed how kind these two people were to each other. Roger was proud and independent. He didn't want to ask for help or admit he couldn't do everything that Gladys needed done. He thought a good son should be able to provide for his mother totally, but he was wearing out and failing at his self-imposed goal of doing it all. Gladys was deteriorating, mostly from loneliness and uselessness. And yet I could tell each one was determined not to blame the other for their misery.

Gladys showed me pictures from her ninetieth birthday party, the biggest get-together in the history of the family. She wore a silver silk dress and a corsage. Nell had died before this party, but Gladys said, "She helped me plan. The last week of her life we sent out the invitations." Molly had come home to help. They made mints together and fixed the nut cups and punch. Her best friend, Amalia, had ridden the bus down from South Dakota. "Over one hundred people were there," she said proudly.

"Mom has lots of friends," Roger interjected, and he winked at her. "Her secret weapon is her pies."

Gladys laughed and told me about cooking for the hospital. Some days she made as many as twenty pies. Her specialty was lemon meringue, but she also made a killer chocolate pie, Roger's favorite. I asked if she still made pies and cakes. She sadly said no, that she couldn't see to read the spice cans. Gladys was now eating mostly TV dinners and pot pies. She said, "I miss my own cooking, especially on holidays."

Roger said he generally ate whenever he felt like it. His work kept him from having a regular schedule, and he thought he saved his mother trouble by eating fast food or microwave meals. I asked Gladys if it was trouble to cook for Roger. She said, "It wouldn't be if I could see."

Gladys said that she still had her eye problems, but maybe not quite as much. She'd had one bad day when her old boss in South Dakota died and Roger couldn't drive her to the funeral. That day she had seen rabbits and weasels running around the living room.

As Gladys told me about the funeral, Roger looked at his hands and mumbled that he was sorry he hadn't been able to drive. I agreed it was too bad, then I asked him how much fun he'd been having lately, a question that clearly surprised him. He said, "I didn't think shrinks cared about stuff like that."

I knew that these two people would live together more happily if both were able to get some needs met. If Roger sacrificed too much to care for Gladys, he might be resentful. Roger needed both free time and the feeling that he was a good son. I thought of the Buddhist Middle Way. Extreme heroics usually don't work over time. People do best with balanced lives in which they care for themselves and for others. On the other hand, if Gladys didn't get out more, she would become increasingly addled. Balancing needs is tricky. When two people live together, either both people win or both people lose. I wanted to find some new resources for Gladys and take some of the burden off Roger.

I suggested that they look for a teenage girl to come in after school to help Gladys make pies and soups. She could read the recipes and labels, and Gladys could orchestrate the cooking. I also encouraged Roger to eat with his mother at least one night a week. He joked that it would be easy to agree to that if she would make him a chocolate pie. I suggested that Gladys spend a little of her money calling Amalia in South Dakota and Molly at least once a week.

## SESSION TEN

Gladys had been coming in for four months. As her eye problem had improved, I had seen her less frequently. Today, the girl whom Roger had hired drove Gladys to therapy. Katie was seventeen, good-natured, and proud of her responsibilites. She explained that she and Gladys had baked ginger cookies for our session.

We left Katie in the waiting area with her homework, and I made tea. The cookies were delicious and took me back to my own childhood, to my grandmother's ginger cookies. I spoke approvingly of Katie. "Oh, you don't know the half of it," Gladys enthused. "She is a good worker and so clean. She reads me my recipes and gets out the right spices. I'm teaching her to can. Just last week she helped put up twenty quarts of pears. I gave her two quarts plus her pay. Next summer I'll teach her to make ketchup."

Katie had made a big difference in Gladys's life. The six hours a week they spent together was all talking time. Afterward, Gladys had her own foods to enjoy and share with Roger, who was now eating with her several times a week. Also, he was dating a woman he'd met when he drove his mother to church. Gladys said happily, "She tells me stuff about Roger that he would never think to mention."

I said that I was glad that she had two new women in her life. She said, "There's more than that. Amalia and I talk every Sunday night. Molly calls me once a week, and I am making friends at church."

I told Gladys about a study that found that old people are not generally lonely if they have three regular contacts. Her isolation had caused the eye problems, but now she had many people in her life. If her daily companion wasn't a television set but rather a real person, I didn't think she would have more trouble.

Gladys always would miss Nell. I encouraged her to keep a picture of Nell handy and to sleep under a quilt Nell had made. (She had been storing it in a closet.) I wrote Roger a note complimenting him on his care for his mother. We hugged good-bye, which is something I often do in my therapy with the old. I walked Gladys out to Katie in the waiting room. As Katie held the door open for Gladys, I heard her say, "Let's stop by the grocery store and pick up some ginger."

Gladys's story illustrates some of the difficulties that arise when everyone has "good intentions and honorable mentions" but are still flawed humans in a culture that doesn't offer much support. Gladys didn't want to be dependent, and Roger was unsure how to help. He didn't want to be intrusive, and he was unable to give his mother all the social contact she needed.

Fortunately Gladys and Roger were willing to seek help. I encouraged them to connect with others, not to carry all the burdens of making things work on their own shoulders. I also helped Roger have reasonable expectations about the situation. He couldn't do and be everything for his mother. I warned him to expect frustrations and misunderstandings. Just because she was old didn't mean she was a saint, and just because he was kind didn't mean he couldn't have bad days too. Even in young people's lives, not everything goes well. Old age is a genuinely difficult situation with lots of sadness and frustration. Many things will not go well.

I tried to show Roger that guilt wouldn't help. I encouraged him to do what he reasonably could and to find others to do what he couldn't do. Mainly, I acknowledged that both Roger and Gladys had needs that shouldn't be sacrificed or taken for granted. Because Roger and Gladys had the money and energy to set a few things up, Gladys was cured of terminal loneliness. She was pulled back from the edge of despair. Roger was able to be a good son, and Gladys had a home where she was useful and connected to others.

* * *

THE OLD ARE segregated not only physically—by their living circumstances and their ill health—but also by their worldview. Language is different. The old may call oatmeal porridge and refrigerators iceboxes. Depression refers to a time when money was tight, not to a mental-health problem. Consumption refers to tuberculosis rather than spending. Metaphors come from communal life or from the war years. My father would say when it was hot, "There's nothing moving out there but the neighbor's dog." My mother, who was in the Navy during the war, talked about "hitting the deck" and keeping our place "shipshape." And many of our elders are shocked by the swear words and sexual innuendo of younger people.

The old are segregated by tempo. Doing interviews for this book, I learned to let the phone ring fifteen times. I learned to wait at doors five minutes after I rang the bell. I had to slow down to work with the old. Their conversation is less linear, and there are pauses and repetitions. Points are made via stories; memories lead to more memories. Details are debated and relished. People long dead are explained at length.

With the old I walked slowly and held hands at intersections or when sidewalks were slick. Many of the old show up early for events and are the last to leave. Many need help getting out of chairs, and many don't go out at night because they might stumble. Because their bones break more easily and mend more slowly, the old are afraid of falling. Many of their homes have upstairs bathrooms and bedrooms, and a broken hip can mean that independent living is over.

Doris Grumbach wrote, "I hear less, see crookedly, lose weight and height, grow crooked and stolid, placid and inept. My age is my cage. Only death can free me."

In health as in wealth, there is no equity. In spite of our very American belief in our individual powers to control fate, people do not always get what they deserve. Nonsmokers get cancer, and people who religiously count grams of fat have heart problems. Simone de Beauvoir understood this when she wrote, "The years do not weigh with the same burden on all shoulders."

Bernice Neugarten at the University of Chicago made a distinction between the young-old and the old-old. She considered the loss of a spouse, retirement, and also changes in physical health to be the critical determinants of young-old versus old-old age. My own belief is that loss of health is what delineates the two stages of old age. Until people lose their health, they are in the young-old category. Until people are ill, many keep their old routines and add some new pleasurable ones. Even if they lose their spouses they still can enjoy friends and family. Retired people travel, do volunteer work, pursue creative activities, and play cards or golf. However, poor health changes everything.

In America, the young-old are mostly in their sixties and seventies. When health falls apart, generally in the mid-seventies or later, the young-old move into the old-old stage. Susan Sontag described the difference between the two stages of old age this way: "Everyone who is born holds dual citizenship, in the kingdom of the well and in the kingdom of the sick."

Recently I told a clerk at my grocery store that I was writing a book on old people. She said rather adamantly that I should interview her. Helen looked about sixty and very vigorous. I answered, rather too glibly, that she wasn't really old, that I was mostly interviewing old-old people, people who were sick and coping with loss. She said, "Last month I would have called myself young, but I have ovarian cancer and today I am old."

For this book I interviewed both the young-old and the old-old. It was particularly striking to me that most people enjoy being young-old. They take pleasure in many things, including grandchildren and opportunities to study and develop new skills. The young-old have time to read, play cards, care for their pets, and visit their friends. My friend Sally practices her violin an hour a day. When Aunt Betty was young-old, she walked four miles each morning and traveled with her church group to China.

Many young-old savor the ordinary. As the poet Issa wrote, "Fiftieth birthday, From now on, it's all clear profit, every sky." As people grow older, time, not money, becomes the precious commodity. They are appreciative. Bert and Nan are an example of a young-old couple.

## BERT AND NAN *(ages 67 and 65)*
*"We're having so much fun,*
*we should be illegal."*

FOR EVERY JOKE about old geezers traveling the country in Winnebagos, there is an actual old couple happily traveling the country in a Winnebago. Nan and Bert are in their late sixties and have been on the road for four years. Since his father's death when Bert was twelve years old, Bert had been the man of the family, supporting first his mother and sisters and later Nan and his own kids. Bert worked long hours at his corner grocery store in Detroit. However, in the last few years, the lifting was hard on Bert's back and he worried about robberies.

When Bert turned sixty-five, he sold the store to his youngest daughter and her husband. He had good health, a modest savings account, and enough money to pay cash for a Winnebago. Nan sewed curtains, and Bert built extra cabinets. They pored over maps and guides to national parks, Bert took fly-fishing lessons, and Nan bought a book on low-fat cabin cooking.

On May Day of Bert's sixty-sixth year, they headed south from Detroit. They camped in state and national parks and KOA campgrounds, and they visited relatives, old friends, and historic sites. That summer they toured Gettysburg; Washington, DC; and Fort Sumter. They fished in Kentucky and walked through Mammoth Cave with hundreds of other tourists. They followed what used to be Route 66 across the Southwest. Nan read novels and bought a small turquoise ring. Bert caught a trout while fly-fishing near Mesa Verde.

In July, they swung north along the California coast. In Big Sur, they watched the sun set over the Pacific and ate cracked crab. In San Francisco, they rode the cable cars and ate pork fried rice at Sam Wo's. They saw whales and seals, redwoods and waterfalls. Nan wrote home, "We're having so much fun, we should be illegal."

In August, camping on the Oregon coast, they met Belle and Stewart. Stewart had been a produce wholesaler all his life. The couples traveled in tandem from one KOA campground to another. Every night they had a potluck dinner followed by a horseshoes tournament.

In September, Belle and Stewart headed south toward their trailer in Florida. Nan and Bert crossed Idaho and Montana. They saw the leaves turn gold in Glacier, and they were on a North Dakota prairie for the first frost. They pulled into Detroit on September 28, just in time for their oldest grandson's birthday party.

At the party, they showed their kids pictures of their trip and of Belle and Stewart, whom they planned to visit in February. They announced they'd had the best summer of their lives. Next year they would leave in April, but they promised to make it home by Thanksgiving. "Thanksgiving," their kids said in unison and dismay. Bert joked, "If I'd known it would be this fun, I would have robbed a bank and retired earlier."

THE OLD-OLD ARE less sanguine. They walk a road filled with potholes of pain, low energy, poor appetite, and inadequate sleep. They lead lives filled with the loss of friends and family, of habits and pleasures, and of autonomy. One of the cruel ironies of old-old age is that often when people suffer losses they must search for new friends and new homes. It's a horrible time to try to "solve problems with a geographical." Yet moves cannot be avoided.

For our elders, many questions arise. Which relatives should they settle by? Should they stay where they are and watch friends move away, or should they be the ones who go? What can they really afford? Will they be a bother or a help to children? Is it better to escape Northern winters and be far from grandchildren, or vice versa? Their search for a home is made more frightening by our deep cultural mistrust of institutions for the aged.

Many people feel they would rather die than be in a rest home. And yet at a certain age, many people need assisted living.

Families have a primal need to be together physically, a need that is now often unmet. I think of Regina, who lives five states away from her mother, who is ill in an assisted-living unit. Regina would like to care for her mother, to bring her flowers and read to her, but she has a full-time job and financial worries. I think of Francine, the head of an independent school in California, a warm-hearted woman whose mother has suffered a series of small strokes. Francine goes to visit her mother every weekend, buys her groceries, cleans her apartment, and refills her prescriptions. Her mother lives in Colorado.

Adult children want to welcome their parents to their communities and even into their homes, but they worry the parents will be unhappy. They may live in homes or neighborhoods not conducive to the needs of elderly people, and they may have children who require all the energy they have. They may work full-time and be unsure how to manage care during the day.

Adult children worry about family tension. Maybe their relationships with parents have worked because of distance. What will happen when there is no distance? Perhaps the family has never been close. What will happen with enforced closeness? And yet, no one wants a three-hour commute or a transcontinental plane trip between them and a needy parent.

Dreams turn into nightmares. A mother moves across the country to be near her daughter, who then is transferred to a job five states away. A couple moves into a retirement community by a golf course, and three weeks later the husband dies. The wife is stranded a thousand miles from home in an expensive apartment near the seventh hole. A daughter welcomes her mother into her home, only to have her mother begin ruining her life. The mother constantly picks on the daughter's son and never allows the daughter a moment to herself. The mother has no friends and is upset when the daughter wants to spend time with anyone else. When the daughter tries to assert herself, her mother goes on a hunger strike.

One of the biggest problems is that the situations that work for people in the young-old stage are not feasible for the old-old. Young-old people may love their mountain cabin or Manhattan townhouse, but old-old people need relatives nearby. Usually it's a crisis that moves a person from the kingdom of the well to the kingdom of the sick. A spouse dies, a wife gets cancer, or a husband goes blind. That's a terrible time to make major life changes. And yet, not to make changes is even harder.

There are rarely simple choices. It's good to move slowly, to think, and to talk things through. It's good to have a test period or trial run before making long-term decisions. I encourage older people to rent before buying and to live a month with a roommate before making a long-term commitment.

My bias is that luxurious surroundings, entertainment options, natural beauty, and good weather are less important than people. As songwriter Greg Brown said, "You can't have a cup of coffee with the landscape." At bottom, I think the search for the right place is a search for the right people. It's a search for love and respect. What's important is a community of friends and family.

## RANDY AND LOIS  *(ages 58 and 86)*
*"I found out how strong and*
*interesting my mother is."*

THE EXPERIENCES OF RANDY and his mother demonstrate the complexities of these American dependency issues. Randy's father died when his mother was in her early sixties. Lois had been a stay-at-home mother who never learned to drive or cash a check. Initially, of course, Lois was overwhelmed by her grief and by her own inadequacies. Randy suggested that she move to his town so that he could help her with finances, transportation, and social life. At the time, Randy had three teenagers and a struggling business, and this was no small offer. However, to his surprise, his mother refused his offer. After a few months of floundering, she rose to the occasion. She took driving lessons, joined an exercise club and a craft guild. After about a year, she sold her house in Cleveland and moved to a condo in Florida.

Randy was surprised but pleased by his mother's independence. He heartily approved her decisions even though Florida was 1,500 miles away from him. A small part of him was even relieved. He had worried that his mother wouldn't be happy with the level of emotional and social support he could offer her had she moved to his town.

This new arrangement worked well for almost twenty years, the years of his mother's young-old age. Lois never remarried. She told Randy that when a man wants a wife her age, it's for a nurse or a purse, and she wasn't willing to offer either. In fact, she did have money, which she now managed very well. She could afford to travel and buy a beachfront condo. She and her women friends formed the "Golden Girls" club and watched that show together every afternoon. For the first time in her life, Lois was a competent, autonomous adult. And Randy was happy with a financially independent, socially active, faraway mother.

Then old-old age caught up with Lois. She had a variety of chronic problems: a thyroid disorder, diabetes, and asthma. In the winter she caught pneumonia and was hospitalized. Her health-care program didn't allow her regular doctor to see her in the hospital. Instead she was assigned a new physician, who was very overworked and had little time to get acquainted. The new doctor changed her medications, and Lois became woozy and incoherent. At first Randy tried to deal with these issues over the phone, but Lois's health and mental status deteriorated rapidly. The new doctor hadn't contacted Lois's regular physician. Lois didn't know where she was, and in fact, no one in the hospital really knew who she was. Randy flew down.

When he saw his mother he was shocked. She looked ten years older and wasn't even sure what year it was or what state they were in. Randy insisted that the new doctor call the original physician and review the medications. After that the hospital doctor discovered that Lois hadn't been confused a month ago. Her original doctor recommended she return to the pre-pneumonia medications, and as soon as she did, Lois became mentally clear again.

Randy was gratified but angry. He said, "If I hadn't been there to push, Mother could have been put in an Alzheimer's unit for the rest of her life and been pumped full of the very drugs that were confusing her."

Randy stayed almost a week. Lois was ready to leave the hospital but not ready to go home. All the assisted-care facilities in the area were full. The family had choices to make. Should Lois stay alone in Florida in a new facility until she returned to her condo? Both Lois and Randy doubted she would ever regain her former level of health. Should she move in with Randy and his wife? They had finally gotten all their children launched and were busy with various projects themselves. Randy didn't really want his mother to move in with them, but he felt guilty. His mother had taken her parents in when they were old. He was the first generation to say no. Well, he wasn't exactly saying no, but his mother could read his mind.

Lois also hated to burden Randy and his wife. She was proud of her life in Florida. She liked the weather and her Golden Girl friends, although many of them had died or moved into assisted-living situations. Yet she felt vulnerable. Until Randy flew down, she'd been out of her head, with no one to represent her. Being confused, ill, and surrounded by strangers had been the worst experience of her life. Lois could safely predict that she would get ill again. Her medical care wasn't consistent, and her health seemed broken. She was afraid to move into a new facility, especially one that wasn't on the recommended list.

In the end, Lois moved to Randy's town—not into his home, but into an assisted-living facility nearby. The move was stressful for both financial and medical reasons, but now it was better. Randy and his wife still traveled and had their projects, but when they were in town, they dropped in to see Lois every day. Randy supervised her medical care and her money. Occasionally it was inconvenient for him, but feeling overburdened was better than feeling guilty and stressed about inadequately caring for a faraway mother.

Randy was surprised by how much he enjoyed his visits with Lois. He told me, "I found out how strong and interesting my mother is." They talked about old times, and Randy realized that she was the only person who remembered his kindergarten teacher and Little League coach, his sixth-grade girlfriend, and his fondness for grilled peanut butter sandwiches. Lois could tell him if his father was good at basketball or allergic to eggs, and she could laugh with him about his grandparents' idiosyncrasies. Suddenly this all seemed interesting and important. Lois missed the ocean and her remaining friends, but she was grateful to have someone looking out for her. Her favorite moment of any day was when Randy walked into her room.

This family made a difficult set of decisions in the absence of optimal resources or good information. The decisions about moving were complicated enough under ideal conditions. But in our culture, we don't even have the language to talk about the interpersonal problems old-old age brings us. Of course, an ill eighty-six-year-old was dependent. She needed someone to check in on her, monitor her health if she was hospitalized, and pay her bills if she could not. However, Lois was fearful of interfering with Randy's life. And Randy was reluctant to ask his wife to make sacrifices and unsure he could keep commitments to his mother. They danced around the issues, respecting each other's autonomy so much that Lois was almost abandoned half a continent away from anyone who loved her.

Lois and Randy's dilemmas are far too typical. Our lack of facilities that truly work for the old puts us in difficult binds. The choices for people who are in the young-old stage may not be the best for people in the old-old stage. Many young-old people prefer to rely mainly on friends for social support and plan lives of activity and autonomy, perhaps far from family. Old-old people often need family nearby. Yet few people have the resources and energy to make new plans when they are ill and in their nineties.

Few of us younger people realize how important relationships with our elders can be. We are educated to segregate. When I began this book, I held the same culturally-induced prejudices about the old as do many Americans my age and younger. For example, I noticed when an old person drove poorly or slowed down traffic, while I didn't necessarily notice all the ones who drove well. I noticed when old people repeated themselves; however, when I repeated myself, I ignored it. Spending time with old people disabused me of my prejudices.

In the last few months, I've felt nurtured and cheered, and I've laughed more with the old than with my younger friends. I've heard lots of corny jokes, but some good ones, too. Aunt Henrietta told me, "By the time people have money to burn, the fire has gone out." One man, celebrating his fiftieth wedding anniversary, told the secret of his marital success. He woke up every morning, looked in the mirror, and said, "You're no prize either."

The women always offered food and tea or coffee. Many were good talkers. They came from a time when conversational skills were highly valued. Sometimes the beauty of their spirits took my breath away. Many had what Hemingway referred to as "built-in, foolproof bullshit detectors." Furthermore, they generally had their priorities in order, and after I was with them, mine were rearranged in more sensible ways as well.

While I enjoyed the interviews, I saw lots of suffering. I saw people waiting in rest homes for calls that didn't arrive and for birthday visits that didn't happen. I met people who weren't served well by their doctors or caregivers. I saw people facing surgery alone, eating institutional food on Thanksgiving, or weeping because they wanted to take a ride on a spring day and see some flowers. I saw old people scrambling to touch a baby, to get near a child, any child.

Some of it was inevitable, but much of the suffering could have been avoided. Younger relatives had lives that kept them away. Misunderstandings made get-togethers unpleasant. For example, when Marie stopped being able to cook Sunday dinners, her children stopped coming by. She didn't feel right asking them to come over when she couldn't feed them. The children knew of Marie's "forced retirement" from the kitchen, and they didn't want to stress her by coming over when she shouldn't be cooking. No one quite knew how to make new plans, so a year went by with lit-tle contact and many hurt feelings. One family-therapy session sorted things out. The family decided to take turns ordering takeout food on Sun-days. As Marie put it proudly, "The most important thing is we are together."

For every sad old person I know, I also know several happy ones who take great joy in their relationships with their families and young friends. I think of my uncle teaching his great-grandchildren to build birdhouses. I think of my neighbor who makes it a point to talk to young children as she gardens. She keeps a jar of cookies filled for anybody in the neighborhood who needs a chocolate chip cookie right away.

I think of a client whose granddaughter was blind. She helped Marissa learn braille and read to her for hours a week when she was young. She took a part-time job so that she could earn money for special camps for Marissa. My client went along on family vacations with Marissa and her mother, and she walked Marissa home from school every day. In Marissa's high school graduation speech, she thanked her grandmother for helping her grow up strong and confident. "I wasn't lucky to be born blind," Marissa said. "But I was lucky to be born with a grandmother."

I think of my client Linda, who takes her mother to Hawaii every Feb-ruary and who drives fifty miles on Sundays to spend the day with her. Linda is an attorney whose mother is her only family. She laughs when she tells me that her mother is always trying to fix her up. Whenever Linda drives her mother to a new doctor, the mother asks if he is married. If he says no, she winks at Linda.

Being with the old, I've learned things about survival. I've come away feeling calmer, more accepting, and more grateful. I don't know if I'll be able to be as courageous and kind as many of the people I have met, but at least I'll have had good role models. I have pictures in my head of courage and dignity under tremendous adversity.

While I was writing this book, people called and wrote me about incredible people in their families, on their blocks, or in their churches.

Many didn't seem to realize that great old people are everywhere. They thought their particular experiences were unique. From these people, I learned that many of us have been saved by an old person, but these stories are rarely told. In our cultural script, heroes are young, attractive, and far away.

Fortunately many of us find our way to the old. I had an acquaintance, Maeve, who was an artist always seeking truth far from home in ashrams and workshops. Just as Maeve was leaving for Europe one summer, her grandmother became ill. The family asked Maeve to care for the grandmother. She protested, but there was no one else and the need was undeniable. Maeve moved to Kansas and lived with her grandmother for six months, until her grandmother died. Maeve handled her grandmother's medical needs, cooked for her, and bathed her. For the first time in Maeve's life, her concern for another person became as great as her concern for herself. This experience changed her life more than all the therapy and gurus had. She grew up and learned to love other people.

We can learn a great deal from the old. They can teach us about the importance of time, relationships, and gratitude. They can teach us how to endure and how to be patient. They can help us put our own pains and problems in perspective. I have a *New Yorker* cartoon entitled "Yuppie Angst." The man is saying, "Oh no, I spilled cappuccino on my down jacket." Old people who have lived through the Depression, the blizzards, the wars, and the deaths of friends and family have a somewhat broader perspective on tragedy.

Freud taught our generation the importance of parental love. We know that parental love is formative, but no one has taught us about the importance of grandparental love. Especially as we get older, the bonding and nurturing go both ways. Connections help our children, our parents, and us, now and in the future. Only by caring for our parents will we be able to ask our children for help later. And only because of our children's love of the old will they be able to say yes.

# CHAPTER 2

# Xenophobia: Our Fears Divide Us

*Few of them made it to thirty.*
*Old age was the privilege of rocks and trees.*
*Childhood ended as fast as wolf cubs grow.*
*One had to hurry, to get on with life*
*before the sun went down,*
*before the first snow.*

—WISLAWA SZYMBORSKA,
"Our Ancestors' Short Lives"

WE SEGREGATE THE OLD FOR MANY REASONS—PREJUDICE, ignorance, a lack of good alternatives, and a youth-worshiping culture without guidelines on how to care for the old. The old are different from us, and that makes us nervous. Xenophobia means fear of people from another country. In America we are xenophobic toward our old people.

An anthropologist could learn about us by examining our greeting cards. As with all aspects of popular culture, greeting cards both mirror and shape our realities. Cards reflect what we feel about people in different roles, and they also teach us what to feel. I visited my favorite local drugstore and took a look.

There are really two sets of cards that relate to aging. One is the grandparent/grandchild set that is all about connection. Even a very dim-witted anthropologist would sense the love and respect that exist between these two generations in our culture. Young children's cards to their grandparents say, "I wish I could hop on your lap," or, "You're so much fun." Grandparents' cards to children are filled with pride and love.

There is another section of cards on birthdays. These compare human aging to wine aging, or point out compensations. "With age comes wisdom, of course that doesn't make up for what you lose." We joke the most about that which makes us anxious. "Have you picked out your bench at the mall yet?" There are jokes about hearing loss, incontinence, and losing sexual abilities and interest. There are cards on saggy behinds, gray hair, and wrinkles, and cards about preferring chocolate or sleep to sex. "You know you're getting old when someone asks if you're getting enough and you think about sleep."

Poking fun at aging isn't all bad. It's better to laugh than to cry, especially at what cannot be prevented. However, these jokes reflect our fears about aging in a youth-oriented culture. We younger, healthier people sometimes avoid the old to avoid our own fears of aging. If we aren't around dying people, we don't have to think about dying.

We baby boomers have been a futureless generation, raised in the eternal present of TV and advertising. We have allowed ourselves to be persuaded by ads that teach that if we take good care of ourselves, we will stay healthy. Sick people, hospitals, and funerals destroy our illusions of invulnerability. They force us to think of the future.

Carolyn Heilbrun said, "It is only past the meridian of fifty that one can believe that the universal sentence of death applies to oneself." Before that time, if we are healthy, we are likely to be in deep denial about death, to feel as if we have plenty of time, that we have an endless vista ahead. But in hospitals and at funerals, we remember that we all will die in the last act. And we don't necessarily appreciate being reminded.

When I first visited rest homes, I had to force myself to stay. What made me most upset was the thought of myself in a place like that. I didn't want to go there, literally or figuratively. Recently I sat in an eye doctor's office surrounded by old people with white canes. Being in this room gave me intimations of mortality. I thought of Bob Dylan's line: "It's not dark yet, but it's getting there."

We know the old-old will die soon. The more we care and the more involved we are with the old, the more pain we feel at their suffering. Death is easier to bear in the abstract, far away and clinical. It's much harder to watch someone we love fade before our eyes. It's hard to visit an uncle in a rest home and realize he no longer knows who we are or even who he is. It's hard to see a grandmother in pain or drugged up on morphine. Sometimes it's so hard that we stay away from the people who need us the most.

Our culture reinforces our individual fears. To call something old is to insult, as in *old hat* or *old ideas*. To call something young is to compliment, as in *young thinking* or *young acting*. It's considered rude even to ask an old person's age. When we meet an adult we haven't seen in a long time, we compliment her by saying, "You haven't aged at all." The taboos against acknowledging age tell us that aging is shameful.

Many of the people I interviewed were uncomfortable talking about age and were unhappy to be labeled old. They said, "I don't feel old." What they meant was,"I don't act and feel like the person who the stereotypes suggest I am." Also, they were trying to avoid being put in a socially undesirable class. In this country, it is unpleasant to be called old, just as it is unpleasant to be called fat or poor. The old naturally try to avoid being identified with an unappreciated group.

IN *THE COMING OF AGE*, Simone de Beauvoir wrote about France in the 1600s, when the average life span was twenty to twenty-five. Exhausting labor, bad hygiene, and undernourishment led to early deaths. Those who did survive longer often gave their homes to their children. Similarly, in Ireland the old were moved into a room called the "western chamber," and the adult children took over the house.

De Beauvoir found a wide range of cultural responses to grandparents. In some subsistence cultures with harsh climates, the old were often left behind or out to die. In Greenland, the aged Amassalik killed themselves so they wouldn't be a burden. When they could no longer keep up, the old Hmong people were left with food and opium along mountain trails. But in most cultures, the feelings between children and grandparents were of great love and tenderness. Elders were considered serene, detached, and holy.

In some primitive societies, old people were valued as a source of stored knowledge. The Aleuts had great respect for their elders, who taught them to fish. The Navahos revered the old singers, who remembered all the tribal stories. The Kikuyu had sayings such as "An old person doesn't spit without a reason," and "Old people don't tell lies." De Beauvoir also found a strong relationship between the compassionate treatment of the old and the caring treatment of the young. Children who grew up well-nurtured tended to love the old.

The Okinawans have great respect for their elders. The old stay in their own homes, socialize with friends and family, and keep working a few hours a day. A ninety-year-old woman still sells fish. Friends will buy a little from her so that she has a useful routine. An eighty-year-old housekeeper will stop over to make sweet potato pancakes and sweep the steps. Many people live to be more than a hundred and stay in remarkably good health. The average age of death for women is eighty-four. Among people who stay on the island, there is little cancer, diabetes, osteoporosis, or stroke, but if Okinawans move away, they have the same mortality rates as others.

Joe Starita, author of *The Dull Knifes of Pine Ridge*, talked about the differences between the way most Americans view the elderly and the way the Lakota view their elders. "For starters," he said, "there is a tremendous difference in the words elderly and elder." The Lakota believe that if the old do not stay connected to the young, the culture will disintegrate. Older people tell stories that teach lessons and keep the culture alive. Because wisdom is highly valued among the Lakota, the older people are, the more they are loved. Older equals wiser equals more respected.

One Sunday afternoon Starita visited Royal Bull Bear on the Pine Ridge reservation. They were sitting at his kitchen table drinking coffee when two pickups pulled into his drive. His three daughters jumped out of one truck with bags of groceries. They greeted their father casually and then got to work. Two of them cleaned his house from top to bottom. They changed his bed linens, swept, and washed floors and windows. The other made him a pot of soup and sandwiches for the next week. Meanwhile the boys from the other pickup mowed his yard, picked up his trash, and changed the oil in his truck. Then they all hugged and kissed him good-bye and drove off. Royal Bull Bear said that this happens every Sunday. It is their duty to care for him.

Starita marveled that in such a "poor" society there is so much generosity of time and money toward the elders. There is a richness of caring among the Lakota that he found missing in most of America. I thought of Mother Teresa's remarks about America being one of the poorest cultures in the world. She had noticed a spiritual poverty here, a lack of connection and meaning.

Sonja is a casualty of our lack of meaning and connection. She needs so little to be happy. And yet that little, a window, a chance to smell the earth after a rain, and time with family and friends, is denied her. Neither her family nor the institution in which she lives is giving her what she most needs. Her story illustrates how small changes could make a big difference in a life.

## SONJA (*age 93*)
*"Who wouldn't be depressed,*
*living with adults who wear diapers or*
*who discuss cremation at the dinner table?"*

WHEN I VISITED Sonja at Shady Home on a misty spring morning, just a few flowers were popping out. The magnolia trees, forsythia, hyacinths, and jonquils gave color to a gray day. Shady Home made a good first impression: It was clean, the staff seemed friendly, and the residents didn't seem over-medicated. Sonja's small space was arranged with an Easter lily, a stuffed cat, and a radio. On her bedside table she had several copies of *Awake* and *The New World Translation of the Holy Scriptures*. Her bed was farthest from the window in a two-person room, and the shades were drawn.

Sonja wore pink nylon slacks and a white sweatshirt that said, "Over the hill? What hill? I don't remember any hill." She was petite, with enormous eyes, and at ninety-three, except for her broken hip, she was in excellent health. She said, "When you get this old you have bad days, good days, and days you'd rather not be alive. But today is a good day."

I rolled her wheelchair into a bright room with big windows looking out onto the parking lot. She explained that she couldn't get to this room by herself and she hated to trouble the staff. She told me that her roommate insisted on keeping the shades closed in their bedroom. All the time we talked, Sonja never stopped hungrily looking outside at the parking lot.

She had moved to Shady Home a year before, when she had broken her hip. Her son, who found this place, came once a week, and her grandchildren dropped in when they could. "They are all busy," Sonja said. "They have their jobs and their own families to take care of." When a friend encouraged her to become a Jehovah's Witness, Sonja did, "just for the social life."

Sonja grew up on a ranch along the Dismal River in the Nebraska Sandhills. She rode a pony to country school. She was the baby of the family, with three older brothers. She grinned and said, "Now don't you guess I was spoiled?" As a young adult, Sonja taught at country schools. She knew all the children in her county. Sonja told me about the sledding and ice-skating, barn dances and threshing parties. She never got tired of looking at the big Nebraska sky.

In 1924, Sonja married Jules, who was from a neighboring Swedish family. Jules had a wonderful disposition and was a good provider. While Sonja managed the kids, the house, the animals, and the garden, Jules built roads. She said, "We made our own fun. My youngsters were easy to get along with because they had a good father."

After Jules died, Sonja never remarried. She laughed and said, "No one else would have suited me after Jules." She stayed in the Sandhills and enjoyed her farm, her family, and her church. She raised one grandson, the son of her daughter, who drank and who "didn't know siccum about raising kids." She sold her last horse when she was in her eighties, and she put in her last garden the summer she broke her hip.

While we talked, Sonja saw a dog outside. She laughed at its hurry. Later she noticed an airplane and clapped her hands with excitement. Sonja had hated to leave the farm, and she missed being outdoors. When she asked her son to take her out of Shady Home for a car ride, he replied, "Wait until it's warmer." She told me, "It's pretty warm already."

She was upset that her roommate kept the shade down, but said, "Leaving the farm was for the best. I couldn't manage things anymore."

Of the rest home she spoke honestly but calmly. She asked, "Who wouldn't be depressed, living with adults who wear diapers or who discuss cremation at the dinner table?" She sighed. "As Bette Davis said, old age isn't for sissies."

She told me that many residents got the flu around the holidays and she believed it was loneliness, not germs, that troubled them. She also told me that many of the old made up excuses about why their children didn't visit them, and they pretended to believe one another to save face.

She said, "I overlook quite a few things. If I don't get along with some-one, I leave them alone. I don't dwell on the negative."

As I listened to her, I wondered how I would cope with all this sadness on a daily basis. I admired the restraint and dignity with which she expressed her feelings. As I said good-bye to Sonja, I thought about all she had lost. She loved her big family and the great landscapes of the Sandhills, walking under the stars and breathing the aroma of tall-grass prairie mead-ows. Now she was alone and confined to a wheelchair in a small room.

Shady Home's first impression belied a real lack of attention to detail, such as windows for people who love the natural world. Sonja didn't have her home, her friends, her work, or her pleasures. She couldn't even control the shades in her bedroom. Yet Sonja remained good-natured and kind. As I wheeled her back to her room, she noticed a plum tree blooming. She clapped her hands again and said, "Oh, isn't it beautiful?"

I wanted to take her out to smell its blossoms, but I had appointments to keep. I made a note to call the home about pet therapy and perhaps a room change. I vowed I would return and take Sonja for a drive in the country.

RIGHT NOW, in the absence of better places and more social supports, nursing homes are what we have for the old-old. They are difficult institu-tions to administer, with hundreds of feeble people who have individual-ized treatment plans that require coverage twenty-four hours a day, seven days a week. Usually there isn't money to hire skilled workers or as many workers as are truly needed. Furthermore, some visitors demonstrate their love for their family members by criticizing everything the rest homes do. As a friend said, "We don't even have a love/hate attitude toward rest homes, we have a hate/hate attitude."

Many people feel guilty and defensive when they put a parent into a home, especially if the parent doesn't want to go, and almost no one does. Of course, people are reluctant to go to hospitals, too, but at least hospitals allow people to return home and they can regularly redeem themselves by saving lives. Rest homes have no such victories. The old go there in desperation, and they stay until they die. The staff's reward for years of good work with a resident is a funeral.

Rest homes are the concrete embodiment of failed social and cultural policies toward the old. What is amazing is that some rest homes manage to function reasonably well under these rough conditions. There are many heroes in rest homes, among the patients and the staffs. Some homes are even evolving into better institutions. This is good, for we desperately need better places for our aging population.

WHEN WE THINK of the old, most of us picture our grandparents. I see my grandmother in her flowered apron, and my grandfather in overalls and a felt hat. But old people today don't much resemble the grandparents of the 1950s. The young-old travel, program computers, study at Elderhostels, and take scuba lessons, or at least they do until they join the ranks of the old-old. Because of economic and demographic changes, as well as technological changes in health care, the old-old have existential decisions to make that our grandparents never had to face.

We know less about the aged than we think we do. There is a lack of good information about the developmental, psychological, social, and spiritual needs of the old. We can empathize with children because we have been young. We remember some of what happened and how it felt. However, we haven't had experiences that allow us to understand the old.

In general there is a tendency to pretend the old are more like us than they really are. We underestimate the differences between adults and children, and we ignore differences in the characters and points of view of our elders. The old-old especially face very different physical, social, and psychological problems than do the rest of us.

Most of us love particular old people, and we want to do the right things for them. But we often don't understand what the right things are. For example, we are encouraged to buy things for the old, but what most older people want is our time. Gifts of attention are much prized. One of my neighbors recently had her eightieth birthday, and I wondered what to buy her. She lives in a small apartment and already has too much stuff. She can't see to read and can't eat candy or most food treats. Finally I decided simply to buy her a few flowers and deliver them. She liked the flowers, but afterward I realized what she liked most was the chance to show me her apartment and have a cup of tea.

My friend Karen travels across our state every Mother's Day to plant a garden for her mother. Louis's mother had a tracheotomy and can no longer talk. He taught her to use e-mail to stay connected to family. Chris attends a university a few blocks from his grandmother's home. He lives with her and does her errands and yard work. She fixes him meals and helps him with his German, which is her native language.

The old also want our honesty. When my client Carmen got a divorce, she tried to protect her grandmother from the news. Grannie was ill in a rest home and, in Carmen's opinion, she didn't need any bad news. Week after week, Carmen chatted away about cooking and window treatments while Grannie watched her closely and said little. Carmen thought she was being kind, but Grannie felt excluded, confused, and frightened. After six weeks, Grannie blurted out her questions: "What's wrong? You're losing weight, and your fingernails are chewed to the bone. Have you stopped trusting me? Do I have cancer? Do you have cancer? Did your husband die?" Carmen realized that she'd been protecting Grannie from honesty, a chance to help, and a genuine relationship—things all sane people want to experience.

Because food and love are so closely associated for our parents' generation, gifts of food can be powerful. Stopping by with a pecan pie or a pot of homemade soup is appreciated as an act of love. People who are in institutions or hospitals particularly welcome the tastes and smells of the real world. Once when my mother-in-law had been hospitalized for several days, I stopped at a Chinese restaurant and bought her a carton of hot and sour soup. I carried it to her hospital room, and that spicy aroma from the outside world revived her. Her spirits and her health improved.

Nothing in our culture guides us in a positive way toward the old. Our media, music, and advertising industries all glorify the young. Stereotypes suggest that older people keep younger people from fun, work, and excitement. They take·time (valuable time) and patience (in very short supply in the 1990s). We are very body-oriented, and old bodies fail. We are appearance-oriented, and youthful attractiveness fades. We are not taught that old spirits often shimmer with beauty.

Language is a problem. Old people are referred to in pejorative terms, such as *biddy, codger,* or *geezer,* or with cutesy words, such as *oldster, chronologically challenged,* or *senior citizen.* People describe themselves as "eighty years young." Even *retirement* is an ugly word that implies passivity, uselessness, and withdrawal from the social and working world. Many of the old are offended by ageist stereotypes and jokes. Some internalize these beliefs and feel badly about themselves. They stay with their own kind in order to avoid the harsh appraisals of the young.

Some people do not have good manners with the old. I've seen the elderly bossed around, treated like children or simpletons, and simply ignored. Once in a cafe, I heard a woman order her mother to take a pill and saw the mother wince in embarrassment. My mother-in-law says she sees young people but they don't see her. Her age makes her invisible.

In our culture the old are held to an odd standard. They are admired for not being a bother, for being chronically cheerful. They are expected to be interested in others, bland in their opinions, optimistic, and emotionally generous. But the young certainly don't hold themselves to these standards.

Accidents that old drivers have are blamed on age. After a ninety-year-old friend had his first car accident, he was terrified that he would lose his license. "If I were young, this accident would be perceived as just one of those things," he pointed out. "But because I am old, it will be attributed to my age." Now, of course, some old people are bad drivers. But so are some young people. To say "He did that because he's old" is often as narrow as to say, "He did that because he's black" or "Japanese." Young people burn countertops with hot pans, forget appointments, and write overdrafts on their checking accounts. But when the old do these same things, they experience double jeopardy. Their mistakes are not viewed as accidents but rather as loss of functioning. Such mistakes have implications for their freedom.

As in so many other areas, the media hurts rather than helps with our social misunderstandings. George Gerbner reported on the curious absence of media images of people older than sixty-five. Every once in a while a romantic movie plot might involve an older man, but almost never an older woman. In general, the old have been cast as silly, stubborn, and eccentric. He also found that on children's programs, older women bear a disproportionate burden of negative characteristics. In our culture, the old get lumped together into a few stereotyped images: the sweet old lady, the lecherous old man, or the irascible but soft-hearted grandfather. Almost no ads and billboards feature the old. Every now and then an ad will show a grandparent figure, but then the grandparent is invariably youthful and healthy.

In *Fountain of Age*, Betty Friedan noted that the old are portrayed as sexless, demented, incontinent, toothless, and childish. Old women are portrayed as sentimental, naive, and silly gossips, and as troublemakers. A common movie plot is the portrayal of the old trying to be young—showing them on motorbikes, talking hip or dirty, or liking rock and roll. Of course there are exceptions, such as *Nobody's Fool, On Golden Pond, Mr. and Mrs. Bridge, Driving Miss Daisy, Mrs. Brown*, and *Twilight*. But we need more movies in which old people are portrayed in all their diversity and complexity.

The media is only part of much larger cultural problems. We aren't organized to accommodate this developmental stage. For example, being old-old costs a lot of money. Assisted-living housing, medical care, and all the other services the old need are expensive. And yet, most old people can't earn money. It's true that some of our elders are wealthy, but many live on small incomes. Visiting the old, I heard tragic stories involving money. I met Arlene, who, while dying of cancer, had to fear losing her house because of high property taxes. I met Shirley, who lived on noodles and white rice so that she could buy food for her cat and small gifts for her grandchildren. I met people who had to choose between pills and food or heat.

Another thing that makes old age a difficult stage to navigate is our American belief that adults need no one. We think of independence as the ideal state for adults. We associate independence with heroes and cultural icons such as the Marlboro man and the Virginia Slims woman, and we associate dependence with toxic families, enmeshment, and weakness. To our postmodern, educated ears, the concept of a psychologically healthy but dependent adult sounds oxymoronic.

We all learn when we are very young to make our own personal declarations of independence. In our culture, *adult* means "self-sufficent." Autonomy is our highest virtue. We want relationships that have no strings attached instead of understanding, as one lady told me, "Honey, life ain't nothing but strings."

These American ideas about independence hurt families with teens. Just when children most need guidance from parents, they turn away from them and toward peers and media. They are socialized to believe that to be an adult, they must break away from parents. Our ideas about independence also hurt families with aging relatives. As people move from the young-old stage into the old-old stage, they need more help. Yet in our culture we provide almost no graceful ways for adults to ask for help. We make it almost impossible to be dependent yet dignified, respected, and in control.

As people age, they may need help with everything from their finances to their driving. They may need help getting out of bed, feeding themselves, and bathing. Many would rather pay strangers, do without help, or even die than be dependent on those they love. They don't want to be a burden, the greatest of American crimes. The old-old often feel ashamed of what is a natural stage of the life cycle. In fact, the greatest challenge for many elders is learning to accept vulnerability and to ask for help.

If we view life as a time line, we realize that all of us are sometimes more and sometimes less dependent on others. At certain stages we are caretakers, and at other stages we are cared for. Neither stage is superior to the other. Neither implies pathology or weakness. Both are just the results of life having seasons and circumstances. In fact, good mental health is not a matter of being dependent or independent, but of being able to accept the stage one is in with grace and dignity. It's an awareness of being, over the course of one's lifetime, continually interdependent.

In our culture the old fear their deaths will go badly, slowly, and painfully, and will cost lots of money. Nobody wants to die alone, yet nobody wants to put their families through too much stress. Families are uneasy as they negotiate this rocky terrain. The trick for the younger members is to help without feeling trapped and overwhelmed. The trick for older members is to accept help while preserving dignity and control. Caregivers can say, "You have nurtured us, why wouldn't we want to nurture you?" The old must learn to say, "I am grateful for your help and I am still a person worthy of respect."

As our times and circumstances change, we need new language. We need the elderly to become elders. We need a word for the neediness of the old-old, a word with less negative connotations than *dependency*, a word that connotes wisdom, connection, and dignity. *Dependency* could become *mutuality* or *interdependency*. We can say to the old: "You need us now, but we needed you and we will need our children. We need each other."

However, the issues are much larger than simply which words to use or social skills to employ. We need to completely rethink our ideas about caring for the elderly. Like the Lakota, we need to see it as an honor and an opportunity to learn. It is our chance to repay our parents for the love they gave us, and it is our last chance to become grown-ups. We help them to help ourselves.

We need to make the old understand that they can be helped without being infantilized, that the help comes from respect and gratitude rather than from pity or a sense of obligation. In our society of disposables and planned obsolescence, the old are phased out. Usually they fade away graciously. They want to be kind and strong, and, in America, they learn that to do so means they should ask little of others and not bother young people.

Perhaps we need to help them redefine kindness and courage. For the old, to be kind ought to mean welcoming younger relatives' help, and to be brave ought to mean accepting the dependency that old-old age will bring. We can reassure the old that by showing their children how to cope, they will teach them and their children how well this last stage can be managed. This information is not peripheral but rather something everyone will need to know.

## Dancing

ONE WINTER EVENING my husband and I drove to the Pla Mor Ballroom on the edge of town. It was an old-fashioned place with wooden booths and a polished dance floor the size of a basketball court. Hundreds of people between sixty-five and ninety-five were dancing. Therapists joke that December is "the season for Seasonal Affective Disorder," but these people hadn't heard of SAD.

As we paid the cover charge, we were inspected for proper dress by a silver-haired lady in white slacks and a Christmas sweater. The Ron Nadherny Orchestra, dressed in matching suits, played "Night and Day." Ron, a handsome man with a mane of silver hair, announced the sets and sang lead. The musicians looked like they loved to play. Making hundreds of old people happy was noble work, and they knew it.

The ballroom was all light, color, and warmth. A silver glitter ball and gold stars hung from the ceiling. White Christmas lights surrounded the dance floor. The women wore velvet dresses with lacy cuffs, black satin sheaths, crisp pant suits, and short evening dresses of red or white chiffon. They wore perfume and makeup and, even though it was icy outside and they'd be on their feet all night, these women wore high heels.

The sets were short, three or four songs, then a break. Women left their purses on the tables, and everyone hit the dance floor for every song. This generation had danced since they were teenagers—through World War I, through the Roaring Twenties and the Crash, through the Depression and World War II. They'd danced through the births of their babies and the college graduations of those babies. Dancing was what they did to have fun. My friend Effie said, "Dancing lasts longer than sex. It's prettier, more graceful, and, unlike sex, it gets more fun as you get older."

At the break, five couples came over by us. The men gallantly escorted their wives to one table and then sat at another. A large bald man unloaded treats from home. Over the course of the evening, he handed out home-made Christmas cookies, chips and salsa, cheese, crackers, and sausages. This group did lots of laughing and not much drinking. They liked sharing food, an important ritual for their generation.

After a ten-minute break, the dancing began again with "Bewitched Bothered and Bewildered," then "Tennessee Waltz." A couple in matching white slacks and red jackets made intricate moves around the floor. They looked as if they'd been dancing together for fifty years. A skinny bow-legged cowboy danced with his short blind wife.

A tall man danced alone, hugging his body close with his frail arms. He wore pink socks and shiny black shoes. He wore heavy, too-blue wool slacks and red suspenders. His hair was badly cut. His eyes were almost shut, and he seemed oblivious to everything but the music and the pictures in his head. He held himself as if in pain, radiating loneliness and stiff with loss. He danced every dance this way all night long.

The dance floor had its share of sad stories. There was a widow out with friends for the first time since her husband's death. She called a cab and went home early. "I'm not ready," she told her friends. There was Iris, with both her legs amputated at the hips, in a chair wheeled by Henry in his faded burgundy suit coat.

Some of the recently widowed were on dates, as awkward as school-kids. Dancers had cancer or diabetes, their hearts were failing or their hearing wasn't good. But tonight they were twirling and swirling. Hospi-tal talk was banished from the dance floor. Some was whispered during breaks at the tables, but the loud talk was of children, food, parties, and snow.

Everyone liked the lively tunes best. Lyrics like "When the sun comes over the brewery, it's time to hit the hay. Sing Auld Lang Syne one more time and then we'll call it a day" really got some endorphins cranking. I watched as a May/December pair waltzed by—but May was in her sixties, and December must have been older than eighty-five, though still a suave dancer.

The couples returned to their tables and passed more treats. Waiters carried big pitchers of water to all the dehydrated dancers. Ron announced that it was Charles and Donna's forty-eighth anniversary, and everyone applauded. The ladies fanned themselves and reapplied lipsticks. The men drank beer and ate sliced sausage. People were warm and well-fed. Tonight there was laughter.

The next set began with Christmas songs, "Here Comes Santa Claus" and "I'll Have a Blue Christmas Without You." With the grace and style of Valentino, the man dressed in white slacks and a red jacket dipped and spun his wife across the floor. Then the band played "Moon River" and the place grew quieter and more somber. This song mainlined to memory, which can be a double-edged sword, the comfort and curse of old age. Memories of happy times and loved ones sustained and cheered, but they also reminded the old of friends and relatives who were dead. Wisely the band followed with the up-tempo "Woodchopper's Ball." As the old man who hugged himself fox-trotted by, Ron announced that Santa would be arriving soon.

Watching the dancers that evening, I thought that music was time. Musical styles divide a century into sections and give each generation its own turf. A song evokes a year; a year evokes a song. Memory is encoded via music. A melody can call up a summer night or a certain embrace. A drum solo can call forth a beach in Southern California or a ride across the desert on a starry July night. A classical piece creates images of children dancing in tutus. A Scott Joplin rag evokes a big man, suit coat slung aside, pounding an old piano. Lyrics from a swing tune bring back a father. The river of time that is music flows through our souls and connects us all to one another.

We left around 10:00, among the first to go. While most of the dancers could sleep in, Jim and I had to go to work early the next morning. As we walked outside, the moon was rising over Shoemaker's truck stop. Its light glittered on the snow in a way that reminded me of the glitter ball and the dance floor. We still could hear the music as we got into our car for the drive home.

# CHAPTER 3

# Time Zones: From a Communal to an Individualistic Culture

*Culture is the shape a place takes when it's inside the head of its peoples—all the habits, attitudes and values they take for granted.*

—FINTAN O'TOOLE

THIS CHAPTER BEGINS WITH TWO STORIES FROM BURT COUNTY, Nebraska, in the Missouri River Valley, north of Omaha. It has been home to my husband's family for five generations. Many Burt County people who were born in soddies or small cabins on homesteaded land are in their old-old age now, and still live among their friends of eighty years. Burt County isn't necessarily the best example of the communal culture that is disappearing, but it is the one I know. Josip Novakovitch wrote that his town was "crisscrossed not with streets but with stories." From Burt County I know eighty years' worth of stories.

I write about this place to explore a time—the early part of the century, when our parents and grandparents were young. People are well rooted in Burt County. Families are interconnected across time and place like prairie grasses. Oakland, where the Darlings live, was homesteaded mainly by Scandinavians who every year have a Swedish festival with a parade, beer garden, smorgasbord, and street dance. Many younger people bike to this festival from Lincoln on what is called the "Ya Shoor Tour."

Burt County folks like connections. Every Christmas in Lincoln, transplanted Oakland families rent a big hall, hire a band, and have a potluck dinner-dance for hundreds of people. Over Memorial Day weekend, Tekamah has a banquet at the high school for all its graduates. Every year, people from all the classes come back to see their friends and family and to visit Cemetery Hill, carrying peonies. These reunions last four days and wind up with a community picnic in the city park.

Many people from Burt County grew up in big families, with extended families nearby. They attended school, shopped, and worshiped with the same group of people. On Saturday night, Main Street was a party. As Sylvia Darling described it, "Everyone took a bath, put on their best clothes, and went downtown. The streets were clogged, and people hopped into each other's cars and wagons to talk. In the summer there was always a band concert on Main Street. Afterwards we went to the cafe or confectionery shop to talk and giggle for hours."

Simone Weil wrote, "To be rooted is perhaps the most important and least recognized need of the human soul." That need was filled in Burt County. Everybody knew your name and your story, and vice versa. Adults looked after and nurtured other people's children, and parents practiced a kind of benevolent neglect of their own kids that is not possible to practice in the 1990s. Those kinds of communities, towns where children owned the streets, have almost disappeared.

Everything we can learn about these old communities must be learned quickly, for soon we will have no one to tell us. Of course there will be records—journals, letters, biographies, and autobiographies. Music and poetry give us clues. But we won't have the voices of our family members, friends, and neighbors.

Children no longer grow up in a familiar matrix of connected people with whom their families work and play. As Alan Durning wrote, "Informal visits between neighbors and friends, family conversation and time spent at family meals have all diminished in the United States since mid-century." Many of us no longer know our neighbors or our cousins. The surface structure of our lives may look the same, but the deep structure is markedly different.

We all have been colonized by a corporate culture. Technology and media have changed us. We are immigrants who have lost our familiar foods, our rituals, our stories, and our communities. In our own land, we lead lives stripped of meaning and history. Older people can help us find a deep structure for our communities. I tell the following stories with the hope of capturing the feeling of what it was like to grow up connected to a place. They are about people who grew up in the communities of Burt County.

## JOHN AND SYLVIA *(both age 83)*
*"They had nothing*
*but a good time."*

WE MET IN the morning of a hundred-degree July day at John and Sylvia's small house in Oakland, Nebraska. When I drove up, Sylvia was waiting at the door and John came out on the porch to greet me. They both looked younger than their ages. We settled into their living room: John in a rocker, Sylvia in the recliner, and I into a deep old couch. The smell of newly mown grass wafted in through open windows. As we talked, I could hear mourning doves cooing outside.

The night before our appointment, John and Sylvia had been to a fancy cafe in Omaha with their kids. It had been their youngest son's birthday, and his wife had treated everyone to an elegant meal. John said the food was pricey and too fancy, that there were dandelions in the salad, and that he was a meat-and-potatoes man. But he and Sylvia loved being with their family.

First we talked about Sylvia's life. Her grandparents had been immigrants from Denmark. Sylvia said, "We were poor, but we made our own fun." She and her cousins played outside all the time—in the corncrib and the haystacks, at threshing parties, and, in the winter, sledding in the fields. Sylvia's father died in the influenza epidemic of 1918. Her mother moved in with her parents in Oakland and, although Sylvia's mother had never eaten in a restaurant, she found work at a cafe, cooking for the train crews.

Sylvia and her brother grew up with strict grandparents. She firmly stated that their discipline didn't hurt her a bit. She said, "Grandmother could give me a stern look that went right through me. Grandfather would take off his cap and hit us over the head. It didn't hurt, but it was a warning."

Sylvia said schools were tamer in her childhood. There wasn't much smoking or drinking, only a little mischief among the high school boys. When one couple had to get married, that created a big scandal. That couple is still married fifty-five years later. Sylvia didn't care much for academics. She preferred gymnastics and described how much she liked to twirl on a beam. She also could "play piano with her hands crossed."

However, her real love was dancing. Starting in high school, she and her friends went to the many dances around Oakland. There were swing bands everywere. She danced at the Lyons' Pavilion, a big building whose sides opened to "let in the air-conditioning." She laughed and told me, "When ballroom dancing went out, things went to hell."

John was born on Yellow Smoke Hill in Decatur. Native Americans still lived in the area, and right after John's birth, Billy Coyote came to the house and remarked that John already had his eyes open. John was the oldest of five. He had two sisters and two brothers, one of whom died of lockjaw. Early on, his father traded his land for a wheat ranch out West. The family later lost that ranch and had to return to Burt County to work as hired help.

John learned to read even before he started school. His brother was athletic, but John explained that "all my muscles were between my ears." Even though he wore overalls to high school, he emceed events and acted in the school plays. He thought rich kids were snobs and avoided them. He laughed and said, "That was pretty easy to do during the Depression. There weren't many rich kids around. Everybody was in the same boat." ·

John's parents were hard workers and good savers, but they were always poor. They had nothing extra—no car, no radio, no phone, and no newspapers. For fun, the family read library books. One winter John read fifty-five books, including all of Zane Grey. John's dad was a big philosopher, and John still quotes many of his sayings, such as, "Don't ever belittle the rich man. We live off what he spills." John's father had strong feelings of loyalty to the animals that kept the family alive. He thought the worst thing the kids could do was to abuse or neglect an animal.

John knew everyone in Oakland, which used to have three grocery stores, a dime store, and a good cafe. He noted that children now weren't as friendly; they had been taught to fear strangers. Kids now have money, cars, and cellular phones, but they aren't as well behaved as kids used to be. John felt his generation had learned good values. They learned to work and "to like whatever came up."

John and Sylvia met at a dance. John explained that his best friend was good-looking and had a car, so usually he got all the girls. Sylvia interrupted to say that she'd liked John fine, but she'd wished he were taller so that she could wear her high heels when she went out with him. John laughed and said, "You can't get rats out of mice." John recalled a time when he and his best friend picked Sylvia up, rolled up the car windows, and smoked big cigars, just to see what she would do. Remembering that day almost seventy years later, John and Sylvia cracked up.

They went to dances all over the area. In the late 1930s, great bands came to small Midwestern towns. Ben Bernie came down from Chicago, and Guy Lombardo played at Hooper. The Orpheum in Omaha had stage shows, and Lawrence Welk played at Bertha. At first, John wasn't a great dancer, but he improved and the Darlings came to be called the "Old Smoothies."

John and Sylvia dated on and off for ten years, but they didn't marry until they were twenty-nine. When John wanted to get married, Sylvia insisted he get a full-time job—no easy task during the Depression. Because of his asthma, John had to stay out of the hayfields. When he could, he worked part-time at the Fontanelle Hotel in Omaha. If he wore a white coat, they'd feed him. After a big event, he'd wash dishes all night. When he saw all the food that rich people wasted, he would get angry. He knew many people who were eating anything, just so they wouldn't starve. Some days John would show up and there would be no work, but the manager would give John a white coat to put on and say, "Go to the kitchen and get yourself a meal. No one will ask any questions." That white coat and an occasional bag of stale doughnuts kept John alive.

John and Sylvia got married in 1941, a small wedding in the house next door to the one they live in now. Shortly after, Sylvia got pregnant and John was drafted into the Army. He liked the Army all right, but he missed his family. Sylvia interrupted him to say that John could be anywhere and be happy. She thought he got it from his family. She said, "They had nothing but a good time."

After John got out of the service, they moved to Oakland. They didn't want to raise their new daughter, and later their three sons, in the city. John bought his milk route for $5,000 and worked that route for eighteen years. He was a well-known character around town. He wore a hat cocked at a jaunty angle, and on the front of his truck he hung a sign spelled backwards so that it could be read through the rearview mirror: "Here comes John."

John had a vast store of sayings, stories, and jokes from the route. He helped housewives hang curtains and turn mattresses. He fed cats and watched over houses when the owners took trips. He got up at 4:00 and took the time to visit with his customers. He'd sit and smoke and give the local news.

John had the virtues most respected in small-town Nebraska—he was a team player, soft-spoken, and friendly. He was funny and adaptable, tolerant and slow to anger. He went out of his way to help. He had been a county supervisor and a school- and church-board member. He winked at me. "I've spent a lot of government money."

Sylvia too exemplified the virtues of her times. She was good-natured, quick-witted, and pretty. Sylvia loved being a stay-at-home mother. She said, "We've never had neighbor troubles. We aren't rabble-rousers." John said, "I was always a lover, not a fighter." I commented on how trusted they were by their community. "We're not rebels or nonconformists," John told me.

Both Darlings still drove and had good memories and quick minds. John retired from his route when he was sixty-eight, but until recently he worked part-time at a parts store. He liked to stay busy. He said he had "seen the rocking chair get too many guys." This year had been hard on John's health. He'd had quadruple-bypass heart surgery, prostate surgery, and cataract surgery. But while he told me about his asthma, the phone rang, and John answered, "Kelly's Mule Barn."

Sylvia had had two hiatal hernias and knee replacement surgery. She suffered from arthritis, but it was better now that she was seeing a specialist in Lincoln. She couldn't garden anymore, but she said, "I still enjoy getting out of bed every day."

John and Sylvia are characters with character. They have been married fifty-four years. They believe they've gotten along so well because they've kept busy. Sylvia joked that John embarrassed her with his teasing. I asked for an example. She told me, "At the alumni banquet, John told everyone that longevity was all attitude. Plus keeping regular."

In the last few years, Sylvia and John had lost a lot of their friends and family. They were slowing down, and both said they want to die quickly and at home. John would like to die the way his father did, gathering wood.

## ROSE AND GERTRUDE   (*ages 85 and 94*)
*"Do you think God would*
*want you to do this?"*

LONG BEFORE I met these two sisters, I'd heard people talk of
"Rose'n'Gertrude" in such a way that I thought it was one name, one person. They went everywhere together. They lived in the modest green
house next to the house where they were born. They had a yard filled with
pink and white roses, orange honeysuckle, and purple impatiens. A sign in
a flower bed read, "The kiss of the sun for pardon, the song of the birds for
mirth, one is nearer God's heart in a garden than anywhere else on earth."

Both sisters wore flowered silk dresses and jewelry. They had snowy
white hair and rosy faces, but Gertrude was much taller than Rose. Rose
served coffee in china teacups that Gertrude had painted. She offered me a
platter of poppy-seed cakes and friendship muffins.

Gertrude began their story. She'd been born at home. Their father
was a housepainter, just back from the Spanish-American war, and their
mother was a housewife. Gertrude said that when Rose was born, their
father told her the truth. "Not the whole truth," she said with a laugh, "but
that Mama had carried the baby in her stomach. For that time he was boldly
honest."

Their mother had been shy and gentle. Their father was "full of the
dickens, peppy, and popular with everyone." He was generous with all the
town's children. If he saw a poor child, he'd buy him candy or give him a
nickel. He never spanked Rose and Gertrude, but if he said something, he
meant it. They referred to their father as "our beloved papa."

Mostly boys lived in their neighborhood, so they played a lot of football and baseball. They had races and played tag, run sheep run, and hide-
and-seek. When their father wanted them home, he'd whistle. Anywhere
in town they could hear him. In the summer, Gertrude spent hours in the
sandy creek and she never worried about being hurt. Halloween was a
great day for kids. The emphasis in their town was more on tricks than

treats. That day kids decorated the courthouse and climbed the water tower.

Rose and Gertrude's grandfather always carried a leather coin purse filled with licorice candy. He opened it for the children and let them take a piece. Even today when they smell licorice, they think of their grandfather.

Rose said, "There was a good atmosphere in the schools. We were all friends. There wasn't much dating. Nobody had cars." Gertrude said there was only one teacher she didn't respect, a teacher who said to her, "Turn around and pay attention or I'll put you in a tub of hot soapsuds." Rose's favorite teacher was her first-grade teacher, who was apparently quite plain. When Rose told her parents how beautiful this teacher was, they laughed. Rose smiled. "She was so good that I thought she was beautiful."

Both girls went to college after high school. Gertrude taught during the school year and took classes only in the summer. Eventually she got a master's degree in education. Rose dropped out of college after her first year because her beloved papa was sick. That year Gertrude sent home money from her teaching. The nurse who lived next door came daily, and their uncles stayed nights to relieve Rose and her mother. The doctor came in the mornings, at lunch, and just before bed. Rose laughed as she remembered going to the creek to chip ice because her father wanted her to serve the doctor a dish of vanilla ice cream every day. Their father's death at age fifty was the saddest thing that ever happened to their family. He died of dropsy, or edema, a condition that would not have been fatal even a few years after his death. Rose said, "I can picture the doctor pacing in our living room the night Papa died. He was broken up."

Rose married and had children. Gertrude worked in the schools for forty-eight years. She encouraged kids to work their problems out, and said proudly that many times archenemies left her office hand in hand. She said to badly behaved kids, "Do you think God would want you to do this?"

After Rose's husband's death and Gertrude's retirement, the two sisters pooled their resources and moved in together. There's no movie theater in town, and Gertrude said, "Our favorite movies are home movies."

Rose is a great-grandmother now, and her granddaughter sends her videos of her great-grandchildren. Rose and Gertrude watch them over and over.

Both women are involved with their church. They describe themselves as happy, and neither really liked to talk about problems. They told funny stories from long ago. Gertrude had a pet chicken when she was a girl. She'd loved this chicken, whom she called Copper, and trained it to do tricks. He lived to be fifteen years old. Gertrude also had a pet pig that her father eventually butchered. Gertrude laughed when she told about her shock and dismay.

I left their house with cakes for my family. On my way home I thought about Gertrude's pig. When I was young, my dad killed my pet rabbit for food. I had felt traumatized and held a grudge against my father for his insensitivity. I never laughed at the story. Rather, I felt sorry for myself. I compared my reactions to Gertrude's. She seemed typical of her genera-tion—not prone to self-pity and more forgiving of parental errors. I won-dered as I drove, What has changed for my generation? Why do we resent, instead of laugh at, family mistakes?

THERE ARE REALLY two kinds of cultural diversity: diversity across distance, and diversity across time. One is called *anthropology*, and the other *history*, and both are connected to psychology. Childhood experiences shape people's relationships to the natural world and their outlooks on work and family. Childhood experiences help us form attitudes about gen-der, authority, and community, and teach us acceptable ways of coping with distress.

Culture also determines much of personality and influences the ways we think, feel, and interact with the world. It allows certain traits to grow while others wither on the vine. Psychologist Irving Goffman believed that a person's location reveals more about his behavior than does his character profile. For example, if you know a person is in a bar at midnight, you can better predict what he is doing than if you know his Minnesota Multiphasic Personality Inventory score or Myers-Briggs category. What Goffman said about place can be said about time. Knowing when people were born allows us to predict attitudes and behaviors. A person from a specific era will have a certain "collective consciousness."

Each generation selects new things to label as good and beautiful, partly because people have a natural human desire to make things new and different. Each generation likes to imagine itself as rediscovering sex, good cooking, fashion, and child-rearing. But mostly, one generation's reaction to the previous one causes the dialectic across time. The grandfather wore boxers, the son wears Jockey shorts, then the grandson "rediscovers" boxers.

Different eras produce different psychological problems. For example, earlier eras produced more perfectionists and overconformers. Our times produce more psychopaths, unsocialized youth, narcissists, and bulimics. Sexual problems are different. In the early part of the century we had foot fetishists; now we have computer-sex addicts. Today we have more compulsive shoppers and fewer hysterics.

Each generation sees the errors of its parents, but not necessarily the errors of its grandparents. Virtues and vices, just like given names, tend to skip generations. Generations tend to overcorrect, so rather than achieve perfection they simply make the mistakes of earlier generations. While my grandparents were frugal, my mother was a big spender. I am frugal, and my children are spenders. While my husband's parents like nice clothes, Jim couldn't care less what he wears. However, our children are fashion conscious. Lax parents create spoiled children who may insist on better behavior from their own offspring. Adults reared in strict homes may want to give their children a softer, gentler childhood and thus may be more permissive. And so the circle turns.

Sometimes, however, there is what looks like a qualitative break. Around mid-century, we moved from being a communal culture to an individualistic one, from being what Martin Buber called an I–thou culture to an I–it culture. We moved from villages into what Cornell West calls a "hotel society." People stopped knowing one another in a variety of roles across time and place. We don't live near our cousins or grow old with the same people we were born with. As we approach the end of our century, we all live among strangers.

This communal culture ended in different places at different times. The causes for its demise are numerous and include demographic changes, technological advances, and housing patterns that favored privacy over community. Communal culture withered as backyard patios replaced front porches, as cars replaced horses, as party lines gave way to cellular phones, and as voters no longer wanted to pay for sidewalks and alleys, which were remarkably good civic spaces. Television, which spread across America in the 1960s, helped destroy our sense of community. With television, people stopped looking toward their neighbors for information and entertainment. The news stopped being only local, and we all moved into a global village.

Community wasn't the property just of rural people. Older people in cities remember knowing everyone in their buildings and neighborhoods. People shared work, meals, clothes, beds, and bathtubs. Many older people grew up with many siblings. One woman described the experience of having eight siblings as having lots of blankets on top of you on a cold winter night. Brothers and sisters enveloped you and kept you warm. In these kinds of families, dynamics were tribal. Cooperation was favored over individuality. There weren't many choices or disagreements about choices. As Henry Ford said of the Model T, "You can have any color you like, as long as it's black."

Recently I sat on an airplane next to an older Southern lady. She was elegantly dressed in a silk suit, heels, a hat, and even gloves. She didn't know the rules of modern flying, which basically are that we act like cattle when we are on planes. We take care of ourselves and ignore the other passengers. Since this lady was unaware of the rules, she introduced herself and chatted about her visit to her son's home. At first I was bugged by her effrontery. To think, she didn't know enough to be quiet! But then I began to enjoy her charming way of speaking. As I laughed at her stories, I felt a little less like a cow being shipped. I realized she wasn't pushing boundaries but that the boundaries had changed during her lifetime. In fact, when she grew up, the word *boundary* meant a fence or border, not an interpersonal protective barrier. She had grown up in a slower, friendlier world in which you had a relationship with everyone you met.

People born early in the century are the last Americans to grow up in a world in which all behavior mattered. Today, autonomy is king. As long as we don't bother anybody, it doesn't matter if we drink too much, spend money foolishly, or are dying of cancer. Most of the people we meet don't know or care about what we do. They may want our money or our services, but not the details of our lives. Their main hope is that we not make trouble or interrupt their work. Without community there is no morality. My brother Jake told me of an old Russian proverb that says, "The tears of a stranger are only water."

Communal people learned very different values from the ones we hold now. Because people lived in close quarters, they had to get along to survive. Sharing, loyalty, and cooperation were held in high regard. Appearance and good manners were important. Because people saw each other every day for lifetimes, reputation was critical. Conformity was a positive virtue. Social training had to do with going along to get along. Wisdom wasn't seen as the property of individuals, but rather as a collective possession. Communities knew how to raise children.

In our "hotel society," a different set of norms is practical. We learn to swim with the sharks, every person for him- or herself. We learn, as Mose Allison sings, that "if you're going to the city you'd better take some cash because people in the city don't mess around with trash." It's better not to get too attached to people one may soon leave. Conformity doesn't matter much in a culture of strangers. The pinnacle of good manners is leaving people alone. Today, wisdom is seen as something each person attains by him- or herself, and self-actualization has replaced being a team player as the highest virtue.

Emphasis on duty and connection made sense in a society in which, day after day and year after year, people were together. The rewards for good behavior were membership in a tribe and lifelong friendships. A person of good character could borrow money on a handshake. People didn't lock their doors.

Of course, communal culture certainly had a downside. Togetherness could create an oppressive feeling of social control. Hurtful remarks were remembered for fifty years. A mistake made in high school might be held against a person until the day he died. Often there was an in-group mentality that led to prejudice against Jews, blacks, Native Americans, gypsies, Catholics, or anyone different from one's own tribe. At its worst, communal meant clannish and intolerant of diversity.

As G.W.S. Trow wrote in *The New Yorker*, "Everyone knows, or ought to know, that there has happened under us a Tectonic Plate Shift, or over us a Cosmic Ticktock. In any case, the buildings are the same: this one a sweet Victorian cottage, that one an old brick tenement out of Hopper. . . . The political parties have the same names: we still have a CBS, an NBC and a Times. But we are not the same nation that had these things before."

Trow spoke about what I have called the difference in the deep structure of the country. Simply put, surface structure is what something looks like, and deep structure is what it is really about. Many things look the same on the surface, but their deep structures have changed. Forty years ago, funerals and graduations were about community, while today the people attending these events may not even know one another. Buildings may have the same surface structures, but the deep structures are different. The difference between a food court at a mall and a small-town cafe early in the century is as significant as the difference between AstroTurf and prairie grasses.

Thinking in terms of deep structure versus surface structure can help family members understand one another. Deep structure is about motives. For example, the deep structure of the question "Do you want some tea?" might be "I want you to feel welcome in my home." Different generations share the same deep structure. Everyone wants to give and receive love, to raise healthy children, and to keep things calm and happy. But the surface structure, the words and actions people use to express their motives, can be very different. For example, the grandparents say yes when a child asks for candy. The deep structure of their message is about wanting the child to be loved and well cared for, and when they were young, food meant survival. The parents say no to a request for candy. They also want the child to feel loved and cared for, but to them that means denying the child sugary sweets.

People are most alike in their feelings and least alike in their thinking. We all may have the same general set of feelings and in the end want the same things. But our place and time determine much of how we think. When family members disagree, it's important for us to ask, "What has your experience been?" The conflicts among surface statements often disappear if deep structures are understood. When people are evaluated in terms of their motives, they are easier to respect and to forgive.

Much of what is said between the generations feels more personal than it really is. Many disagreements are caused by our misunderstanding of different cultures, by what I call time-zone problems. Only by understanding what things mean to people in other time zones can we truly communicate with them. For example, Great-aunt Martha's concern about what the neighbors think isn't necessarily superficial, as we tend to view such concerns in our independence-loving 1990s. Rather it is about respect and connection, about having a proper place in a communal universe.

Attitudes toward food vary according to generation. Partly these differences are about preferences and experiences—Dorothy Lynch French dressing versus sesame-rice dressing; corn meal mush versus polenta. But our attitudes about food go deeper than preference or convenience. Our parents grew up in a world in which frog legs were called "mountain chicken" and wealth was often defined simply as having enough to eat. As Uncle Max put it, "There's no such thing as too much food."

Older people often associate food with security. Many are hoarders. Even though as an adult my mother had plenty of money, she would never throw away leftovers. She would save a teaspoon of peas or half a biscuit. She would cut the mold off cheeses and eat a half-rotten apple. She had an enormous basement pantry stocked with jars of Karo syrup, bags of flour, and cans of pork and beans. She would have needed to live to be 200 to eat all that food, but just walking into that pantry gave her pleasure.

My generation grew up with plenty of food. As adults we worry about our weight and our health. We don't eat sausage for breakfast or make pounds of peanut brittle when we have time to spare. We don't always associate food with love; sometimes we associate it with gluttony or heart attacks.

This difference in experience can lead to misunderstandings. Parents cook giant meals and are hurt when their children don't seem grateful. They urge them to eat and then eat more. The deep structure of their message is "I love you and want to show my love." The adult children may refuse politely, but they're thinking, *That kind of diet can kill me and probably is killing you.*

To our parents' generation, sharing food is a metaphor for sharing community, for being in I–thou relationships. When they were young, sharing food meant, quite literally, "I will go hungry so that you can have something to eat." On hearing that a niece didn't feel loved by him, an old neighbor said, "Of course I loved her. I gave her a bushel of fresh-picked corn."

Communal people were raised to trust those in authority. The older generation tends to trust police, politicians, and scientists. They have a hard time believing a president could lie or that police could be arbitrary and brutal. They tend to see scientists as problem solvers, not problem creators. They don't question their doctors. Many of my friends get frustrated by their parents' unwillingness to confront their doctors. I think of a neighbor who had an infected arm. She visited a quack who mistreated her infection and she ended up hospitalized. She never questioned this doctor's treatment or even called him to say that she was getting worse. Her exasperated daughter told me, "When I confronted Mom, she said, 'The doctor knows what he is doing.' "

I think of Millie, who showed up at the emergency room in terrible pain. She was given pain pills and sent home with no diagnosis or treatment. Now she lives in fear that the pain will return. Yet she said nothing critical to the doctor at the emergency room.

Behavior was what counted. Older people didn't necessarily seek authenticity or congruence between feelings and actions. Saving face was a positive virtue. Reputation was all many people had during the Depression. It wasn't easy to appear respectable when the family was barely surviving. I think of Aunt Grace living as a newlywed in a chicken shed, but, as she proudly told me, "It was a clean and neat chicken shed."

Actions spoke louder than words. In *Nothing to Do But Stay*, Carrie Young wrote about how her family showed love by doing. With her first paycheck, Carrie's older sister bought her a beautiful red dress trimmed with green velvet. Carrie's mother made quilts constantly. An enormous number were needed to keep eight people warm through the North Dakota winter. Carrie wrote that so many quilts were piled on the bed that all the girls had to turn over at once. In 1927, Carrie's father spent all day shoveling out of snowdrifts to get his girls home from town school for Christmas. Her mother watched at the window. Late afternooon she spotted them in a drift five miles away and she tracked them for hours until they arrived. A father who fought a blizzard all day didn't need to say much about his feelings.

Our generation is schooled in the language of feelings, and we wish sometimes that our parents could talk more about their feelings and about their relationships with us and each other. Sometimes we attribute their lack of talk to a lack of feeling. Usually, but not always, we are mistaken. There are a few people who don't have many feelings for others. I had a friend, Mandy, who helped her grumpy, judgmental father write his memoirs. He wrote a 200-page book about his war exploits, hunting trips, and civic activities. Mandy's birth merited one line, and she never appeared again. She told me, "This gave me a sense of what was important to my father, and I wasn't it."

Mostly, our parents just are not comfortable with our openness. Clients often tell me stories that would be funny if they weren't so sad. Robert traveled across the state to visit his ill father. He wanted to talk about their relationship, while, as usual, his dad wanted to discuss football or interest rates. Robert tried to hug his father, but his father made a joke about "queers" and shook his hand. Robert later told me woefully, "I've had more intimate conversations with the carry-out boy at my grocery store."

People born early in the century were taught to keep their feelings to themselves. For example, World War II veterans didn't come home and talk about the war. They were shell-shocked and didn't necessarily understand their own psychological states. They also thought that their friends and families wouldn't want to hear the truth.

This generation learned to buck up, make the best of it, and look on the bright side. They were warned not to go looking for trouble. Slights, annoyances, or upset feelings didn't carry much weight. Good women didn't swear, get angry, or express dissatisfaction. They definitely did not state their own needs. In my experience, it is hard to get older women to say what they want. They have been trained to be indirect. They will say things like, "I think we had better . . ." or, "It isn't done this way," or, "We should . . ." or, "I don't care, you decide."

Men could express at least their anger in private, but not the "softer" emotions such as sorrow or self-doubt. Men often were so emotionally constricted that it was hard for them to parent. Many never hugged their children or said "I love you." Many adults of my generation are hungry for touch, for "I love you"s from their fathers. Modern dads often work hard to give their own children the warmth and praise they didn't get as kids.

I don't mean to imply that older men were not kind. As young men, many risked freezing to death to bring home wild game for a meal. Or they worked long hours in coal mines or far from home in city sweatshops to feed their families. Many showed great tenderness toward animals, women, and children. As old men, they work endlessly on family cars or gardens. They fix what is broken in the house, and run errands. They show love by being useful but are unschooled in the language of connection. They are ignorant and afraid of "feelings talk," but they give away homegrown tomatoes and pumpkins.

Gender roles were different. Earlier, being a good father simply meant being a good provider. Now, being a good father involves being a nurturer and a good listener, and being physically and emotionally available to children. Earlier, fathers were expected to support their wives' efforts to raise well-behaved children. In the past, women's roles were about enabling others to succeed. Women defined themselves by their service to others. Today, women have gone from basking in reflected glory to seeking their own glory. Sometimes this shift causes friction between women my age and their mothers.

My client Lydia bemoaned her relationship with her mother: "All Mom wants is to be loved. She's devoted her life to others, and even today she lives for compliments. She'll work all week on a meal for the twenty seconds' worth of praise she receives."

Lydia sighed. "That puts me in a bind. I want her to feel good, but I also want her to get a life of her own. I resent her thinking I am selfish because I don't worry about pleasing others. What I see as developing my potential, she sees as ignoring the family. On the other hand, Mother told me recently that she didn't know who she was. She's seventy years old and I find that tragic. I am proud that I know who I am."

Often there is tension between generations about gender roles. Younger women don't want to do all the cooking and the dishes at holiday meals. Older women are sometimes disappointed that their daughters-in-law don't sew or do laundry. They believe a good wife does these things, and they forget that the good wife is now working at a fifty-hour-a-week job. Fathers expect their daughters to wait on them like their wives did, but the daughters have read Gloria Steinem and say, "Dad, get your own coffee."

Younger people also are troubled by the sexism of their parents—jokes about lady drivers or dumb blondes. They wince when women are called "girls." They notice differences in the ways the generations evaluate women. Some older men feel it's only good manners to compliment all women on their appearances. I've been amused by the lengths to which they will go. I once showed up in a grocery store wearing old sweats, my hair wet from rain, only to be told by an older gentleman that I looked lovely that morning.

In the past, sexual attitudes were a complicated mix of Puritanical and ribald. People didn't talk much about sex, and when they did, it was in euphemisms. Legs were "limbs," for example. Female teachers couldn't teach after they got married. In Tekamah, it wasn't considered proper for pregnant women to be seen in public. When she was pregnant, my mother-in-law could leave her house only after dark. Phyllis described walking late at night with her mother, eager just to get out of the house and exercise. On the other hand, there is a certain earthiness to many older people. Sexual humor at shivarees was expected. A friend of mine took her eighty-year-old grandmother to the ballet. On seeing Baryshnikov, she remarked, "That young man has a full bag of groceries."

Sex had a valued place in the lives of most people. Sexuality had not been used to market products and was still connected mostly to love and relationships. Sexual innuendo was rare compared to now, when virtually any statement can be viewed as having a sexual meaning. Sex was private and sacred.

Older people also are more likely to see men and women as very different from each other. The genders had separate spheres. Many older women never learned to drive or write checks. Marital bliss was largely a matter of staying busy. People had lower expectations about what a marriage should be, and they had fewer options.

Early in the century, women couldn't vote and children had few legal rights. At the end of our century, relations between children and parents and husbands and wives are less authoritarian. For the most part, families today are more democratic. Intimacy is expected, and couples are encouraged to communicate their thoughts and feelings. People feel freer to follow their dreams. There is room for more conscious choice in almost every area of life—living situations, relationships, work, religion, and leisure-time activities. However, there is less form to fall back on, and there is more existential angst. With higher expectations for marriage, there is more disappointment.

THE WORD *DEPENDENCY* has a very different deep structure for older and younger generations. A communal culture assumed dependency on family and community. It wasn't good or bad, just necessary and therefore unquestioned. When our parents were young, many had grandparents or great-aunts and great-uncles living in their homes. They were liked or disliked according to their temperaments, but their right to care wasn't in doubt. As Aunt Henrietta said of my father after his stroke, "He couldn't be trouble; he was my brother."

In mainstream psychology, healthy development has been conceptualized as a process of increasing autonomy and independence. As we became a therapized culture, dependency grew to imply something weak and pathologicial. Closeness became enmeshment, obligations became resentments, and requests for care were labeled attempts to control. What had been an expectation—that the old will need their children—has become a shameful secret. What was a necessity—that children care for their parents as they age—has become a choice.

This change in the meaning of dependency, from a natural to a shameful condition, has turned our elders into elderly. The old don't want to be dependent in our dependent-phobic culture. And we young are afraid to get sucked in. We've been educated to the dangers of closeness and well warned about entanglements. What we haven't learned about is the serenity and safety that come from extended family and community.

Over the course of the century, the relative values of dependence and autonomy have been totally reversed. John and Sylvia and Rose and

Gertrude were proud to fit in with their families and communites. While most people from their era were happy to be part of the group, almost no one in my generation wants to be seen as a conformist. We like to see ourselves as free thinkers, as individuated, autonomous adults.

Early in the century, parents wanted children to work hard, complain little, cooperate with others, and respect authority. Richard Low wrote about these attitudes in *Childhood's Future*. He cited a Middletown study of Muncie, Indiana, in 1924. Parents were asked what quality they most desired in their children. At the top of the list were obedience and comformity. In 1974, the same question was asked, and the list was exactly reversed. What modern parents most desired for their children was autonomy and independence.

In the early 1900s, the view of children was Hobbesian. Most people thought that children were born evil and needed to be indoctrinated into the good. Although there were exceptions, physical punishment was an accepted part of child-rearing. The punishment could be harsh—whippings with a belt or razor strap, slapping, or depriving children of food. Most parents believed "Spare the rod and spoil the child."

Praise wasn't considered good for children. It made them swell-headed and stuck on themselves. Parents didn't brag about their children. Acting uppity was met with the hostile question "Who do you think you are?" As if, my friend Karen jokingly put it, "the greatest crime was having high self-esteem."

Parents believed that children should be seen and not heard. Frustrated children were not considered traumatized but as receiving a lesson in patience and endurance. Robert E. Lee expressed this philosophy when he said, "Teach your children to deny themselves." Children were raised to joke about upset feelings. Children who complained were told, "I'll give you something to complain about," and children who were bored were told, "I'll put you to work."

Then in 1943, Arnold Gesell wrote *The Infant and Child in the Culture Today*. Parents were urged to follow rather than force their children, and to respond warmly to their needs. Affection was stressed over discipline. Dr. Spock's book on baby- and child-care followed in 1947. Like Gesell, Spock believed that babies needed friendly, accepting adults, and he urged parents to love and enjoy children for who they are.

Many time-zone issues arise with child-rearing. Again the deep structure between generations is similar, but the surface structures are different. Everyone wants children who are well adjusted, well behaved, and productive. Yet most modern parents would never talk of "breaking a child's will." What seemed like discipline to our parents' generation may strike us as abuse.

While time-zone issues can cause conflict and tension in families, they also offer children a diversity of viewpoints. Under ideal conditions, diversity enriches experience. While grandparents teach children skills and manners, parents teach children to express their feelings. It's good to teach children to endure pain, but also to acknowledge and communicate feelings. Children who are with grandparents and parents can learn independence and also communal cooperation.

In *The Optimistic Child,* Martin Seligman integrates the best ideas of the century on parenting. He argues that up until 1960, children were reared in an achievement-oriented culture, and after that time they were raised in a feel-good culture. He thinks that the emphasis on feelings has made children more depressed and less optimistic. Children are less vulnerable to depression if they are focused on skills and behavior. He thinks that honesty is better than flattery. Children need help formulating reasonable assessments of challenges and their likelihoods of success. They need skills and specific strategies for succeeding, not empty words of reassurance.

Seligman believes that the more we achieve and the less we expect, the higher our self-esteem. Children can feel better either by succeeding more or by downsizing their hopes. His new ideas include some very old ideas. Parents in the 1920s emphasized good behavior and limited expectations. They also advocated the prudent use of praise.

It's important not to idealize past eras. No virtue is absolute. It's good to know when to be loyal and when not to be loyal, when to discipline children and when not to discipline children. Any modern parent who has been badgered and bullied by her child can occasionally wish for the good old days when kids didn't talk back. However, there was a stiffness and reserve that came from too much emphasis on good behavior. Modern children are more likely to tell their parents their experiences and to joke around with them. Family meals are less formal and more fun.

In the past, humility was highly valued, and praise was delivered sparingly if at all. Thus, people were modest and low-key, but they also had low self-esteem. Family loyalty was a virtue, but too much loyalty kept mothers from reporting sexually abusive fathers. Keeping a stiff upper lip didn't always work. Sometimes people kept their lips stiff all the way to the insane asylum.

## Lawrence Welk

LAWRENCE WELK, bandleader and TV-show host, was hard-working, community-oriented, and unsophisticated. He smiled and danced his way through the Depression, the war, and even the death of the big-band era. Rural people all over the Midwest watched him as they would a little brother who'd made good.

Welk was born in a soddie on a farm near Strasburg, North Dakota. His parents were German immigrants who brought only their prayer book and an accordion to the United States. Lawrence was the youngest of six, and he never took to farming. He had a fourth-grade education and didn't learn English until he left home at age twenty-one. His father didn't want him to go into music because he was afraid Lawrence would lose his Christian values. When Lawrence left the farm, his father said, "You'll be back begging for a meal in six months."

With his chocolate-brown suit, slicked-back hair, and big teeth, Welk could have come only from the Great Plains. Even dressed in a suit and dancing around a ballroom, he still looked like he had the mud and straw on his boots, the farmer's tan, and the sun squint.

Welk scraped by for years. Once a band fired him because they thought he was such a dunderhead that he was holding them back. He said of that incident, "I was pretty low." But he hired another band and played the next weekend.

Welk liked the phrase "champagne music" to describe his light frothy sound. He flashed his big smile and laughed at all the jokes. He kissed the pretty girls who sang on the show, and danced with ladies from the audience. He was known for his bloopers. Once he introduced "Take the A Train" as "Take a Train." Instead of saying "feather in his cap," Welk always said, "That will be feather in his head."

His band was his "musical family," and he was involved with the lives of its members. He hired many musicians for life, including Myron Florin, Big Tiny Little, and the Lennon sisters. He loved musicians who practiced, and he fired only complainers. He figured out that people who complained constantly could never be satisfied and they soured others.

Everyone predicted that Welk would fail on TV, but he was on for twenty-seven years and reruns of his shows are still watched in 1998 on Saturday nights. His critics, most of whom fled the Midwest to escape people like Welk, were relentless. Not only was he a mediocre musician, he wore lederhosen. One of the kinder critics wrote, "He's got a shy, clodhopper charm and heaven knows he's sincere." Another wrote, "Nobody likes him but the public."

Welk was the musical equivalent of comfort food, the vanilla pudding and chicken noodle soup of big-band music. He said musically, "There, there, you'll be okay." He was the poster child for resiliency. He said, "Don't even think about your troubles. Let's dance." His show was a safe cocoon, a diversion from hard times, at least for the hour it was on. He cheered up many shell-shocked Americans. Maybe that's why his show is still being broadcast.

Welk was born in an era when stoicism and cheerfulness were much respected. People learned to put on a happy face, to let a smile be their umbrella. A healthy attitude meant accepting things at face value and leaving well enough alone. Mature adults were expected to spare one another their feelings.

The music of the time expresses those values. During the hard years of the dustbowl and Depression, the music was happy. The Mills Brothers, Bob Wills and the Texas Playboys, and the Glenn Miller Band all cheered people up. Bluegrass singer Bill Monroe worked at WJKS, a station whose initials stood for Where Joy Killed Sorrow.

My generation was raised with an almost opposite set of rules. Openness is much valued, and stoicism is now called denial. A person who bounces back too quickly, like Welk did after his band fired him, isn't processing his feelings. The modern person never "holds his tongue." As a therapist, I've received calls from people worried because family members were not depressed by certain events—not a big worry of pre-Freudian families.

Communal people coped by working, by praying, by socializing and dancing. As Edward Robb Ellis wrote in *The Diary of a Century*, "Now that we're in a Depression, clowns are important." Aunt Henrietta was so hungry she would eat a stick of butter if she could, but she laughed about this and said, "We had everything but money." Work and religion were considered the great healers. People read poetry and their Bibles in times of despair. Many people held their lives in place by enjoying books, music, relationships, or the natural world.

The emphasis on accepting fate, on making lemonade from lemons, produced hardy personalities. Less resilient people didn't survive the harsh life of the early 1900s. Death, pain, and calamity surrounded people. Women had their babies at home, often with no medical help. Infants died of influenza or cholera. People learned to handle suffering or they didn't make it.

One summer when my mother was a girl, her family's entire wheat crop was wiped out by hail. After the damage was assessed, her father said,

"There is nothing we can do here. Let's take a trip." The family drove across the country to Niagara Falls, camping and visiting relatives and friends along the way. Except for visits to her grandparents, this was the only vacation of my mother's childhood.

My daughter-in-law's grandfather also had his crop hailed out one summer. He stood quietly on the porch looking at the ice-filled fields and the stripped plants. Then he said to his family, "Gather up those hailstones and let's make some ice cream."

The people who survived this century have much to teach us about resiliency. They know how to laugh, to dance, and to share meals with one another.

## The City Cafe

ON CHRISTMAS EVE in Tekamah, everyone in town was invited to the City Cafe for free soup and pie. My husband and I went with his parents, Bernie and Phyllis. Outside, light snow fell on the icy streets and the wind howled down from the north. Inside the cafe, evergreens and ropes of tinsel decorated the tables. Paper snowflakes and glittery stars hung from the ceiling, and I was taken aback by the tree blasting out carols. Even the dartboard sprouted holly, and the auto-parts calendar had poinsettias painted beside the swimsuit-clad models.

The City Cafe was owned by two sisters, Norma and Lucille, who were great at keeping things homey. They baked cinnamon rolls for local people on their birthdays, and saved tables and slices of pie for their regulars. It took us fifteen minutes to get across the room. We stopped to visit the farm couple Jim worked for in high school, the florist who lived next door to his parents, one of Jim's schoolteachers, and the parents of one of Jim's high school buddies. We stopped for clam chowder served in two sizes, regular and JP size, so named for a local man, John Peck, who liked a big bowl of soup. Lucille, who dished it up, wore a Santa Claus cap and a sweatshirt that said, "I want it all." She'd gone to school with Phyllis, and as she passed me a bowl of soup, she told me that they had both been "ornery."

We carried our soup to the back room. Norma surprised us with four pieces of pie that were four inches tall and spilled off the sides of the dinner plates. Jim's best friend was Norma's nephew, and she had known Jim since he was a baby. He praised the meal lavishly, but not any more lavishly than it deserved.

This time of year, Tekamah was cold and dark. The cafe was filled with elders, many now widowed and/or infirm. Almost all lived on small fixed incomes and worried about their propane bills, property taxes, and health-care costs. They worried about slipping on the ice and about losing their marbles before their hearts stop beating. But in here it was light and warm, loud and joyful.

As we ate our soup and pie, our relatives came over to greet us. Actually almost everyone in town was related to us through Bernie, whose mother's family had eight kids, most of whom stayed in Tekamah and had big families of their own. Norma came back to see if we liked the pie. In answer, Jim dropped to his knees, waved his arms up and down, and shouted, "I am not worthy." Bernie told about a sliver of cheesecake he'd had in Omaha for $4.25. He said indignantly, "People around here won't put up with that kind of thing."

An old man in a felt hat and a coat with a fur collar stopped to kid around. We joined in singing "Happy Birthday" to Wilma, who every year baked Jim's family a Christmas pastry. We looked at pictures of grandchildren and heard about the basketball team and the Mistletoe Ball. The cafe almost made us forget how cold it was outside and how early it grew dark.

*Once in East Africa, on the shores of an ancient lake, I sat alone and suddenly it struck me what community is. It is gathering around a fire and listening to someone tell us a story.*

—Bill Moyers

Community is like wilderness, a concept that grows more dear as its reality vanishes. Over the course of the century we have gained autonomy at the expense of this connection. Today there are fewer nosy neighbors, but those neighbors used to watch our children when they played. It's hard simply to have people around when they are needed and not around when they are not needed. But we are beginning to see the terrible limitations of hotel society, especially for children and the old.

Fortunately, there is a new generation of psychologists who are rethinking our definitions of mental health. New definitions are being formulated that take into account our need to be connected to family, to the people who live near us, and even to animals and the natural world. Communal people always have defined themselves in relation to their village. For them, maturity hasn't been about autonomy as much as it's been about working well with all the people in one's community. Modern relational theory suggests that a mature person is one who is deeply connected to his or her world and who moves toward greater complexity in those relationships. Ecopsychologists suggest that those relationships should extend to the entire planet.

The dialectic across generations applies to community as well. One generation flees the tight connections, and the next generation longs for roots. Perhaps our move away from being a tribal culture wasn't such a qualitative or permanent break after all. Perhaps, as the century ends, the circle is turning back. Once again many of us yearn for a culture of connected people with shared histories and identities. Without social connections, school bond issues don't pass and nobody votes to fund the senior center. We are realizing that life without community is "life lite."

We live in a time when community reconstruction is what will save us. If we give our elders our time and our respect, they can teach us how to do it. They can teach us about civility, accountability, and connection. Their knowledge of how to tell stories, how to live together, how to nurture children, and how to share the work will help us build better communities in the future.

We can look to the past for ideas about constructing communities. Size was important. Thomas Jefferson preferred towns of 1,000 people. It was possible to really know 1,000 people and their relationships to one another, yet 1,000 people create enough diversity to display the human condition in all its forms. We are realizing that bigger is not always better. People do better in smaller, human-sized spaces.

Old communities involved a lot of walking. Children walked to school, and elders walked downtown for the mail and a cup of coffee. Most people weren't automobile dependent, and that made talking to neighbors easy. There was usable civic space everywhere. Sidewalks and front porches connected families. Public squares, parks with benches, libraries, dance halls, churches, and community centers gave people places to meet. Old communities organized around reunions of all kinds—class reunions, band reunions, club and family reunions.

Our great hunger for communal life is being satisfied in many ways. Churches are filled with families seeking community. Reading groups are another manifestation of this need. Walking paths; craft guilds; and art, music, and literature festivals are about community. Bookstores and cafes with comfortable chairs, drinks, and meeting areas build community. Reunions of all kinds are blossoming across the land.

I like the idea of co-housing, which was originally a Scandinavian concept for intergenerational, self-designed, and self-managed communities. Today we actually have more than 180 co-housing developments in the United States, mostly on the coasts. Co-housing is multigenerational, and cars are kept on the perimeter of the shared land. Most co-housing communities are made up of individual homes, a meeting hall, and lots of shared indoor and outdoor recreational space. They all have common areas for cooking and eating. That's another definition of community: cooking and eating together.

Some of us baby boomers lived in communes when we were younger. As our children grow up, we once again find the idea of group living appealing. Many friends have talked about their desire to live with or at least near close friends, to share expenses and housework, and to care for one another. People of my generation tend to trust friends more than institutions to treat us well. We would like to be interdependent. Already in Los Angeles there is an experimental interdependent-living community in which older people live together and help one another. I think there will be many more communes for elders.

The essence of rebuilding community is creating opportunities for relationships. We can introduce ourselves to others and speak on planes. We can learn the neighborhood children's names. Creating community means mainly slowing down and paying attention.

Individual families can work at building community. For example, I know a couple who decided that after dinner they would walk around their neighborhood with their children instead of watching a television show. At first the children protested, but then they started liking the people they met, the dogs, and the special places they were able to find. They learned the names of people on their street, and they learned where to watch for birds. One night the son had a friend over, and he accompanied the family on their neighborhood walk. The next night after dinner, the little boy was waiting on the front porch for them. By now there are a half dozen kids who wait to go on these walks with the family. They are the Pied Pipers of their neighborhood.

We often eat at a small neighborhood Asian restaurant. On Wednesday night there's a big table open for any teachers or students from our nearby high school. Sometimes fifteen people show up; sometimes ten. But the important thing is that there is an open invitation to join this group for anybody at the school who wants to come. It's a small thing, but it gives teachers and students a sense of connection, an oasis of I–thou sanity in an enormous system.

Local businesses often allow time for communal relationships. Like pilots—the most accountable businessmen—local business owners are "flying on the same plane" as their customers. My pharmacist knows his customers and is endlessly patient with questions and concerns. I have seen him visit for a half hour with an old person concerned about bunions, or a young mother whose baby has diaper rash. His way of working is not cost-effective, but his bottom line isn't money. It is knowing people well enough to be truly useful.

The Mill, a coffeehouse downtown, is always packed with people. The coffee and snacks are great. The atmosphere is the right combination of quiet and stimulating. On Saturday mornings, a men's group meets there. Christians meet for Bible study beside environmental activists. Poetry readings, benefits, and acoustic music concerts happen on a regular basis. Students from the university have study groups, and journalists conduct interviews there. It is a hub, a cultural center for our downtown, a place where I can walk in and know twenty people. We all need places like this in our lives, places where people know our names and the names of our children and parents.

Margaret Mead defined an ideal community as one that has a place for every human gift. An ideal community would somehow keep the best of the old ways and add the best of the new. We would have a mixing of races, generations, and viewpoints. We could enjoy the intellectual and cultural stimulation of cities and the safety of friendly neighborhoods. We'd have privacy and potluck dinners, freedom and civic responsibility. All the adults would take responsibility to help all the children. We would have connection without clannishness, accountability without autocratic control. The ideal community would support individual growth and development and foster loyalty and commitment to the common good.

A modern community that has many of these qualities is the Omega Institute in New York. When I arrived there to teach, I was assigned a cabin in the woods next to the massage tent. As I checked in, I heard the music of drums and Peruvian pipes and smelled the aroma of nasturtiums and freshly baked bread. When I walked onto my porch, I stumbled over a sleeping raccoon.

Omega is a learning center that offers weekly classes through the summer to about a thousand adults at a time. The classes range from writing and psychology to meditation and dance workshops. The setting is lovely. There is a creek, a forest with deer, a garden that has vegetables and flowers, and a pond for swimming and sunrise viewing. There is a large field for games, a basketball court, and a communal hall that serves great meals. There is a central hall, a bookstore, and a coffee shop that has Ben and Jerry's ice cream. In a small navigable space, everything humans really need—people, the natural world, books, food, culture, religious life, and music—exists in a simple form. There are no TVs, radios, or cars. No drugs, alcohol, or tobacco are allowed. The brown toilet paper is coarse, undecorated, and unperfumed, but it works. It's possible to walk everywhere. Children are safe. The kitchen staff audit philosophy classes. Old people study with their grandchildren. Things aren't locked up.

When people get off the bus at Omega, they look tired, stressed, and hyped up. However, after a few hours, the worry lines fade from their faces; their bodies relax. They begin laughing and singing. Omega works because the people there know the meaning of the word *enough*. It's built on a human scale to meet very old human needs for social and intellectual stimulation, for exercise, natural beauty, art, peace, and spiritual renewal. Humans can handle the amount of information available to the sense organs; no one is overwhelmed. Omega gives a glimpse of what a community could be. It is a human-sized place that provides autonomy, diversity, and safety. People stop hurrying and talk to one another. They look at the stars and listen to the wind in the trees.

# CHAPTER 4

# The Great Divide: Psychology

*Say! You've struck a heap of trouble—*
*Bust in business, lost your wife;*
*No one cares a cent about you,*
*You don't care a cent for life;*
*Hard luck has of hope bereft you,*
*Health is failing, wish you'd die—*
*Why, you've still the sunshine left you*
*And the big, blue sky. . . .*
*These, and none can take them from you;*
*These, and none can weigh their worth.*
*What! you're tired and broke and beaten?—*
*Why, you're rich—you've got the earth!*
*Yes, if you're a tramp in tatters,*
*While the blue sky bends above*
*You've got nearly all that matters—*
*You've got God, and God is love.*

—ROBERT SERVICE,
"Comfort"

NOBODY WRITES POETRY LIKE THIS ANYMORE. IT RHYMES, IT
has exclamation points, and it is utterly without irony. Many old people in

the Midwest can recite "Comfort" by heart. It's instructive to compare the Service poem to verses from "America" by a popular modern poet, Allen Ginsberg.

> *America I've given you all and now I'm nothing.*
> *America two dollars and twenty-seven cents January 17, 1956.*
> *I can't stand my own mind.*
> *America when will we end the human war?*

> *Go fuck yourself with your atom bomb.*
> *I don't feel good don't bother me.*
> *I won't write my poem till I'm in my right mind.*
> *America when will you be angelic?*
> *When will you take off your clothes?*

## Paradigms Collide

WHEN I BEGAN writing this book, I thought what would most separate my generation from earlier ones was technological change. But, in my experience, the "great divide" turns out to be psychology. With Freud, the psychological climate of the world changed and our self-reflective generation was born. It isn't that difficult to grasp the technological changes that people who grew up in soddies—making their own clothes and growing their own food—have experienced. What's hard to comprehend is their pre-Freudian way of processing reality.

Mine was the first post-popular-psychology, post-communal-culture, and post-TV generation. When we were teenagers, our parents really didn't understand us. We were the ones from another country. Now our parents are old and we don't understand them, that their experiences have led them to a different set of conclusions about the world, conclusions that keep us from communicating easily and clearly with each other. When we were young, we wanted and needed their understanding, and now they are old and they need our understanding.

Many of the tensions between generations are not personal. The difficulties are nobody's fault. We can't change our histories, but we can educate ourselves about them. We can be aware that surface-stucture differences do not always reflect differences in deep-structure motivations. We need translations and interpreters rather than declarations of war. If we can work through these time-zone issues, we will learn from each other. All our lives will be richer.

When did the study of psychology come to America? Psychology greatly influenced urban sophisticates and intellectuals in the 1910s and 1920s, but most Americans knew nothing about it at the time of World War II. The Midwest was slower to catch on than the East Coast, and since many writers were heavily influenced by Freud, readers were familiar with psychology sooner than nonreaders. My grandmother was a contemporary of D. H. Lawrence and Georgia O'Keeffe, yet she lived in the old country. She was a Victorian, and the artists were post-Freudians.

When I graduated from high school in 1965, I had never heard of psychotherapy. Now psychology is everywhere. Small-town people talk about low self-esteem, depression, panic disorders, and Freudian slips. Truck drivers go to therapists and waitresses analyze one another's dreams.

Progress has rolled across the Plains. The whole culture has become therapized. We've gone from Minnesota, Land of 10,000 Lakes, to Minnesota, land of 10,000 treatment centers. Many issues such as alcoholism, once either denied or thought of as sinful, are now considered mental health problems. We have become the "I'm dysfunctional, you're dysfunctional" culture. People who claim to be happy are viewed either as in denial or as hypocrites. If you say you had a happy childhood, you are less likely to be believed than if you say that you were traumatized by cruel parents. We now believe that there are no well-adjusted people, only those who are skilled at masking their pathologies. We now live by a topsy-turvy model of mental health, where the sick are well and vice versa. We trust the miserable and doubt the perky.

By the early 1990s, popular psychology was on radio and TV talk shows, in women's magazines and presidential speeches. *Reaction formation* and *projection* were household words. Recently I saw a cartoon in which a doorman says to a little girl, "Your mother must have a hidden agenda, the way she gave you those extra cookies." As my friend Pam put it, "We baby boomers seem obsessed with taking our emotional temperature at every turn." To many of my generation, therapy is the answer to everything. I think of writer Spalding Gray, a thoroughly modern man, who proposed in front of his therapist.

We've slid over a cultural waterfall. Even when we have the best of intentions, moving across generational boundaries is hard. We think our parents are ridiculous for worrying about appearances, manners, causing offense, or what others think. We worry more about meeting our own needs and expressing our feelings. Our parents see us as selfish. Their generation is less analytical than ours. To them, hello means hello, a rose is a rose is a rose. There is less self-reflection and picking apart of motives. We see them as uncommunicative, and they see us as endlessly massaging our fragile egos.

While our parents considered self-sacrifice a virtue, we associate it with being a martyr or a chump. When our parents talk about all they have done for us, we wince. On the other hand, our parents are likely to view our efforts to be independent as heartless. I once heard a psychologist describe a client who had no goals for herself, who lived entirely for her family. He said grimly, "That makes her a dangerous person." A professor who introduced me to a woman who had made many sacrifices for her family said, "She stands for everything I have learned to despise: a life of selfless devotion to another person."

# SISTER THERESA *(age 64)*

*"I have not been educated
to do my own thing."*

## SESSION ONE

Sister Theresa's story is an example of paradigms colliding. She came in
stressed by an old-fashioned values system and the pressures of the 1990s. I
tried to give her some modern tools to help her cope with those pressures
and still be a good nun.

Theresa was in her late sixties, a petite woman in a gray habit that fell
below her knees. She was friendly, but clearly anxious. Throughout our
first session she perched on the edge of the couch, never smiling, and when
I asked her questions about her feelings, she actually winced. She had come
on orders from her Mother Superior, who'd noticed she was crying easily
and having memory problems. Recently she had experienced panic attacks.
Theresa had tried to cope with this situation through prayer and meditation, but for the first time in her life, these methods of gaining peace
failed her.

Theresa worked as a nurse in a busy Catholic hospital. In this era of
managed care, she was being run ragged, doing more work for more
acutely ill patients and getting less support. Theresa was physically
exhausted and ill from working fifteen-hour days, but the work had to be
done. She couldn't leave her floor when things were in crisis, which was by
now pretty much all the time.

There were other problems as well. Theresa lived in an apartment with
Sister Josephina, who had been assigned to her because Theresa was so stable. Josephina was emotional and intrusive, talking all the time when
Theresa desperately needed quiet. However, Theresa had no skills for
asserting herself with Sister Josephina. In fact, she didn't even have the
notion of asserting herself. When I asked, "Have you confronted her?" she
answered, "Sisters don't confront. We accept."

When I asked her what she did to relax, she stared at me. I repeated the question. She said, "I used to love to swim. I was on a swim team in high school, but we nuns aren't allowed to wear bathing suits. The last time I was in a pool was 1959."

Theresa had been raised in Iowa by parents who had emphasized stoicism and duty. They had decided that their plain-looking, serious child would make a good nun. Theresa herself wasn't sure that she wanted to be a nun. Then, in high school, she read the mystical Catholic writers, such as St. John of the Cross and Teresa of Avila. This exposure, along with her parents' enthusiasm and her notable lack of success with boys, convinced her to enter a convent. "I wanted a life of faith and sacrifice," she said. "I wanted a life with God."

Theresa was a novice for one and a half years. It was a hard life, up at five and to bed at ten. She read, prayed, and cleaned. She said, "The happiest day of my life was the day I became a nun." Later she got her nurse's training at the University of Iowa and was assigned to work at the hospital. She'd been a leader in the religious community, hard-working, devoted, and obedient. She was embarrassed to be causing trouble now.

As we talked that first session, it was clear to me that we weren't using the same language. I asked how she took care of herself, and she answered that God took care of her. I asked if she had talked to Josephina about their conflicts, and she answered that Josephina was her cross to bear. I asked what she thought caused her anxiety attacks, and she said that she needed greater faith in God.

Psychology has language for self-analysis and self-care, one that leads mostly toward freedom and the actualization of the self. Sister Theresa's language was all about the loss of self for the greater good, about duty, submission, and community.

Our conversation would have been amusing if Theresa hadn't been so depressed and anxious. When I suggested that she take better care of herself, she said that she believed in putting her own needs last. I offered to get permission for her to swim as a treatment for depression, but she protested that she couldn't challenge her Mother Superior. The low point of our work was when I said in exasperation, "You have self-sacrificed yourself into a major depression." She answered primly, "I have not been educated to do my own thing."

## Session Ten

Slowly things got better between us. Even though Theresa thought I was a heretic, she was stressed enough to keep coming in. She had thought about suicide, which her church teaches is a sin. I learned to frame suggestions as good for the order and for her job, not just for her. I'd say, "If you are relaxed and healthy, you can work even harder for Christ." Theresa realized that the anger she felt inside for her roommate wasn't all that Christian and that perhaps they should have a talk. She saw that the anxiety that kept her awake nights didn't just make her miserable, which was okay, but that it interfered with her functioning. We realized that we wanted the same thing for her—a productive, religious life, but one in which she was rested, healthy, and sane.

Over time, I convinced Sister Theresa that it wasn't a sin to care for herself if that self-care allowed her to do Christ's work. Her Mother Superior came to one session and was wonderfully supportive. She suggested moving Sister Josephina back to the mother house and allowing Sister Theresa to live with another sister who was a close friend. She also agreed to work with the hospital on staffing problems.

The finest result of that meeting, though, was that Theresa got to swim. I told the Mother Superior that swimming was an essential stress-management tool. Otherwise, I said, "Sister Theresa might need tranquilizers." So Theresa bought a baggy swimsuit with a skirt and began swimming early mornings at the YWCA.

She came in looking ten years younger, glowing with enthusiasm, and laughing for the first time in our relationship. When I asked how she was, she hugged me and shouted, "I love to swim." She laughed at her own booming voice, and for fifteen minutes she described the pool, the cool water, and the way swimming made her body feel. "My tensions just fade away, and I'm revived and refreshed."

She told me that she was sleeping well, crying less, and having fewer anxiety attacks. Sister Josephina had moved out, and her friend moved in. Work was still overwhelming, but now it was the only overwhelming thing in her life. With my coaching, she became more assertive about getting help on her unit. The Mother Superior had even ordered her to take a vacation and go home for a visit that summer. She said, "I haven't been home in ten years."

In our work together, our time zones collided. We both learned from the crash. I observed the joy and sense of purpose that being a nun gave Theresa. I came to appreciate her supportive community, even though its emphasis on caring for others sometimes came at great expense to its own members. Theresa saw that to cope with the demands of life in the 1990s she needed some of the skills of modern people. She needed to know how to assert herself, manage her stress, and set limits on her work. She learned she could be a good sister and a good therapy client. At that last session, she said about swimming, "I can't believe God would object to my doing something that helps me this much."

To THE OLDER GENERATION, therapy is an odd concept. One woman was quoted in a *New Yorker* story as saying, "You'd have to be out of your mind to give a psychiatrist money, when you could go out and buy a pair of shoes." I remember talking to a widow about therapy. "Would it bring back my husband?" she asked me.

My client Kelli wanted to help her mother, who was stressed by her delinquent grandson and her son's bankruptcy. Kelli felt her mother might stop having anxiety attacks if she discussed these things with a therapist. After considerable coaxing, she got her mother to see a good local therapist. After the first appointment, her mother proudly declared that she had passed her mental-health checkup and didn't have to go back. "Did you tell the therapist about the bankruptcy, about your grandson, or about your panic attacks?" Kelli asked. Her mother answered indignantly, "No. It was none of his business."

Most elderly people don't recognize therapy as part of their world. When they do see therapists, they don't necessarily benefit. Some work so hard at putting a good face on things that it is impossible to figure out why they came in.

Leo was referred to me by his physician for addiction to prescription medications. When I asked him about his life, he said everything was wonderful. Leo had a great wife and family, a great job, and great friends. When I asked him about the drugs, he said his doctor thought he had a little problem, but really he was just super. Finally, in exasperation, I asked, "Is there anything not great in your life?" He looked shocked and said, "Young lady, everything is just fine, thank you."

Why don't older people like therapy? First of all, the idea rarely occurs to them. When they were young, they either kept their problems to themselves, prayed, or talked to relatives. In the rare event they talked to people outside the family, they sought out ministers for spiritual guidance, close friends, or doctors, bartenders, or hairdressers. Most likely, they did other things to deal with stress. Some people drank and beat their kids, but the majority coped in relatively healthy ways. My dad fished. My grandfather went to the pool hall and played checkers. Aunt Grace gardened and raised songbirds. Aunt Henrietta joked around.

Not only does this age group have no experience with the "talking cure," they have training in just the opposite. They learned to whisper words like *cancer* and *divorce*. They were taught that even to speak about an event somehow made it more real. Thus, one way to protect oneself from painful events was not to talk about them, to pretend they didn't exist. Psychotherapy flies in the face of this theory.

So when older people are in therapy, they often participate in quite idiosyncratic ways. A father attended a family session with his son and demanded I tell his son to stop screwing around and stay in his marriage.

One lady told me that her previous therapist was terrible. She said, "The damn fool just sat there and said nothing."

Family therapy sessions with the different generations are interesting. Many times, parents consider betrayal what kids consider hard, honest work; and parents consider family loyalty what kids consider stonewalling. Face saving can cause problems. I think of Danny, who had alcoholic parents. He tried to talk about their drinking, and they claimed they just had a glass of wine now and then. When he protested that they passed out at his son's birthday party, they explained they were just tired. Danny couldn't get his folks to deal with their alcohol problems. He continued to visit them, but he eventually decided that his children must stay home. He didn't want them hurt by drunk grandparents.

My client Darlene came in because her mother was having an affair. Actually she'd had affairs her entire life and denied them all. Darlene had accepted her mother's adultery and even her dishonesty. She didn't love her, but she tolerated her for her father's sake. However, as her own children grew up, Darlene questioned whether it was healthy to expose her children to a grandmother who was so dishonest. She said to me, "If she would just admit her problems and get help, I think I could forgive her. It's when she pretends everything is rosy that I feel crazy."

When a doctor recommends therapy, older people worry about the stigma. The older generation grew up in a time when mental illness was much feared and hated. Most decide that they would rather suffer than face the shame, the labels, and the admission of defeat that therapy implies.

Many can't afford it, or even if they can they are appalled by the price—one hundred dollars an hour just to talk to someone, especially someone fifty years younger and still wet behind the ears, a *pisher*, as one client put it. So they rarely show up in therapists' offices, and if they do, they feel awkward. A few really take to it, but many remain deeply uncomfortable with the whole idea. My physician mother had little respect for "complainers" and "malingerers." She respected my work with seriously disturbed people, but she wondered at my patience in listening to "all those people contemplating their navels."

## VICKY AND ANN *(ages 35 and 68)*
*"Before I talked to Vicky,*
*I thought I was happy."*

VICKY CALLED to make an appointment for her mother, whom she felt needed to work through some issues with a therapist. I asked how her mother felt, and Vicky laughed. "Well, let's put it this way. She'd rather have a root canal."

They came in the next day. Ann wore a pale pink suit and low heels and carried a snap-shut purse that matched her shoes. Vicky wore linen slacks and a silky Indian top with lots of jade jewelry. She was thin and pretty, but she had a tense face.

Ann was polite, slow-speaking, and prim. All her life she'd been an executive secretary for a local insurance company. She worked in an era when women trained men to be their bosses. Ann was clearly uncomfortable being in my office, but eager to do the right thing. Vicky, on the other hand, told me within seconds that she lived in Nashville with her two teenagers and that she attended virtually every support group known to humanity—Overeaters Anonymous, Gamblers Anonymous, Narcotics Anonymous, and Debtors Anonymous. Vicky said that her former husband was a poor provider and that she attributed her money problems to Ann, who had taught her that men supported women. She noted that it hadn't turned out that way for either of them. Sentences tumbled out of Vicky, while her mother sat with her hands crossed in her lap and a distressed smile on her face.

At some point I interrupted to ask how I could be helpful. Vicky said that her mother had low self-esteem and she wanted her to work on her issues. "What are they?" I asked Ann gently. She hung her head and said miserably, "I don't know. Before I talked to Vicky, I thought I was happy."

Vicky said, "Mother, you're deep in denial. Trust me, I can recognize it." When Vicky told me that her mother had never healed from a bitter divorce, Ann said softly, "I thought it was amicable." When Vicky described her parents' marriage as loveless, Ann said, "Well, it wasn't totally loveless." Vicky sighed. "You need to face up to your past."

Vicky described various fights her parents had, the harsh words between them, and even an affair her father had when she was in kindergarten. "Vicky remembers so much that I don't remember," Ann said. "I am amazed when she tells me all that happened."

Vicky said that because of her parents, she'd had poor relationships with men. She alluded to abuse and spoke harshly about her father and her grandfathers. Ann coughed politely, but Vicky ignored this signal of distress and poured out her dilemmas. As a single mom, Vicky had really struggled. Her daughter was mouthy and rebellious; her son experimented with drugs. There wasn't enough money or time. The schools weren't safe.

Ann was clearly embarrassed by her daughter's outpouring. Every now and then she'd interject a soft "Is it that bad?" which bugged Vicky, who deeply believed in the importance of openness.

I felt awkward, caught between two women from two culturally conditioned time zones. They had different memories, comfort levels regarding self-disclosure, and ideas about how to deal with pain. Ann grew up in a world that taught her to keep family problems in the family. Vicky grew up in a world where "denial isn't a river in Egypt." I needed to speak to each person in her own language.

They had different paradigms for who was a mentally healthy person. Ann was taught to be docile, cheerful, and a silent sufferer; Vicky was taught that healthy people emote. Invariably they clashed. What Vicky called processing, Ann called complaining. What Vicky called working on family issues, Ann considered betrayal. Of course, their individual personalities entered in. Vicky was more assertive and outgoing, while Ann was quieter and more low-key. But their personalities were shaped also by their times.

At one point, Vicky threw up her hands and said to me, "Thank God I am here to tell you what really happened. Mother makes her life sound like a Doris Day movie." Ann was too polite to object to her daughter in public, but she said mildly, "I think you exaggerate."

I wanted to take a generational perspective that was respectful to both women. Both women were partly right. The past probably was worse than Ann remembered and better than Vicky did. In an ideal universe, Ann would process more honestly and completely, and Vicky would buck up and not dwell so much on the negative.

Vicky was what Robert Bly calls a "perpetual adolescent," always seeking gurus. Vicky defined her mother with her modern constructs, and Ann obligingly agreed to be so defined. Her daughter's unhappiness was what brought Ann to a therapist; her daughter's memories, not hers, were the ones that rankled. She loved her daughter and would do anything to keep close. If Vicky were happier, Ann would be baking cookies for her two grandkids and gardening.

I identified with both women. I was between them—chronologically, literally, and figuratively. When my mother was alive, I grew irritated at her because she, like Ann, denied the troubles of the past. She liked to remember only that we were a happy, golden family, at least until my father's stroke. Her distorted memories frustrated me. And I can feel sorry for myself in a way that resembles Vicky more than Ann. Neither Vicky nor I was exactly conditioned to make the best of it.

I liked Ann's politeness and gracious courage, and I understood Vicky's need to talk about the past. My job was to make sure that neither woman had a monopoly on storytelling about the family. No matter how whitewashed, Ann's version of history should be respected. I hoped I could teach each the skills of the other generation. Ann could use more processing skills and openness about her feelings, and Vicky could benefit from letting a few sleeping dogs lie.

Vicky had a difficult life in a tough town, and Ann was growing old alone. These two women needed each other. Beyond their surface-structure differences, they clearly cared about each other. They shared a deep structure: the desire to have a strong, close family for Vicky's children. However misguided her plans for Ann might be, Vicky sincerely wanted her mother to have high self-esteem. And Ann would do anything for Vicky, including enduring this far-too-personal therapy.

At the end of our session, I asked if we should reschedule. Ann looked at Vicky, who said, "Yes, of course. We're just getting started." I asked Ann what she wanted to do, and she surprised me with an honest statement. "I never think about what I want to do. I think about what I should do."

Vicky said, "Mother, that's not healthy. That's why we're here."

I said, "You two are here partly because you disagree about what is healthy. My job is to help you talk these differences through in a way that allows you both to feel good about each other."

As they left, Vicky hugged me and said, "Mother is in pain, and I'm struggling to get things right. I think therapy will help." Ann smiled uncomfortably at me and said, "Have a nice afternoon."

IN ANN'S GENERATION, loyalty and restraint were highly valued. Sometimes these qualities were heroic, and other times they covered up serious problems. For example, members of an earlier generation might label Uncle Martin as having "a little touching problem," while a modern person would say that Uncle Martin committed incest.

Queen Elizabeth and Princess Diana are good examples of paradigms colliding. Both women exemplified the virtues of their time zones. Diana was open, spontaneous, and authentic. Elizabeth is restrained, stoic, and dignified. Diana was raised post-Freud, post-Spock, and post-Maslow. She was a psychologically-minded woman who could process feelings, share her pain, and analyze her reactions to any event ad infinitum. Elizabeth keeps her feelings to herself and does her duty. She can't share her pain any more than she can Rollerblade or program a computer.

My client Abby's mother, who has many health problems, lives with Abby. Abby doesn't consider caring for her to be a burden but rather a privilege. Still, occasionally Abby has a bad day in which too many things go wrong at work and home. She'll complain a little about stress or say she feels overwhelmed. Her mother will immediately become upset and insist on moving into a rest home. Abby will have to calm her mother down and reassure her mother that she wants her with her. Abby said to me, "What I consider harmless processing, mother considers rejection. She feels obligated to act."

Our parents' generation handled pain and trauma in an understated way. When my mother-in-law was seriously ill, I wanted to talk about the stress, to emote, and to say "I love you." My parents-in-law joked and avoided discussions of the serious situation. Phyllis watched TV and played cards in her hospital bed. They were kind to me, but I am sure they thought I was overly emotional. I felt they were ignoring important issues.

The different ways of handling emotions lead to misunderstandings. Older parents are angry at their grown children's complaints. Parents label their children whiners. To them it looks like their children have so much more than they had as kids and yet they don't appreciate it. On the other hand, children are skeptical of their parents' protests that their families were happy. Adult children sometimes confront their parents about abuse, when the parents felt they were only providing good discipline.

There are many fractured families as a result of such collisions. Adult children want to acknowledge and forgive, but not pretend that bad things never happened. Older people view their children as hothouse flowers who distort history and remember only the bad. We say we want to know the truth. Our parents ask, "Now, why do you want to bring that up?"

These differences make for some comedy and tragedy. I was chairing a discussion on family issues in Kansas when an older woman announced that no one in her family had any serious problems. Perhaps that was true, but no one born after 1950 believed her. And only in the 1990s could the following happen. I was interviewed by a radio journalist who recently had been divorced. On the air, she told me that after therapy, she confronted her parents for raising her in such a conflict-free family. Because her parents had never argued in front of her, she felt they had let her down. She didn't learn to handle conflict and despair from them.

I don't want to eulogize or romanticize the past. Real abuse—sexual, physical, and psychological—occurred then as it does now. Denial can keep serious problems from being solved. Sometimes a lack of psychological sophistication gets people in trouble. Repression and attention to duty at the expense of self can lead to depression and fatigue. Holding in feelings over the years can lead to wounded relationships, backstabbing, and somatic symptoms. Tensions end up getting expressed through headaches, passive-aggressive behavior, or fights over wills.

People who are silent about disagreements aren't necessarily loving. Silence can make simple problems unfixable. Many older people would have better relationships if they could ask for what they want. They seethe with resentments that might fade if they were expressed. People who can't communicate directly about their needs are set up for bitterness. The older generation has more than its share of martyrs, sulkers, and emotionally constricted adults.

Many things that should be discussed are not. When Bess Truman's father killed himself in a Richard Cory kind of suicide, Bess's mother fell apart. She was a "prisoner of shame" and almost never left the house again. Bess cared for her invalid mother the rest of her life, and Harry Truman hesitated to run for vice president because this suicide might come up. Perhaps if the mother could have talked through her grief, she could have returned to the land of the living and made her own and her family's lives easier.

However, the situation is more complicated than it looks. There are different ways of acknowledging pain. People were given a great deal of support in the past, only it was via pies, jokes, and offers to work. Today people in trouble may be more exposed but not necessarily more supported. They may actually get less concrete support.

## MONA AND JUNE *(ages 93 and 60)*
*"I try not to dwell on it."*

JUNE CALLED to make an appointment for her mother, Mona. Six months earlier, Mona's only son had died in a car accident. Since then Mona had been slipping away—she wouldn't eat, and she slept most of the time. Mona's doctor attributed this decline to old age, but June felt Mona was depressed. I warned June that many older people don't take to therapy. She said, "We'll be in tomorrow."

The next day June brought Mona, who wore a black silk kimono and slippers and had short stylish hair so silver it looked white-blond. I complimented her haircut, and Mona said proudly, "June did it." June smiled and said, "When I was a girl, I liked to play with Mother's hair, and I still do."

When I asked about Mona's health, she said, "I have no aches or pains. My only complaint is low energy."

June wore a flowing dress, Birkenstocks, and a necklace made from snake vertebrae. She was an administrator at an arts institute, on leave right now to care for Mona. She said, "I came home three months ago for a visit and realized Mother needed help. She weighed ninety pounds and had stopped going out. She was acting like she was ready to die."

Mona said, "I told June I was getting old, but she wouldn't accept that."

"Mother, you're depressed."

Mona brushed that judgment away with her hand, but she said, "June is a good daughter."

June said, "By now I'm Mother's personal trainer as well as her cook, chauffeur, housecleaner, and social secretary." June said she had tried to interest Mona in her old friends, in dance recitals, or in concerts—all the things Mona had loved—but Mona wouldn't perk up. June said, "You don't know how unusual this is for Mother."

June prepared delicious soups and salads and invited people in for dinner. Mona would say, "Oh, don't make me eat. I'm not hungry." Once, Mona had said sharply that a veggie burger June had fixed looked like a dead mouse. Finally, June lectured her. She reminded Mona of something Mona had taught her: "If you can't change your life, change your attitude."

"Mother, why are you so negative?" June had asked. "Why don't you say, 'I'm so lucky to have this delicious meal prepared by someone who loves me. I will enjoy eating it'?"

June laughed. "I had never lectured my mother before, but I'm glad I did. After that, she stopped complaining."

"I am better now," Mona said. "June has brought me back to life."

"You still have a ways to go," June said.

As a young woman, Mona had many adventures. Her family loved both the great outdoors and the cultural life of the cities. She grew up speaking Czech and English. Once she danced in front of the Prince of Wales. Mona liked her rural childhood, her years as a student and dancer, and her time as a wife and mother. She lit up when she talked about the past. Only when she spoke of her son's death did she seem old-old.

June said, "After Frank died, Mother lost her interest in living."

Mona said simply, "Losing Frank has been the hardest thing."

I asked gently, "How have you tried to deal with your loss?"

Mona floundered: "I try not to dwell on it."

"Mother, you think about it all the time," June said.

Mona needed to talk about her feelings, but I was unsure whether it was fair to ask this of a ninety-three-year-old woman who preferred "not to dwell on it." Like many other old people, she had tried to ignore tragedy. This method had worked with earlier losses, but it wasn't working now. Mona could actually benefit from some modern-day coping skills.

I said I thought Mona would do better if she came in and talked about Frank. I asked her to bring pictures of him. June said, "Mother has kept all his letters. She could bring those in." Mona winced but nodded in agreement. I said, "Next time you come we'll talk about your son. I want you to have at least a few sessions where you express your sadness."

Mona ended our session by saying that she has had a lucky life, that she was born into a beautiful family and later had her own beautiful family.

June interrupted her to say, "Mother, you have not had a lucky life; you have had a hard life. Your brother was killed in the war, and you lost your father when you were young. When you were only fifty, you lost your husband, and now you have lost a son."

Mona thought about what June said, and then responded, "Everybody has those kinds of experiences, but I have always had good people in my life. I have always found things to enjoy."

June said, "Mother tends to deny her sorrows." Mona said, "June is more emotional than I am."

"You are both right," I said. "Mona, you have been able to weather losses by focusing on the positive. However, this time you lost your ability to find things to enjoy. I think if we talk this through, your charmed life can regain its charm."

Mona said, "I hope June realizes that none of this is about her. I love her very much." June's eyes teared up. "I love you too, Mother. That's why I want you to talk to a therapist."

MONA HAD MANY of the problems the old-old face: loss of loved ones, waning health, and depression. Her ways of coping, which worked when she was younger, were not adequate for the pain and trauma of her developmental stage. She needed some of the processing skills of our generation. Gutting it out alone wouldn't get her through this grief.

Both generations know something important about handling pain. It's good to be able to face problems, and yet sometimes the best way out of an impossible situation is through the door. Sometimes it's better to share sad feelings; other times it's better to joke or get to work. There is a golden mean, a proper balance.

Parenthetically, one good thing about aging is that it sometimes frees people to tell the truth. People who might object to a story are dead, or even if they are alive, the statute of limitations runs out. Many adult children report having good, serious conversations with their parents about family history. As they approach death, many people decide to come clean with facts about abortions, divorces, suicides, and other skeletons in the closet.

Many people older than age eighty are able to say, for the first time in their lives, how much their children mean to them. My aunts and uncles tell me that they love me, something they didn't do when we were younger. Often grandparents can be much more expressive with their grandchildren than they were with their own children. Old men can cry when they are deeply moved, and they are moved more easily and more often.

One of the difficult truths we eventually came to examine in my family was my grandfather's mental illness. Early in the century there was almost no knowledge about mental illness. Both diagnosis and treatment were in primitive stages. Superstition and prejudice substituted for information. People with schizophrenia or manic depression often were left to wander about as the town loonies, or were locked up for life in horrible institutions.

My paternal grandfather was a victim of this ignorance. When I was a girl, I knew only that as a young man, my grandfather had committed himself to a mental hospital, where he spent most of his adult life. Before he became ill, he was bright and handsome, a cattle trader and inventor, much respected in Christian County, Missouri. When I met him, he had a broken hip from crudely administered electroshock therapy and he walked with a limp. My parents had taken me to see him, but he asked them not to come back. He said, "It's so much trouble for you, and it doesn't matter that much to me."

My father talked of his own childhood poverty and his many stepfathers, but he never mentioned schizophrenia, a word I first read in a college textbook. When my dad was middle-aged, he told me that he had spent his whole life trying not to go crazy. Even as a teenager, I realized that trying to be sane all the time was a kind of craziness itself.

I think with sadness of my gentle grandfather, who died before we knew much about the etiology and treatment of mental illness, before we had any psychotropic medications. Today, properly diagnosed and medicated, my grandfather could have worked and could have lived most of his life at home. His family could have had support from therapists and other families with similar problems. His children would have felt less fear for their own futures. Today our theories about mental illness are kinder. And no one gets a broken hip from shock therapy.

Whenever I feel critical of the mistakes that have been made in my field, I look at my own family and feel grateful for modern psychology. In the Ozarks in the early part of this century, there were no therapists. Myth and malarkey filled in for scientific fact. The family of a mentally ill person felt great shame. Today there is less shame and more dignity, less ignorance and more openness. I am glad for psychotherapy and modern medicine.

## DR. GEORGE (age 77)
*"Hard times,*
*but good times, too."*

GEORGE HAS THE VIRTUES of pre-Freudian, communal people and of post-Freudian individualists. He is hard-working and a team player. He can reflect on his life and yet put his reflections aside and act on behalf of others. He can sacrifice and take care of himself. Most important, he can deal honestly with painful reality and yet be positive and good-natured. George is a psychiatrist who came from a family of Japanese immigrants. On a cold November day, I drove to his place. Even though he had been a doctor most of his life and had four children who were doctors, his home was a modest ranch-style house in an old suburb. His wife, Chiyo, who met me at the door, was lovely, with shiny hair and bifocals. George was slim and dapper.

As we sat in the living room, Chiyo served us coffee in small porcelain cups. Her seriousness and grace with this ritual reminded me of a tea ceremony. When I told them that I would be going to Japan, George gave me advice about rail passes and hotels. He said, "You can leave your purse on the chair on the bullet train. Japanese people don't steal or lie." He also said, "Take plenty of business cards and tell that husband of yours to wear a dark suit. The Japanese are formal."

When I asked George, who usually interviews others, to tell me about his own life, he seemed almost shy. His father had come to Southern California after the turn of the century to study but soon found himself married. He and his wife lost their first son at birth. George was the second born, followed by a brother and sister. Early in life, George spoke only Japanese, but things changed in kindergarten. The principal of his school couldn't pronounce his name, Kioshi, and she said, "From now on you're George." George laughed when he told that story but he remembered the principal's name after all these years.

His dad had been making a good living driving a truck when he rented land and began farming. Then, to quote George, "He lost his pants." Once a friend asked him why he had sold his truck and gone into farming. "I didn't want my boys to be truck drivers," his father replied simply. Even during the Depression, his mother always managed to put a few dollars a week in a jar. She said, "This is so George can go to Berkeley." George smiled. "Japanese children are obedient, so that's what I did," he said.

"The Depression was hard on the Japanese," George continued. "We were the slaves of California, doing the hardest work for the least money." He said that the Japanese dealt with their misery in two ways: *enryo*, which refers to a tendency to deny oneself in public, to turn down a cup of coffee or a second cookie, to take pride in not needing and not taking anything; and *gaman*, which translates loosely as "grin and bear it." Instead of becoming bitter and paranoid, most people took the attitude that it could have been worse, and they made do.

George played sports during high school. He faced little discrimination, but he said it never would have occurred to him to date a Caucasian girl. George focused on positives. For example, George told me he should have been drafted earlier, but the draft people gave him the time he needed to finish his studies. He found something good to say even about the time right after Pearl Harbor. George was a student at the University of California, living in Berkeley with six Caucasian guys who all supported him against Japanese-bashers.

After Pearl Harbor, Japanese-Americans were punished. Young men were classified 4C, enemy alien, not qualified for the military. George was taken out of school and sent with his family to Heart Mountain Relocation Center. While there, George finished his degree from the University of California through correspondence courses.

George chuckled as he remembered what his mother had said in the camps: "If I were a man, I'd jump this fence and leave." George didn't jump the fence, but he was the second person to leave. He was accepted to a graduate program at the University of Nebraska, one of the only schools to accept Japanese-American students during the war.

The camp people dropped him off at a train station with a sack lunch and a small bag of clothes. He felt self-conscious on a train filled with unfriendly-looking people, but after a while a retired railroad man came over to talk to him. This man had worked with Japanese people for years. He cheered George up and even invited him to visit his home in Wyoming. Then, when the train pulled into Lincoln, many students met him at the station. He felt secure and good in Nebraska. He received his master's degree in economics at UNL, but afterward he picked sugar beets in Idaho. He told me, "I was a well-educated beet picker."

In 1945 he joined the Army. He went to Officer's Training camp in Fort Benning, Georgia, and then to military intelligence school. While he was an adjutant to the Kyoto Post Command, he met Chiyo. Her father was a silk maker, and like most Japanese families during the war, they almost starved. Chiyo said that she was always hungry. Whenever he could, her father sold beautiful silk kimonos for sacks of potatoes.

Because Chiyo was a Japanese citizen, George had to get an act of Congress passed in order to marry her. George was with his troops in Korea when he was notified that he could marry. The Regiment Commander granted him a seven-day pass to Japan. After a brief honeymoon he returned to his unit. He and Chiyo had a Japanese wedding on May 10, and an American wedding on November 11 at the U.S. Consulate in Kobe. They have been married forty-seven years.

After the Army years, George returned to Nebraska. Chiyo missed her family and Japan, especially in springtime. They lost their first child but soon had four children, and Chiyo was too busy to feel homesick. George worked his way through medical school with the GI bill and by driving a taxi. He earned all the money because he wanted his children to have their mother at home to help with their studies.

George picked psychiatry because he couldn't handle the deaths of his patients. He blamed himself when anyone died. He said that even in psychiatry, he'd been emotionally involved with his patients. His bill collections never ran higher than 50 percent. He said, "I had sympathy for the people I saw. I didn't want to hassle them for money."

In the early years his clinic was next to his home, and at night his patients would come and visit on his back porch. He took the kids along when he made nursing-home visits. This combination of the old world and the new was typical for George. He practiced modern psychiatry, but he related to his clients as if they all lived together in a small village. His kids often were around him as he worked.

George spoke with rare insight and honesty for a man of his time and culture. He said, "I was a workaholic and I took my stress out on the family. They knew that I loved them, but I shouldn't have done it." He felt that he'd been too authoritarian, "like most Japanese men are," and he'd tried to mellow out as he got older.

George had a gift for remembering kindnesses. When he was serving in Korea he went to visit his friend Tanji in another unit. While Tanji's group had double-lined sleeping bags, George's unit had single-lined bags, and they were always cold. When George teased Tanji, "How did you guys get these?" Tanji gave him his bag.

Another happy memory was of his unit's reunions in Hawaii. George noticed how expensive his room was and asked to move to a smaller room, but Tanji had taken care of everything. At one of those reunions, George's friends had talked of heart troubles, cancer, and the deaths of other vets. When George returned to Nebraska, he had a panic attack. He went to a fellow psychiatrist to discuss his anxiety. They agreed that, like everyone else, George must accept that he is mortal. He felt much better after that talk and never had another panic attack.

About ten years ago, though, George had a heart attack. Before his heart surgery he asked to see a priest. He confessed his sins and was baptized. At that moment all his anxiety about death left him. Now he is a religious person and does volunteer work for human-service agencies. He likes his work and feels fully compensated by the thank you's of his patients.

George showed me a picture of himself, his brother, and his mother during the Depression in Southern California. They are standing by a road with an orange grove in the background. Their clothes are tattered, and they are barefoot. George holds a straw hat for working outdoors. His mother has her arms around the two boys, and they all are staring directly into the camera. Although his mother looks proud of her strong sons, only George is smiling. Under the picture, George had written, "Hard times, but good times, too."

In general, George and Chiyo are enjoying their lives of family, friends, work, and travel. The past year their eldest son, John, was killed in a car wreck. George said, "It was tough, but we are over his death. We now have a new mission in life: to help our daughter-in-law with the children."

George is a soft-hearted guy who has helped people all his life. In his young-old life stage, he is having fun. He watches his diet and exercises regularly. He and Chiyo often visit Japan, and he goes fishing with his sons and grandsons. He showed me a picture of himself in shorts and a T-shirt with a giant tuna he'd caught. Then he added, "Look how young I look when I'm fishing." He said, "With a fish this big I don't feel sad if it gets away. I feel the best contender won."

George's mother taught him *gambare*—to do your best, go for broke; *giri*—the importance of character; and *gimu*—responsibility. After the war, the prejudice against Japanese-Americans was so strong that the only way to make it was through education and hard work. George said that he, like most Japanese-Americans of his generation, had feelings of inferiority. As a psychiatrist, he liked Adler, who wrote about the pleasure humans take in overcoming their fears.

From modern psychology George learned to be honest and open about his feelings. He is sensitive to others but expects good behavior. He has found Buddha's Middle Way—how to work hard for others and then go fishing. He has even learned to see losing a big fish as a victory.

George doesn't deny pain, but he can rise above it and turn sorrow into wisdom. He has the knack for converting pain into a mission, like his new mission to care for his grandchildren. George knows the great secrets of life: Find good work and people to love, focus on the positives, and appreciate small things. He can make conscious choices about whether he will be a modern American psychiatrist or a pre-psychology Japanese-American.

*To keep every cog and wheel is the first*
*precaution of intelligent tinkering.*

—ALDO LEOPOLD

As we approach a new century, psychologists must synthesize the best of both models of coping. Many of us already are returning to "old-fashioned" methods of coping. In the early part of this century, humor was the big survival skill. My dad, who had grits and gravy week after week during the Depression, joked about how his family had a different name for that meal depending on the day. Sunday they called it "turkey" and Monday it was "roast beef." Modern healers, such as Norman Cousins, recognize the value of laughter; Frank Farleigh's provocative therapy gets people to loosen up and laugh at their problems.

In the 1960s, Fritz Perls wrote, "To say 'I feel obligated' is to say 'I

resent.'" Many therapists encouraged their clients to break free of responsibilities and obligations: "If it feels good, it is good." But in the 1990s, we are
realizing that being useful is an excellent mental-health tonic. Frank
Pittman's questions to clients exemplify our changes. He used to ask,
"What are others doing to you, and how are you feeling?" Now he is asking, "What are you doing for others, and how are others feeling about
you?" Also in the 1960s, we told clients to "get in touch with your anger,"
or "let it all hang out." Now we are saying that anger is generally not productive and that anger control is an individual responsiblity.

Cognitive-behavioral therapists teach that anxiety, depression, and
other self-defeating behaviors are the results of illogical thinking, that "you
feel the way you think." They emphasize self-control, good mental attitude, and not dwelling on things. In *Feeling Good*, David Burns recommends old-fashioned strategies—maximize the positives, be optimistic, and
focus on what is working well. Burns writes, "Don't overwhelm yourself
with too much at one time." This advice sounds like "Don't cross your
bridges until you come to them." He advises people to stay busy, which is
not unlike "Idle hands are the devil's playground."

Rather late in the day we are realizing also that some things are best left
unsaid. Therapists no longer encourage their clients to share every emo-
tion. I think of the current saying "Don't go there," which is really a warning not to process a particular experience.

We are learning that neither generation has a monopoly on good mental health. The older generation had their flaws, but they were good at
dancing during the Depression and at joking about their hungry bellies. My
generation has helped parents become more gentle and open with children
and more reflective about relationship issues. We are more sophisticated
about human motivation.

Flexibility works best. Teaching people how to talk about the suicide of
a family member is good, but so is to teaching them to tend flowers. Talking
to an abused teen about her feelings is good, but so is teaching her to rock

climb or quilt. A well-timed chocolate cake or pot of chicken soup can soothe many an aching heart. They could in 1904, and they can today.

*I learned from my mother how to love*
*the living, to have plenty of vases on hand*
*in case you have to rush to the hospital*
*with peonies cut from the lawn, black ants*
*still stuck to the buds. I learned to save jars*
*large enough to hold fruit salad for a whole*
*grieving household, to cube homecanned pears*
*and peaches, to slice through maroon grape skins*
*and flick out the sexual seeds with a knife point.*
*I learned to attend viewings even if I didn't know*
*the deceased, to press the moist hands*
*of the living, to look in their eyes and offer*
*sympathy, as though I understood loss even then.*
*I learned that whatever we say means nothing,*
*what anyone will remember is that we came.*
*I learned to believe I had the power to ease*
*awful pains materially like an angel.*
*Like a doctor I learned to create*
*from another's suffering my own usefulness, and once*
*you know how to do this, you can never refuse.*
*To every house you enter, you must offer*
*healing: a chocolate cake you baked yourself,*
*the blessing of your voice, your chaste touch.*

—JULIA KASDORF,
"What I Learned from My Mother"

# Part Two

# Discovering New Lands:

## *Relationships Between the Generations*

# CHAPTER 5

# Traveling Together: The Things We Carry

*The older we grow, the greater become the ordeals.*

—GOETHE

*Old age is like a plane flying through a storm.*
*Once you're aboard, there is nothing you can do about it.*

—GOLDA MEIR

THE ONLY THING WORSE THAN HAVING AGING PARENTS IS NOT having aging parents. The old-old die by inches. At first, Father can no longer jog, then he can no longer take long walks or do heavy lifting. Later, he gives up foreign travel and flying, with all its stresses. Finally, he can't drive the car. At first, Mother is no longer the best cook in the country, then the children worry she will poison herself with spoiled food or burn down the house. Families must adjust to each new lost "inch."

It's hard for an adult child to watch the mother who gave her birth grow old and helpless. It's painful to witness the father who always knew what to do become a confused and uncertain old man. As children care for ill parents they face certain universal problems—sleep deprivation, workload pileup, no time for themselves, and the sense that nothing is being well handled. Most experience the "I am guilty wherever I am" syndrome, as well as oscillations between guilt and rage about the whole situation. They often burn out and feel ashamed that they have burned out.

The role reversal is hard on parents, too. No father wants to ask his daughter to help him go to the bathroom or explain to his son that he forgot to ask the doctor an important question. Parents worry about burdening their children. They fear losing their dignity and autonomy. Everyone is off script.

Adult children are anxious about doing too much, and worried about doing too little. They fear parental disapproval or embarrassment, and they are nervous about making the wrong decisions at a time when decisions really matter. A bad call can mean death, squandered resources, or lifelong regrets. Information isn't adequate, and everybody desperately wants to do the right thing.

All kinds of problems crop up. My client Reena, a loving and conscientious daughter, put her brain-damaged mother in a rest home at her mother's request. But when she visited the next day, her mother shouted at her, "How dare you leave me in a place like this?" Another client, Leonard, had a father who suffered from myasthenia gravis. He asked Leonard to help him commit suicide, but Leonard refused. The next day his father swallowed 300 Aleve and lay in bed until he was discovered by Leonard's daughter. She called 911, and her grandfather was taken to an emergency room and given liquid charcoal to induce vomiting. Now he has liver damage in addition to his myasthenia gravis, and he feels betrayed by Leonard and by his granddaughter.

Ellen Goodman wrote about a man who had to return home and take the car keys from his father, the person who taught him to drive. She wrote of our sorrow and confusion about how to handle such delicate and painful issues, and mourned that there is no Dr. Spock to tell us what to do for our parents.

Out of a misguided respect for privacy, family members may not help one another enough. Adult children try to walk the fine line between being overbearing and neglectful. They may not ask, "Is someone abusing you?" "Do you need money?" "Are you taking the right amount of medication?" Their parents may not ask, "Do you think I'm losing my memory?" "Would you help me cut my toenails?" "Can I come live with you?"

Loss of functioning is difficult for everyone. People have different "idioms of stress." Uncle Benny eats too much, Aunt Tillie cries, Uncle Walter withdraws, and Dad yells at people. Big sister may overmanage, little brother may slip out to the garage to smoke marijuana. People's coping methods crash into one another. The talker corners the withdrawer. The pot smoker is discovered by the grand-aunt, who came out to the garage to cry. People's needs don't mesh. Father is depressed and withdrawn when the daughter feels a desperate need to connect.

As families struggle with new and complicated issues, tensions arise. No one can be on their best behavior for months at a time. A grandmother who is constantly nauseated is impatient with a self-absorbed teenager. Adult children arrive for a visit stressed about pink slips from work or failing slips from school. A child gets lost in the sadness and confusion of moving her grand-aunt to the rest home and has a temper tantrum. Grandfather cries at the dinner table. A usually mild-mannered son shouts at an insurance-company employee about a bill for his mother's hospital stay. A harsh word elicits a day of the silent treatment from a befuddled uncle. A faulty phone connection to a dying grandmother seems like the end of the world.

People want things to go well, but they are human. Everybody steps on everybody's toes. There is baggage from the past as well as trouble in the present. Our parents weren't perfect parents, and we weren't perfect children. Nobody becomes a perfect person with age. Even when everyone wants things to end on a good note, problems come up. How could they not in such difficult and unknown territory? Loving people means being disappointed.

Old-old age can be a time of great sorrow, but also of great healing. One of my clients was raised a strong Catholic, but she had broken with her faith as a young woman and become a Buddhist. Her father had taken a second job when she was a girl to keep her in Catholic schools. He could not believe his oldest daughter would reject the religious teachings that meant everything to him. He sincerely believed that she would not go to heaven. He couldn't forgive her.

My client went home to care for her father the last weeks of his life. She read him his Bible and prayed with him, something she hadn't been willing to do for years. He asked her questions about Buddhism. The last day of his life, he said to her, "I think Buddhists and Catholics go to the same heaven. We will be together in the end."

My client Belinda was disowned by her rural Kansas parents when they learned she was gay. She kept in touch with one of her sisters, but otherwise had heard nothing from her parents or brothers for twenty years. She worked in a city far away. Her letters were returned unopened. Belinda was in her forties when her sister called to report that her father had developed tongue cancer. Belinda called her mother and offered to help.

Much to Belinda's surprise, her mother broke into tears and accepted her offer. Her mother agreed partly because over the years, and especially since her husband's illness, they had changed their attitudes toward Belinda. Impending death has a way of putting things in perspective. After all, Belinda was their daughter. Partly, too, her mother accepted because all the other children were tied up with jobs and children. Belinda was a freelance writer who could work anywhere.

Within weeks, Belinda had moved her office into her old bedroom on the farm. Her brothers came by to see the folks, and while at first they were skeptical about her, when they saw how kind Belinda was to their father, they softened. They began joking and horsing around with Belinda like they had as kids. Her sister relaxed too when she had Belinda to share the burdens of her parents' old-old age.

Belinda's parents felt she was their savior. It's hard not to love and appreciate someone who is helping with driving, insurance forms, bedpans, and back rubs. At one point in his six months of dying, Belinda's dad said, "I'm sorry about the cancer, but I am glad it brought you home."

These long, hard years can work only if everyone can agree to tolerate imperfection and to stay the course. This stage in the life of a family requires the skills of both the older generation and the baby boomers. It requires courage, forbearance, stoicism, and the abilities to laugh and to forget problems. And it requires the abilities to assert needs, to communicate openly, and to process pain. Successful resolution of this stage allows the old-old to feel respected and at peace with their families. They learn to accept the nurturing that children offer. The young get the chance to grow up and truly be adults.

## THE SWENSON FAMILY
*"I know she is lonely, but she even
follows me into the bathroom."*

BEVERLY HAD SCHEDULED this appointment for herself; her teenage daughter, Abby; and her mother, Zella Mae. She was determined to have family counseling, even if it meant lying and bullying that first time. She'd told Zella Mae the session would be mostly about Abby. And she'd said to Abby, "You come, or I'm going to leave you alone with Granny."

I didn't meet a happy group at our morning session. Outside it was May Day, with flowers and blue sky; inside it was gray and cold. Beverly began by telling me she was divorced and had been since Abby was five. She worked at an insurance office as an administrative assistant. She turned to her mother and said, "Do you want to talk?" Zella Mae glared, and Beverly said, "Mother is unhappy to be here. She lives with us and helps out with the bills. She has diabetes and is on dialysis. Just this year, her health has gotten worse. She's had some heart trouble, and her vision is failing."

Zella Mae interupted to say, "I thought this was about Abby." Abby sighed elaborately, and Beverly said, "We'll get to Abby. The doctor wants to meet all of us."

Zella Mae mocked her daughter, repeating in a nasty tone, "The doctor wants to meet all of us."

Abby rolled her eyes and asked, "Why did we even come?"

When I asked Abby about herself, she looked at her mother, who signaled her to talk. "I don't know. I'm in ninth grade. I hate school."

Once again Zella Mae interupted: "Tell her you're failing math. Tell her how you smart off to your mother and me and how you won't do your chores." She turned to me and said smugly, "The chickens have come home to roost."

"Mother, that's enough." Bev said wearily.

"That's enough." Again, Zella Mae spoke in that mocking tone. "I thought that's what we were here for, to work on Abby."

"Did you tell her that?" Abby asked angrily.

Within five minutes, everyone was mad at everyone else. I slowed things down with a few ground rules: No interrupting; everyone gets to talk; it's best to talk about yourself, not other people.

I turned to Beverly. "Perhaps you should explain why the family is here."

Beverly looked tearful and nervous, but plunged into her story. "I called you after a bad week. Mother was fighting an infection, and I got Abby's math grade in the mail. Work was stressful, and every night I came home to Abby and Mother arguing. I knew it was time to call when Abby threatened to run away from home and I thought, *That's a good idea. Maybe I'll go, too.*"

Zella Mae crossed her arms over her chest and said, "Let Abby go. You've spoiled her rotten. No one can live with her."

Abby jumped in: "Granny yelled at me all the time, but I ignored her until I couldn't take it anymore. I'm patient with her, and you know it."

Beverly sighed. Zella Mae glared at Abby, who looked ready to bolt. I repeated my guidelines, and we continued doggedly on.

By the end I understood a few things about this family. Zella Mae almost never left the apartment except for her doctor's appointments. She probably had never been a sweet-natured person, but the loss of her health, her home, and her husband had left her permanently depressed and demanding. She was venting all her ire on her family. Abby was a typical teen, mouthy and less than studious, but really not a big troublemaker. In spite of her bluster, I could tell Abby loved Beverly and wanted to please her. I thought Abby's relationship with Zella Mae was about dead. Both were at a developmental level where they had little to give, and they had hurt each other too much for things to improve without time and major changes.

Beverly was caught between a stressful job and a stressful home life. She couldn't get any time or space for herself, and her role as mediator between a teen and a sick parent was complicated by her lack of assertiveness. Beverly had been raised to be deferential and respectful to her mother. She didn't know how to stand up for herself. While Abby and Zella Mae were hot-tempered and aggressive, Beverly was a conflict avoider who had trouble saying no. She was being eaten alive.

I suspected she could handle Abby if she didn't have her mother to deal with as well. However, the combination was wearing her down. She wasn't sleeping well, cried almost daily, and had migraines.

I ended the session by asking how the three of them would like the family to look a year from today. Abby said, "I'd like Mother and Granny off my back." Zella Mae said, "I just hope my granddaughter isn't pregnant or on drugs." Beverly said miserably, "I want us to get along." Abby sniffed. "Fat chance." I had to agree with her, but I scheduled another appointment for them the following week.

## SESSION TWO

Beverly came in alone. She looked exhausted and said she had a migraine coming on. I offered to reschedule, but she said no, she needed to talk. I asked about the others, and she said sadly, "Neither of them will return. You don't want to know what Mother said about therapy. Abby got mad this morning and punished me by refusing to come in. I probably could have made her, but I wanted time alone with you."

I listened while Beverly poured out her troubles. She had a difficult boss and no chance for advancement at her company unless she took computer classes. She couldn't do that while her daughter and mother were at the apartment. When she walked in the door at night, Zella Mae followed her around, complaining. "I know she is lonely," Beverly said, "but she even follows me into the bathroom."

Beverly explained that her mother had no friends or interests and did nothing to take care of herself physically or emotionally. "If I take her out to dinner, she complains about all the choices and the prices. Then, when the food comes, she says the portions are too big. She interacts by criticizing." Beverly looked at me sadly. "As I watch Mother, I'm making mental notes on what I don't want to do when I'm old."

She continued. "About once a week when I am stressed about Abby, Mother announces loudly that she will not abandon me. I think to myself, *Abandon me, please, abandon me.*"

We laughed, and Beverly seemed to breathe more deeply. I asked about Abby. She said that Abby was basically a good kid in the throes of adolescence. She alternated being sulky and demanding. Beverly knew Abby needed more nurturing and more help with her social life and homework right now, but she didn't have any more energy. She was almost out of family-leave time and unsure how she could keep driving her mother to dialysis. She worried about money and about holding her job with her migraines. I asked her what she did for herself, and she stared at me. "What do you mean?"

"I mean, do you have friends, do you exercise or go to movies?"

"What's a movie?" she asked.

I smiled, and she said, "What I really need is permission to put Mother in a home."

"I can't give you that permission," I said, "but I'll talk the issues through with you."

Mostly I listened as Beverly talked about how upset Zella Mae would be and about her guilt at not doing what either Zella Mae or Abby wanted. She also was fearful of her mother, whom she'd never successfully challenged. In fact, Beverly had tried only once before and she had lost her voice during the argument.

I encouraged her that she was stronger now and could do what needed to be done. I encouraged her not to think of a home as an either/or decision—"Either I am a good daughter and let Mother ruin my life, or I abandon her to a death trap." She could relocate her mother and still visit her, care for her, and be a dutiful daughter. I quoted her an old saying about power struggles: "Either avoid them or win them."

I said, "Talk to your mother about what you are doing. Be firm but kind. Make sure she knows you will visit her wherever she is. Take her along when you tour the different homes. Give her as much control as you can in this situation."

By the end of the hour, Beverly had decided to start looking for an assisted-living facility. We rescheduled for a month down the road. Beverly said, "I'm almost out of sick time. I'd better use what little I have left to look at housing for Mother. But I'll come in and tell you what happened."

## SESSION THREE (TWO MONTHS LATER)

Much to my surprise, Beverly and Abby came in together. Beverly looked a little more rested, and Abby too seemed calmer. Beverly announced, "The deed is done. Last weekend mother moved into Cherry Hill Manor. It's the place she selected."

I congratulated Beverly on standing firm. She said, "I knew I needed to take charge. It was time to be a good mother. It's too early to tell if Mother will like it, but she hasn't complained as much as we thought she would."

Abby said, "Granny never likes anything. If she doesn't complain non-stop, that means she likes it."

"I go by every day to check on her," Beverly said. "It's clean, the staff is caring, and the residents are talkative. She has her own room and TV. I actually think she is getting better medical care there. They drive her to dialysis and monitor her blood sugar."

I asked Abby if she had been by to visit, and surprisingly she'd stopped by twice after school. By way of explanation she said, "It helps Mom feel less guilty if I visit."

"I wanted Abby to understand that it's not her fault that Mother is in the home."

I asked Abby if she felt guilty. She hovered on the edge of a smart-ass response, but finally said, "I don't think Mom would have had the guts to do this unless I was flunking math."

"I have been worried about you. I know we need time together, but I did this partly for me. I want a life, too."

I asked Beverly if she felt better since Zella Mae left. "Let's put it this way," she said. "My migraines have settled down, I've signed up for a computer course, and Abby and I went to the movies."

"For the first time in about ten years," Abby interjected, but without much venom.

*The fatal metaphor of progress, which means leaving things behind us, has utterly obscured the real idea of growth, which means leaving things inside us.*

—G. K. CHESTERTON

*We were going to leave a mark on the world but instead the world left marks on us.*

—WALLACE STEGNER

While adolescence is about the loss of childhood, old age is about the loss of adult status and power. Cultural myths rarely tell the truth about either stage. Both stages involve major physical and social disruptions and psychological stresses. In both stages, the true self is often isolated: in adolescence by a poisonous peer culture, and in old age by the death of those who have common memories. Much of what is happening inside is kept secret. It feels socially unacceptable to tell the truth.

It helps to view adolescence and old age from developmental and cultural perspectives. In our elders, grumpiness can be about physical pain. Depression may relate to the isolation the old feel in our youth-oriented culture. "I hate this birthday card" or "I won't eat this soup" isn't necessarily personal. Moodiness comes from loss of control.

Just as the parents of teens often feel hopeless in the face of cultural pressures and developmental imperatives, so do the children of old-old parents. Many of the problems stem from our culture's letting us down.

Today, most people live into their seventies and eighties, and many live into their nineties. In the past, an arthritic aunt moved in with a niece and her husband, or a widow lived in a bedroom off her daughter's kitchen. Now there are more choices; however, people aren't necessarily happier. More choice can mean more stress, more possibility of disagreement, and more opportunity to make bad decisions.

We need a new way of thinking about old age. One developmental challenge is keeping horizons open. A businessman friend told me how boring his retired friends are. "When they worked, they traveled, they solved problems and dealt with all kinds of people. They had opinions on social issues. Now they are stagnant." I think of Belinda, who woke up the same time every morning and had the same breakfast of stewed prunes and toast. She then carefully proceeded through the same schedule day after day, year after year. She was calm and well organized, but not learning much about herself or the world.

It's good to have routines, and it's good to violate those routines. I know a man who had sixty-five different ways to walk to the post office for his mail. He was an alert person, "green on top," as my aunt Margaret would say. The old must search for the right mix of comfortable habits and new experiences. Without the former there is chaos; without the latter there is ossification.

Just as toddlers and teenagers cause certain kinds of family crises, so do aging and ill parents. Crises make everyone more who they really are. The pessimists become "lethal pessimists." The optimists drive everyone else nuts with their cheeriness. People get rigidly locked into roles they might be able to jettison in less extreme situations. The introvert won't speak, the extrovert "extroverts" all over the place, and couples don't see things the same way. Delicately balanced relationships can topple under the new weight of crisis.

As my client Harriet said, "I'm being a good daughter right now, but a lousy wife." Harriet's mother had recently lost her eyesight, and Harriet was helping her in all the ways she could. However, because she had a full-time job, Harriet was rarely at home. Her husband was increasingly critical of her behavior. She said sadly, "Instead of pulling together in this crisis, we are pulling apart. Andy is a high-maintenance husband. I have always organized my life around his needs, and now I can't." She sighed. "I walk into the house about nine at night, exhausted and hungry. He is waiting for me. I desperately want alone time, and he is this awful combination of clingy and grumpy, needy and angry. And guess what happens. We have a big fight."

My client Patsy had a somewhat different problem. Her husband, Dan, loved her mother and, in fact, gave Patsy a hard time when she talked about the stresses of having her mother live with them. "I love Mother, too, and I want to help her through her last months," Patsy said. "But I need to complain just a little to someone. Mom is a lot of work. She has fifteen pills a day that must be carefully monitored. She can't feed or dress herself." Patsy got tears in her eyes. "I can't complain to Dan, who reminds me of my duty and of what a saint my mother is, or to Mother, who would feel so guilty that she would insist on leaving. I don't want her to leave; I just want to be able to express a few of my feelings."

Good information helps families make good decisions, have reasonable expectations, and communicate honestly. Good information helps families feel less alone, less guilty, and more forgiving of one another. Some of this information is about things like money, time, health care, community resources, or diet and exercise for elderly relatives. But some of it is about the feelings of family members.

Every family with an older member faces certain emotional tasks. The first task is sorting out what is personal and what isn't. With an ill parent who grew up in a different culture and who has experienced loss, it's hard to know what causes what reactions. Some issues are time-zone issues; others are related to posttraumatic stress. An old person may be upset about the cost of long-distance phone calls, an enormous expense fifty years ago but a relatively small one in today's world. Grandmother may want to speak only a few minutes on the phone. A grandchild may be hurt by this abruptness if she doesn't realize that Grandmother's reaction stems from attitudes developed long ago.

Many old-old people repeat instructions over and over. They may arrive at events early and worry if others aren't there on time. These tendencies to double-check and arrive early come from overcompensating for their physical or mental frailty. They feel vulnerable, and they worry that others are vulnerable, too.

Sometimes we just need to cut old people some slack. It's not fair to be mad at a great-aunt who is unreasonable because she is brain-damaged. It makes no sense to be hurt by the remarks of a grandfather who is doped up on painkillers, oxygen-deprived, or frustrated because he needs a feeding tube. It is easier to forgive a great-grandmother who gives your child sweets before meals if you know something about the Depression. It's easier to forgive a compulsive talker if we remember that 90 percent of her favorite people now rest in the cemetery.

## NAOMI AND JONATHAN  *(ages 45 and 79)*
*"I love my father,*
*but I don't like him."*

NAOMI IS a good example of someone who had trouble sorting what is physical, cultural, and personal. Last year her father lost his wife of fifty years. This year he had a stroke and lost his ability to walk. Naomi made arrangements for him to move from his neighborhood in New York City to a handicapped-accessible health-care facility in our town. Even though she had a full-time job and two teenagers, Naomi visited him every evening.

Those visits were difficult. Her father was frustrated by his loss of mobility and control, and he held one-sided conversations with his dead wife while Naomi was in the room. All he did was complain. As Naomi said, "He could make coffee nervous." She wasn't sure if his bad moods and poor manners were related to the stroke. What could she call him on? What wasn't fair to criticize?

Jonathan had always been difficult. He was a Holocaust survivor, and when he looked back on his life, he remembered only the terrible tragedies. When Naomi visited her father, he wanted to talk about his relatives who didn't make it. Sometimes it made Naomi mad. She wanted to shout, "Enjoy your grandchildren; look out at the spring flowers; taste this marvelous roast I made especially for you."

Her father's moodiness and impatience isolated him from the family. When he went to Naomi's house for Shabbat, he complained about the rest home and criticized her children. His complaints about her children hurt the most. He had always been proud of them. When Naomi's oldest daughter was born, her father had said, "This is my victory over Hitler."

Naomi sighed. "I hoped the kids would cheer him up. They love and respect their grandfather, but now they fight with him, too. They are hurt by his lack of real interest in their lives.

"I love Father, but I don't like him," Naomi said. She looked earnestly at me. "I don't even know what to be mad about. Of course, he's depressed. Who wouldn't be, after losing his wife and his health? But the bitterness does him no good. He won't do the things that could help, like socialize at the rest home or laugh with my kids. I'm not sure how much he can change at this point. I want to push him to do what he can, but it's not fair to push him to do what he cannot do."

I suspected Naomi's father was having a sorting problem, too. He may not have known whether his wife's death, his ill health, or the behavior of his grandchildren was causing his depression. He may have been blaming his family for things that were not their fault. He probably wished that his daughter were more attentive and that his grandchildren were more respectful. He may not have been aware of the difficulties Naomi had balancing her work and family. He didn't grow up in a world of professional women who have no servants. He may not have understood that manners for teenagers are more casual in the 1990s than they were in Poland in the 1930s. When his grandchildren don't introduce him properly to their friends or wait to start eating until he has begun the meal, he may take it personally and blame his daughter for what are essentially cultural differences. So his depression gets even worse.

A friend told me about a terrible lunch she'd had with her eighty-year-old grandmother. On one hand, it seemed as though they had nothing to say to each other. And yet everything they did say seemed to set off a chain reaction of emotional responses. Bea said that later she figured out what went wrong. They were looking at each other with old pictures. She viewed her grandmother as she had been twenty years earlier, a married club woman with interests and friends. In fact, by now, her grandmother was lonely and isolated in an elegant condo.

Bea realized that her grandmother probably saw twenty-year-old pictures of Bea, too, of Bea as a radical and footloose college student. Now Bea was battling her way up the corporate ladder during the day and caring for a friend with AIDS in the evening. She was nothing like the college student her grandmother thought she was talking to. While the two women looked at these old pictures of each other, they couldn't have a real relationship.

When dealing with aging parents, we view them as powerful authority figues and as people who were competent to handle any situation. We also may see ourselves as we were as children—scared, vulnerable, and incompetent. Being around our parents can call up unpleasant feelings about them and about us, feelings we would just as soon never admit we had.

Every little discussion rests on a mountain of history. When Mom asks petulantly, "Why are you late for dinner?" many ghosts are in the room—Mom's mother, Mom as a young mother, her adult daughter as a young child, and perhaps even Mom's husband and the daughter's current mate. A remark echoes through decades of family experience. It's no wonder small discussions can seem earth-shattering and skyscrapers get built on meringues.

Barry's mother always tells him to wear his seat belt and drive the speed limit, even though he is fifty years old and has never had a fender bender. Marissa is forty-five and a good cook, but her mother only lets her set the table for family dinners. Antonia's mother calls her "baby" and "little darling." When Antonia is in a good mood, that's okay, but when she is tired and defensive she wants to say, "Mom, I am a doctor now; don't call me a baby."

Perhaps the most difficult challenge for parents is to realize that their children are adults now. Parents may have trouble relinquishing both control and "worry rights." When parents are in pain, ill, or lonely, staying relaxed about their children is tough. People who have experienced loss are conscious that the smallest things can change everything forever. They are more likely to be alarmists and worriers.

As parents age they need more help from their children. Yet they may remember this son as the one who forgot his schoolwork, or this daughter as the rebel who wouldn't do what was expected of her. These old pictures may keep parents from seeing clearly the adults before them and acting accordingly. Some adults, however, regress around their parents, which makes it harder for everyone to update. When adults are with their parents, it makes sense to do the chores without being asked, to curb the impulse to respond as a snippy adolescent, to avoid slobby or lazy behavior, and to say "please" and "thank you."

One of the best ways to update old pictures is to ask open-ended questions about the present and then really listen to the answers. When a child senses that a parent isn't aware of who she is now, it's okay to update her parent. It's okay to say, "Mom, I haven't collected stamps for twenty years now," or, "I don't drink, so I don't need wineglasses, but I want to tell you about the volleyball team at my church," or, "I know I used to like roast beef sandwiches, but I have high cholesterol now and don't eat red meat."

Old pictures of gender roles also can interfere with problem solving. Traditionally, women did most of the housework and caregiving. However, in an era when most women work outside the home, domestic burdens must be shared. Families work better when things are fair. Adult children bring different skills to a crisis. What is fair and practical are the important questions, not what gender is the caregiver.

Old relationship conflicts can reenter the scene. Well into our middle years, it's easy for us to have leftover adolescent issues with parents. We still may stiffen up when we are criticized about our spending habits or asked where we were last night. Parents also have memories of tough times with us. They may see certain behaviors as similar to childhood behaviors, and may say things like, "You always pout when you don't get your way." That may be true, but nobody forty-five years old wants to hear it.

Most families have suffered hard times. Maybe there was a messy divorce or the son was in jail as a young man. Perhaps the youngest child was a prodigal son who dropped out of the family for years and then reentered in his thirties. A parent abandoned the children, had a public affair, or gambled away a college fund. Maybe there was abuse or alcoholism.

Unpleasant memories don't disappear just because a parent is ill and dependent. And in fact, glossing over the past takes an enormous amount of energy.

Usually it is better to acknowledge past pain and to forgive, but not necessarily forget. I think of the things my friend Bill said about his mother. They'd had a stormy relationship, but in the end they said honest and loving things to each other. As she died, they reached some closure on their relationship. Her last words to Bill were "How are you doing?" At the funeral, Bill acknowedged that "raising me wasn't an easy task." He smiled and said, "I'm sorry that time doesn't permit me to elaborate on that subject." He recommended that his mother's tombstone read, "Not a whiner."

Denial is really another way of holding on to old pictures long after their realities have disappeared. It's an understandable and totally forgivable quality. Children don't want to curtail their parents' functioning, and they don't necessarily want more responsibility themselves. Most of our elders also ignore early warning signs that they aren't coping well alone because the implications are staggering. They don't want to give up their homes, their cars, or their checkbooks. They don't want to stop traveling or walking downtown alone.

Changes tend to happen gradually, and there may not be one precise moment when a line is crossed. Children will be vaguely worried, and parents will be defensive about their functioning but insist they can handle things. Usually it's a crisis that brings families out of denial. Because he can't see, Dad drives the car across a yard and into a living room. Grandmother falls down and lies on the floor for a day because she is too weak to get to her phone. Uncle Louis is found drunk on a sidewalk. Aunt Jennie gives $10,000 to a telemarketer for shares in the Brooklyn Bridge. Mother swears that Russians are following her and calls the police to report them.

An incident triggers the reaction "We must do something." Awkwardly and reluctantly, the issues are faced. Denial is temporarily not a problem. Plans are made that fit the current situation, and everyone slowly adjusts. Dad stops driving at night. Mom no longer cooks when she's alone. Things go pretty smoothly until there is more deterioration. Then another crisis occurs.

The saddest families are those in which the generations are estranged and the parents dare not ask for help. Old pictures can't be updated because there is no communication. Sometimes the adult child has not forgiven the parents for earlier mistakes. Other times the child is simply uninterested in the parents. They have drifted too far apart to even pretend a connection. Or perhaps years earlier the parents disowned a child because he or she married outside the faith or disobeyed some other major family rule.

Sometimes there is no justice in who gets an appreciative, helpful child. Parents who were neglectful and abusive sometimes have marvelous children. Sometimes loving parents have children who hold grudges and punish them for hurts thirty years old. Many parents have some children who come to their aid but other children who do not. Lucky parents have children who appreciate the burdens and stresses of raising them and are eager to return the favor.

A client came in to talk about her father, who recently had moved back to her town. He had lived far away for years and kept in touch only via postcards and rare phone calls. But when he got ill, he moved to our town to be near my client and her family. She said, "He wants all this togetherness, but he abandoned me years ago. When he complains I should visit more often, it's hard not to resent him. When my first child was born, he didn't even call."

My friend Emilia invited her eighty-year-old mother, Maria, to move into her home. She and her husband fixed up a nice room for Maria. Over lunch, Emilia told me how weird the role reversal is for her. Her mother needed help getting dressed and balancing her checkbook. When her mother was out at night, Emilia worried just like she worries about her teenagers. She said, "Mother was a fashion model in Mexico City when I was a girl. Now before bed she wants me to tuck her in and read a story."

Many middle-aged adults drive their parents to appointments and help them with their shopping and house and yard work. They manage their money, remind them to brush their teeth, and make their difficult phone calls. They accompany them to the doctor because the parents can no longer give and get the right information.

As roles reverse and needs change, there are many new issues. If these issues are handled in a timely manner, families can be planning with, not for, their parents. Adult children need to know the names and phone numbers of their parents' friends, neighbors, lawyers, stockbrokers, and doctors. Holiday rituals many decades old may no longer work and need to be renegotiated. Parents may need to tell where they keep their secret papers—their journals, love poems, or certificates of deposit. When my mother died, we couldn't find her address book, so we couldn't notify her lifetime friends of her funeral. We also couldn't find her money, which she had scattered across many banks and offices. Planning sessions could have solved these and many other problems.

Money, not sex, is the big secret of our time, and it must be discussed. Children need to know about financial resources for long-term health-care planning. Parents must disclose their secrets. Family crises can occur around these revelations. Sometimes parents must reveal that they are wealthy. Children sometimes react angrily: "You mean you had a million dollars and you didn't offer to send our kid to camp that summer I lost my job!" Other times parents must confess that they have lived beyond their means and are saddled with debts. The son says, "All these years you've driven new cars and traveled while I scrimped and saved. And, dammit, now you want my financial help."

Physical boundaries change, too. All of a sudden, children may be helping their parents with intimate physical acts. Many adult children report their discomfort at seeing their parents naked, and at washing, dressing, and administering certain medical treatments to their parents. Parents are embarrassed as well. Carla told me of needing to change her father's diapers. He was tearful and apologetic. She said, "You changed a lot of my diapers. Now it's my turn."

These issues are about what to give and not to give. Wealthy people usually pay for more services, which isn't necessarily a good thing for either generation. A back rub from a child may feel better than one from a professional masseuse. A ride to the bank from a granddaughter offers more than just a ride to the bank. A daughter who helps her mother sort through the attic gains something from this experience. A grandson who helps his grandmother with her physical therapy learns something important about perspective. Too much hired help can hinder the growth of both generations. Some things are done ideally by those who love each other.

While my client Elena's father was still in an ICU, her mother fell and broke her hip. Elena said, "I hate to ask my sister, who is taking her law-school exams, to come back. My brother has a new baby, and his wife isn't doing too well. My brother offered to pay for help back here. But most of what needs doing needs to be done by a family member. I can't hire someone to talk to my mother's doctor, or tuck my kids in at night, or reassure my husband we will survive this month. My father will not let anyone but me help him with his meals."

In new situations, families have decisions to make about time, money, and space. How often do we share meals with the folks? Do I dare ask my son to drive me to church? Will Mother be offended if I offer to brush her hair? Should I tell Aunt Connie she has bad breath? Will my grandchildren be upset if I can't bake cookies anymore? Should we ask Mother to move nearer to our town? Is it time to offer to handle the money?

Relatives who help too much step on other family members' autonomy. Some grandparents interfere with their children's discipline of their own children. A daughter behaves like a "little Hitler," pushing her mother around in the worst way. Or sometimes children help too little and are neglectful when they meant only to be kind. Sometimes autonomy must be violated. Sometimes it's necessary to say, "I'm taking the car keys before you have an accident," or, "You must get treatment for your infection."

One of the common boundary issues is time. Often older people have time on their hands. Some elders love to play Monopoly with their grandchildren or spend an afternoon shopping for a birthday card. They don't always understand that their children are under different time pressures. Penny hated to go home because her parents always made her feel guilty for not coming more often and staying longer. She visited once a month out of a sense of duty, but she left feeling manipulated and unappreciated. Nobody had much fun. In truth, duty isn't the best motivator. People go where they feel accepted and relaxed. She and her folks were caught in a vicious circle.

John and his boys visit his mother regularly at her retirement village. Her place is well set up for family visits, with an ice cream store and a court-yard with basketball, croquet, and shuffleboard. While he and his mother visit, they can watch the boys play. Because the experience is a joyful one for all involved, John comes to visit as often as he can.

However, it's more complicated than that. Sweet-natured elders like John's mother are sometimes abandoned by family. Adult children can be busy with jobs and educated away from the joys of connection with their families. I've met many good-natured older people whose best friends are elevator men or the people who bring them Meals on Wheels.

My generation tends to be peer-oriented. We hang with our friends. Our parents came from a family-oriented generation. They have trouble understanding that we could enjoy friends as much as family. A client told me that his mother wanted him to come to dinner on his birthday, and he explained that he was having a party with his friends that day. He told me, "I would have invited her, but I don't think she would have liked watching *Spinal Tap* and Van Morrison videos." She was hurt and said, "You mean you'd rather be with your friends than your mother?"

Busy adult children, if they are under time pressures, should call fre-quently and regularly, albeit briefly. The same thing goes for visits. Fish and visitors start to smell bad after three days. Going home for twenty-four hours and enjoying the visit is better than gutting it out for a week.

For families with elder relatives, good-byes also are important. They are metaphorical and must be done carefully. It's important that we touch, say words of love, talk about the next time together, give one last small gift of a joke, kind words, or smiles. I encourage families to take plenty of time with good-byes. The good-bye is what lingers for good or ill. A well-done good-bye can salvage a difficult visit. A well-done good-bye can warm the cockles of the heart until the next visit.

Having a schedule of visits and calls that can be maintained over the long haul is essential. People can be in crisis mode only so long, and sometimes old people are ill for years. I have seen sad situations in which family members who always have been loyal and caring get "burned out" and abandon their aging relative. That person is then left to go through the roughest times alone.

Especially when parents live far away, it's hard for us to know when something is a crisis. Children can't take time off and fly to their parents' for every little thing, but with a ninety-year-old parent, every little thing can be fatal. While it's easy to second-guess mistakes later, it's impossible to know the right thing at the time when a decision must be made. Many children desperately want to be with parents when they die. They'll be at the hospital for their two weeks' vacation, then leave, only to hear days later that their parents died alone.

We often assume that old people need less help or more help than they do. We may inflict help or not be there when we are truly needed. Boundary issues require honest talk, negotiation, and compromise. Dad may need someone to go to the doctor with him but be perfectly capable of mowing his own yard. Mom may need help shopping but do just fine cleaning and gardening. Every few months it's good to set aside some time to talk about how the situation is working. Parents may need to ask for more, and children may need to explain changes in their own lives that will affect the parents. It is imperative to ask frequently, "How is everybody doing with this situation?" The important thing is to listen closely and keep in mind that no one is to blame for things being difficult. With all the complexity, how could they not be difficult?

As much as possible, elders need to make decisions about their own lives. It is important not to do things for the old that they can do for themselves. It is important also to let them do what they can for others. The common response to loss of choices is depression. However, at some point, getting old is like that game in which you fall back and trust that others will catch you. That game goes better if the person falling is relaxed and if the person doing the catching is strong and loving.

In some families, the relationship an adult child has with his parents isn't that good. Maybe what has worked is that they lived two thousand miles away from each other. All of a sudden the parent wants to live nearby and have daily contact. The son is nervous that old quarrels will resurface and old tensions erupt. The parents are anxious that they will disrupt their child's family or that he will try to boss them around.

Sibling issues can rear their ugly heads. Old rivalries reemerge. Old pictures can again pose problems. Mom trusts the oldest child but not the youngest. Dad and the boys are close, but he ignores the daughters. Little sister is anxious that her older sister will want to control things like she did years ago. The twins always present a united front and outvote their younger brother. These leftover sibling issues can get in the way of problem solving and make everyone anxious and upset. Siblings may have different ideas about who should do what and a host of other issues. These disagreements may be hard to settle for people who have a long history of fighting over who will clear the table or feed the dog.

Although some of the bitter disputes over wills are about money and simple greed, more often they are about who Mom and Dad loved the most. A lawyer once told me, "If you really want to know someone's character, share an inheritance with them." He had seen incredible battles over land, silverware, and even baby pictures. Siblings can be upset about who the parents chose to live near, who is the executor of their will, and who is allowed to drive Dad's car. A fight over who gets a wedding ring or the kitchen table is a fight over who did the most for Mom. Siblings who have always competed for parental approval now compete for the sailboat or the linen tablecloth.

One particularly distressing problem arises when a parent remarries late in life. Scott and Sue came in to talk about their father, who was leaving all his money to his new wife. The father felt he needed to do so to demonstrate that she was number one in his life. Scott and Sue knew their mother would want the money she earned working as a clerk to go to her grandchildren, not the children of a woman she had never met. Sue said, "Mom worked hard for her money, and she would turn over in her grave if she knew what was happening." Scott said, "This money business is keeping us from liking our new stepmother."

I suggested all four people involved come in for a session. I hoped the stepmother would do the right thing and insist the father save his money for his grandchildren. Scott and Sue agreed to ask their father and his new wife to come in. Later, things did go better, thanks to some honest talk.

When things get tense, old patterns are likely to appear. Accents get stronger. People use less grammatical language and more phrases from their childhood. Big sister gets bossy. Little brother expects everyone else to do the work. Middle child searches desperately for his role in the proceedings. The baby of the family has a temper tantrum, only now the baby is fifty-five years old.

Adult children may be afraid they aren't up to the task of being really helpful. Jerry wanted to be there for his mother, who had Parkinson's, but he worked sixty-plus hours a week and had two teenagers. He told me, "I miss visits with my mother, miss my kids' ball games, or skip out on work. Whatever choice I make, I am in trouble with someone."

Julie was a banker in her mid-thirties when her father had a major heart attack. She worked from eight to five and had a three-year-old, a newborn baby, and a big house. Julie was on the school board, a volunteer for the YWCA, and took a tai chi class. After a few weeks of visiting her father and her distraught mother, Julie realized something had to give. She said wryly, "My life worked fine if I gave up sleep."

My client Cheryl had a mother with a history of mental-health problems. As she aged she was on many kinds of medication—for depression, psychosis, sleep problems, and various somatic complaints. Toward the end of her life, Cheryl's mother lived in a sanatorium in New Jersey and Cheryl flew in to visit her every three months. She described those visits to me as "missions of mercy." They were horrible trips. Her mother complained nonstop and accused Cheryl of stealing her money and furniture. If Cheryl left her side for even a few hours to see an old friend or go swimming, her mother would accuse her of running away. Cheryl told me, "After a few days with Mother, I feel like I'm losing my mind. If I weren't able to get away from her, I'd need to check myself into a room at her facility."

Some adult children have fears of abandonment. When we care for an aging parent, we are caring for someone who will leave us. Living close to parents and really seeing them through their deaths can set adult children up for more pain. Nothing is abstract and distant. Everything hurts. The more we love, and the more open we are to those parents, the more pain it seems we will feel at the end. Aging parents have their anxieties as well. They are afraid of losing control and being a burden. They are frightened of becoming trapped in bodies without minds, or with minds without functional bodies. They don't want to, as my aunt Betty put it, "lay around in their own crap."

Anxiety is infectious. Many family feuds erupt around medical crises and funerals. These times are high-risk for families, but humor, exercise, good food, and rest can keep anxiety levels lower. People need to use every coping tool they have at their disposals. Those who don't have healthy ways to cope with stress will have unhealthy ones.

Aging parents force their childen to admit they have limitations, that they can't do everything. Adult children don't have the money, the time, the living situations, the psychological sophistication, or the medical knowledge to handle things perfectly. In the end, they can't do enough. They can never repay parents for the gift of life. They can't save their parents from pain, sadness, and ultimately from their deaths. However, with honest talk, planning, and good intentions, children can make things better. They can feel they did what they could. Everyone can learn something new about love.

Al did a good job helping his father. When he had to put his father in a home, Al carefully researched places and found one on a lovely river. Before he moved his father in, he brought the staff pictures of his father as a boy and as a younger man. He wanted the staff to see his father as the active, interesting person he was. He wrote a letter introducing his father to staff. He told about his father's life, work, and religion. He ended the letter: "I hope you will find my father a man you will be happy to know. Like the other residents, he will need your help, but he still has much to offer. I hope you will encourage him and motivate him to find pleasure in his life. Thank you for becoming part of our family. I look forward to meeting you soon."

Al's dad lived less than a year at the home. Al spent a lot of time with him. They talked about both of their lives, and also about Dad's upcoming death. Al wheeled his father down to see the river. He even helped him go fishing a few times. One of his father's last happy afternoons was spent catching three small perch.

As parents age, families wrestle with the great questions about meaning, purpose, God, and the afterlife. During the old-old stage, people need to talk about their beliefs. Ideally, differences are balanced by tolerance. Not all families are so lucky. I know a couple in their seventies, both in poor health, whose only daughter belongs to a religious cult. This cult teaches that its members must avoid all those who don't belong to the cult. So the daughter lives six blocks from her parents but has no contact with them. The couple haven't seen their grandchildren in decades. The daughter sends her parents religious tracts filled with hellfire and damnation and dire warnings about the Apocalypse and the Second Coming. She includes notes saying that only after her parents' souls are saved will she allow them back into her life.

The parents considered joining the cult just to be with their daughter and her family, but pride and common sense stopped them. The mother told me, "I am upset that she has chosen to believe in such an ungenerous God. It hurts that my grandchildren believe we will burn in hell for eternity."

A common concern is whether or not to protect older family members from bad news. Children don't know whether to tell them about a faraway friend's death, or about money or family problems. In general, it is a mistake to keep secrets. People tend to get "protected" out of mainstream adult life. When old people sense what is happening, they feel isolated and suspicious. They also feel incompetent and demeaned. Honest information and honest feedback are what keep us all in touch with reality. To leave people out, whatever the motives, is to do them a disservice.

In American culture we find it acceptable to give children feedback. We say, "Don't chew with your mouth open," or, "It's not polite to burp in public." Children may not always like this feedback, but they learn from it. However, we consider it rude to give feedback to any adults except our mates or our employees. This custom can be harmful. We all have bad habits and nasty traits, and at the age we stop hearing about them, they are likely to get worse. Without feedback, people are likely to become rude, self-centered, eccentric, and out of touch.

It's an art to give honest feedback in a kindly way. It's important to say, "I tell you this because I care about you and I value our relationship." Finally, it's good to tread lightly, to not repeat oneself or state things too dramatically. It's better to say, "Mother, I would come more often if you would ask me about the children. I want to share their lives with you," than to say, "I can't stand being with you. You never let me get a word in edgewise." Constructive criticism is more likely to be heard if it is preceded and followed by a compliment.

It's okay to ask older relatives not to use words that are racist. Share honestly why certain language is painful to you. Ask about their experiences with people of different races, and then talk about yours. Watch history documentaries and read history books together. Talk about the kind of society you want to raise your children in. Be respectful but firm. A friend insisted that her father stop telling racist jokes. When he told them at Sunday dinner, she left the table, and eventually she was able to get him to stop.

While older people are often excellent conversationalists, they may need a little help getting started. Ask questions, converse slowly, give them time to remember and to develop their ideas. Ask about the places the family has vacationed, then ask what happened in those places. Ask about stories that connect the old person to the political and cultural world of their times: "Where were you when FDR died?" "What was the first movie you ever saw?"

Ask about the way things were done: "How did you make butter?" "How did you read before you had electric lights?" Ask about objects and people: "What kind of car did you drive during the war?" "What did your house look like?" "What do you remember about your parents? Your grandparents?" "What is your favorite kind of tree or favorite song, and why?"

Work projects are a good way to relate. Many old people talk more easily while cooking, shelling peas, knitting, or fishing. Sorting through and labeling old family photos is a good way to hear many family stories. It's a terrible mistake to be too busy for this activity. When an old relative dies, the younger person is left with a drawer of unlabeled pictures and the knowledge that there are many good family stories he or she will never hear.

Remember that the older generation appreciates action. When my sister-in-law Pam helped her grandmother freeze corn and can tomatoes, they had some of their best talks. When my neighbor Marlene and her father cleaned out her garage, he told her about his first marriage. When my client Rhoda and her dad refinished furniture, they had their first and only talk about their relationship.

Gifts also can be important. Aunt Betty appreciated a bed light so that she could read when she had insomnia. My father-in-law likes crossword-puzzle books. Most older people love fruit from Florida or California, garden vegetables, and homemade treats. My mother-in-law loves cassettes of John Wayne movies. Nothing makes Great-aunt Myra happier than a gift of dog biscuits or chew toys for her much-loved dog, Cookie. While giving pets isn't always practical, bird and squirrel feeders and even trips to visit animals are great gifts. Drives in the country or to visit old hometowns also are wonderful presents. Plants are good gifts—they are young, alive, and need care.

It's good to watch old movies and play old music. It's also good to keep older relatives updated on the world. Make sure they see new books, movies, and concerts. Talk about current politics and cultural events. It is especially rewarding to help people do things for the first time. My grandfather waterskied in his seventies, and until he died, he carried a picture in his wallet of himself on skis. Uncle Randall is in his eighties and learning computer graphics. My friend Lucy began taking piano lessons at age seventy-eight. I know many women who become writers or artists in their seventies.

Old people generally love to tell and hear jokes. Many a tense situation has been rescued by a good laugh, and many a sad conversation has been redeemed by ending on a funny note. Say good-bye in such a way that the last memory is of laughter.

Expect some language differences. Don't swear or use psychobabble. Don't insist on feelings talk, and accept love that is shown rather than spoken. As Holden Caulfield noted long ago, a mother can show love with a bowl of consecrated chicken soup. On the other hand, it's okay for adult children to talk about their feelings, especially the positive ones. Old people like to hear they are loved and respected. Almost no one minds being told they are appreciated.

Express what you feel should be expressed. Time is running out, and it's not a good idea to wait until later to discuss the really important things. Don't be afraid to show physical and verbal affection. Touch, hug, hold hands, give back rubs, say "I love you."

Every family situation is different, but there are a few good rules of thumb. Treat people as you would want to be treated in their situation. Encourage family members to have friends of all ages, partly so that everyone doesn't get old at the same time. With old-old people, expect disappointments, misunderstandings, and bad days. Even in the lives of healthy young people, not every event goes well. Old-old age is a genuinely difficult situation with lots of built-in sadnesses and frustrations.

Everyone involved in a family crisis needs a little time alone every day. When my mother was ill, I walked at sunset. No matter how stressful the day had been at the hospital, I found that I could handle things better if I watched the sun go down. My client Becky lived with her mother, whose Ménière's disease kept her chronically nauseated and dizzy. Becky was a caring and dutiful daughter, but she made sure that she got alone time in the evening to have a glass of wine and listen to National Public Radio.

Unite with family members around what all of you like. While surface-structure communications may be stressful, deep-structure meanings are likely to be shared. Everyone wants everyone to feel loved and valued, and everyone wants time to pass pleasantly. Whenever possible, talk about what all of you enjoy and appreciate. Share happy memories and hopes for the future. Believe that all family members can grow until the moment of death. Be alert for changes in attitudes and behaviors. Even in a worst-case scenario like the one below, good things can come from horrible situations.

*You must do the thing you think you cannot do.*

—ELEANOR ROOSEVELT

*Courage is the price life exacts for granting peace.*

—AMELIA EARHART

## THE KLEIN FAMILY *(Gordon and Edna are in their late 60s; Louise is 43.)*
*"Edna may look like an old brain-damaged person to strangers, but she is my wife and I love and respect her."*

LOUISE CAME INTO THERAPY just after her mother was diagnosed with Alzheimer's disease. Reaching this point had been a long, hard process. Several months earlier, Louise had noticed that her mother seemed easily confused. If Louise told her a story with lots of details, Edna would forget the beginning before Louise reached the end. When she went shopping, Edna would forget where she parked her car. She lost purses, jackets, and books, and she asked the same questions over and over.

At first Louise denied the problem, which was easy because Gordon, her father, covered for Edna. Gordon began spending more time with Edna, driving her places and writing down the details of her day. When Louise asked her father if he noticed changes in her mother, he was uncharacteristically touchy. He denied it vehemently and told Louise to ease up on her mother.

Louise had great respect for both her parents. Gordon had taught chemistry at the university, and Edna was an English teacher and one of the smartest people Louise had ever known. She told me, "My respect for my parents kept me from confronting the situation sooner. I just couldn't believe they had problems they couldn't solve.

"Mom especially was a dynamo," she continued. "She loved Willa Cather and could quote from all her works. When I hated my first job as a secretary, she sent me a note with a line of Cather's: 'You can't know how crushing office work is until you have been crushed by it.'" We both laughed and shared thoughts on Cather. Louise then continued, "Mom once said to me, 'If you ever see me in front of the boob tube, shoot me. You'll know whoever I am has disappeared.'" She paused. "At the time I laughed because it was impossible to imagine her watching TV."

Louise started to cry. I handed her a box of Kleenex and waited. "Things got worse this year. Mom grew more emotional and weepy. She needed my reassurance that she was loved. She'd call me at work to ask if I would be coming over. My mother, who was the most independent woman I'd ever known, wouldn't do anything alone."

Meanwhile, Gordon grew more defensive. When Louise brought up concerns, he told her she was overreacting and disloyal. For the first time, Louise felt distance developing between herself and her father. Louise had never argued with her folks—there had been no need. They were kind, rational, and excessively concerned with her rights. But now, in one emotional scene when Louise wanted her mother evaluated, Gordon called her a traitor.

Finally, when Edna got lost, there was a crisis. She'd gone outside to find the cat and didn't return. Gordon looked for her alone for an hour, then called Louise at work. Louise called her husband, and they all looked for another hour. Then they called the police. When the sun set they were panicked. The three of them sat in Edna's kitchen, drinking coffee and jumping whenever the phone rang. At dawn the police brought Edna home. She'd been found on a country road, cold and confused.

Tests were ordered. Louise clenched her fists. "Those tests were so humiliating to Mom. She could answer questions about our family, and history questions, such as, 'Who spoke at Gettysburg?' But when the examiner asked her who was president now and what day was it, she was lost. She couldn't remember numbers or new information. Mom was ashamed, and Dad was livid."

She sipped some coffee. "It's been hard, but we now know the truth. In a crazy way, everything makes more sense."

I asked how much her mother understood. Louise said, "Last Tuesday mother looked in the mirror and said, 'This is not me.' She asked about euthanasia."

We talked about the stages of Alzheimer's disease, how the failing body loses functioning in roughly the reverse order that a baby gains abilities. I told Louise about a support group for her and Gordon. We agreed to meet again in a few weeks, and Louise said she would bring Gordon. "I need to take more care of Dad now, too," Louise said. "He has grown old overnight."

As the session ended, Louise told me, "My daughter is pregnant with her first child, and we wanted this to be a happy time for the family."

She told me about a dream she'd had one morning, that she was an old lady with long gray hair and saggy cheeks. She called to tell her mother the dream, and Edna had dreamed that she was young again, with blond hair and soft skin.

## SESSION TEN (ONE YEAR LATER)

Louise and Gordon left Edna at adult day care and came in for a session. I'd seen them off and on this last hard year. They attended a support group, which was good and bad. They were learning more about the disease and sharing their sorrow with caring people. But they got depressed by stories of people whose relatives were farther down the road. As Gordon put it, "Most people would rather die than face Alzheimer's." Louise said, "We don't even know what tense to use when we talk about Mom. She is still alive, but so different. The Edna who was an English professor and an excellent mother and wife is gone. The new Edna watches daytime TV."

Gordon shook his head and said sadly, "You lose them before you lose them."

Today we talked about perseveration—when Edna got an idea in her head, it stayed there. She called Louise at work as many as twenty times a day. Louise said, "Just like Picasso had the Blue Period or the cubist period, Mother has periods. She had the 'garbage disposal is broken' period. For over a month, until the repairman came, I heard about that garbage disposal every day. Then it was the birdfeeder period. Mom wanted me to buy Dad a birdfeeder for Father's Day. She must have called me about that a hundred times. I could hardly get any work done. On good days I'd be able to laugh, but other days I wanted to cry I was so frustrated."

Edna wrote the same checks over and over, and Gordon learned to hide the bills and the checkbook from her. Gordon never left her alone, but every now and then something would happen. When she went to work in the garden, Edna had left the stove on. She often plugged up a sink or the tub, turned on the water, and promptly forgot what she'd done.

Louise said that Edna continued to need lots of reassurance that she was loved. She praised her father for his unwavering affection. Gordon said, "Edna may look like an old brain-damaged person to strangers, but she is my wife and I love and respect her."

Gordon had hung in with Edna amazingly well. He was heroic in a way that thousands of people are heroic: He took responsibility for the welfare of people he loved, for better or for worse. However, the stress had taken a toll. His Parkinson's disease had worsened and, although he was endlessly patient with Edna, he sometimes snapped at Louise or his granddaughter. He blew up in stores when clerks were slow or unfriendly, and he even had an attack of road rage. He had dreams of being dragged behind a car that Edna was driving. He shouted and shouted, but she wouldn't stop and no one noticed his dilemma.

Louise continued to struggle with her new parents—a TV-watching, insecure mother who needed constant supervision, and a sicker, sadder father than she'd ever expected to see. She also worried about her own memory. Was she developing Alzheimer's? There were tests available, but did she want to know? She had nightmares of a big tree falling on her house and crushing it.

Today Louise and Gordon discussed moving to assisted living. They had visited the assisted-living facilities in our area and found one that might work. Gordon and Edna could move into an apartment. They would have medical monitoring, housecleaning, and communal meals. Edna could be on an Alzheimer's day unit and return to the apartment with Gordon for evenings and bed. Eventually Edna could live on the in-house Alzheimer's unit.

By now Edna didn't always recognize Louise or her granddaughter, although she always recognized Gordon. Sometimes she thought Louise was her little sister or that her granddaughter was Louise. Once Edna asked Louise, "Do I know your name?" Louise answered, "You gave me my name."

Sometimes Edna would be teaching, telling students about an upcoming test, or scolding students who hadn't read their materials. Sometimes Edna, who had wanted to read all the great books before she died, simply stared at the Jerry Springer show. She was heartbreakingly unpredictable. There were times when she knew Louise and tried to make plans to go to a bookstore. Other times she'd shout at Louise, "Who are you, anyway? I didn't order a pizza."

Louise said, "I am not angry at Mom, but I hate the disease. This has cost me my belief in God. How could a merciful God do this to my mother?"

Gordon and Louise dreaded moving Edna. Change was upsetting to her. She loved her house and garden. I struggled to find a positive topic with which to end our work. I asked about the new baby. Louise smiled. "Mother loves to cuddle with her namesake. Edna Two never fails to brighten her days, and ours as well."

SESSION TWENTY

Louise came in alone today. She looked better than the last time we had met, calmer and healthier, even younger. She began by showing me pictures of her mother with toddler Edna. They were in a day room with bright yellow flowers. Both Ednas looked happy and beautiful.

Louise reported that things seemed temporarily stabilized. Edna had adjusted to the move and indeed seemed to enjoy the attention and people. Gordon was less isolated. He loved the new grandbaby, and this afternoon he was out playing golf.

Louise told me about the Alzheimer's unit. At first she could barely stand to visit. The calendar in the communal room was generally a month or two behind. Residents had missing teeth or stains on their clothes. They shuffled past one another, lost in their own heads. One woman carried a doll that she rocked as if it were her baby. Another was always calling her children in from play. A sweet well-dressed lady said over and over to Louise, "I would like you to like me as much as I like you."

Many of the residents thought their parents were still alive. They would say, "I'll call Mother. She would enjoy this cake," or, "Dad will be in from the field soon. He'd like to meet you." Many wouldn't recognize their own children, who they imagined as toddlers or schoolchildren, but they would recognize sons- and daughters-in-law.

After Louise got used to the place, she managed to find small victories and even jokes. She loved making the residents smile or laugh. She liked the day children visited from a nearby school. She said, "That's when everyone really perks up."

Louise told me of a time she sat with a large group of women. She asked one what her favorite flower was, and the woman couldn't remember any flowers. To be helpful, Louise said she liked red roses best. The woman said, "That's my favorite flower, too." Then they went around the circle and fifteen women solemnly declared that red roses were their favorite flower as well. Louise told me, "I might as well laugh as cry."

She said the philosophy has changed for Alzheimer's patients. At one time the recommendation was to bring patients back to reality by correcting their misconceptions. Now the rule is the opposite. As one staff member put it to her, "If you can't bring them back to a better reality than they are experiencing in their heads, leave them be." That is what Louise did with Edna. They would play games for hours. If Edna asked how Louise's math test went, Louise would say, "I made an A." Edna would say, "I'm so proud of you."

Louise noted that things would get worse. Just when they thought they had adjusted, there would be more deterioration. Each loss brought new grief. But for now, things seemed under control. Louise was again working without interruptions. She didn't lie in bed nights worrying about her parents. Her nightmares had subsided.

She called her mom daily and visited several times a week. Louise said that her mother liked visitors, especially the baby, but anybody, really. Now and then a student would stop by, and that meant a lot to the family. Edna remembered things from long ago—nursery rhymes, the alphabet, how to count, the Pledge of Allegiance—but she wasn't sure where she was now. Louise liked to sing with her because while they were singing it felt like old times. She took some satisfaction in the fact that her mother was physically and emotionally comfortable. Edna got chilly easily but otherwise seemed healthy. She suffered less now than she had earlier. Edna was beyond knowing about her disease.

"Mom can't remember much, but her emotional system is intact. She can give and receive affection. She loves to laugh and be touched."

Louise had attended a lecture by Nebraska writer Lela Shanks, whose husband had Alzheimer's. She quoted her to me: "'People with Alzheimer's are people to be loved. They are our mothers and fathers, our grandmothers and grandfathers.'"

I asked Louise if she was still angry with God. She was quiet for a while. "I have grown from this experience. After this hard thing, I can handle anything. I am learning that I cannot separate the good from the bad; everything that happens makes my life."

She looked out the window. "This disease has given me a chance to see how strong my father is and how strong my daughter could be. I learned some things about myself as well. I learned that if I choose love, not indifference, then I can stay the course. I still can't forgive God for Alzheimer's. The cost of these lessons is unforgivably high. But I am not angry. The same God that gave us this awful problem gave us the strength to handle it."

CHAPTER 6

# *Homesick for Heaven*

*The tragedy of old age is not that one is old but that one is young.*

—OSCAR WILDE

*If I'd known I was gonna live this long,*
*I'd have taken better care of myself.*

—EUBIE BLAKE

WHEN PEOPLE ARE IN THEIR THIRTIES, THEY WORRY ABOUT losing their looks. In their fifties, they worry about losing capacities. By their seventies, people worry about losing everything—control, relationships, and their very lives. Old age isn't for the faint of heart. Aging people lose hair, muscle power, memory, strength, and agility. They lose taste buds, libido, and the ability to sleep soundly. Many people lose their work, which, for all its stresses, is what gives many lives meaning. The old lose their health and finally their hope. As Aunt Grace put it when I asked about her health, "Let's face it, I'm going downhill and any improvements are temporary." Or as Phyllis said, "The golden years aren't so golden. There is a lot of brass."

This chapter is the field guide to another country. It explores what old people are feeling, and why; it puts some of their behavior in a new context. It shows what they are up against—all the losses and fears. It's the saddest chapter in the book.

In this chapter, I compare old people to victims of posttraumatic stress disorder. I examine the psychological toll of this developmental stage as well as its salvation. The stories are PTSD stories. The old don't suddenly develop bad personalities; they are overwhelmed by events. Hemingway wrote, "The worst death is the loss of what formed one's center." Many old-old people lose that which formed their centers. Their lack of interest in others, their irritability, and their complaints are PTSD reactions.

*I feel like an aeroplane at the end of a long flight,*
*in the dusk . . . in search of a safe landing.*

—WINSTON CHURCHILL, ON RETIREMENT

## *Metaphors*

OLD AGE LENDS ITSELF to metaphors. If life is a sky, then the lucky young have mostly blue sky with a few clouds that clear rapidly. As one ages, the clouds increase, and by the end, the sky is overcast. The barometer drops, and a storm rolls in from the west.

Hippocrates was the first to compare life to seasons and old age to winter. Long ago, Horace wrote, "Sad age comes. Farewell to laughing, happy love and easy sleep." Chateaubriand called old age a shipwreck. On his sixty-ninth birthday, Whitman called himself "an old, dismasted, gray and battered ship, disabled, done." In 1936, Freud wrote to Stefan Zweig, "I still cannot get used to the grief and afflictions of old age and I look forward with longing to the journey into the void."

When May Sarton was in her sixties, she wrote optimistically, "The joys of my life have nothing to do with age. They do not change. Flowers, the morning and evening light, music, poetry, silence, the goldfinches darting about . . ." But after her stroke, when she moved into old-old age, she wrote, "I am learning that any true cry from the heart from an old person creates too much havoc in the listener and is too disturbing, because nothing can be done to help the person on the downward path." She couldn't listen to music because "it opened the locked places in my heart and all my unstoppable tears flowed."

Sarton struggled to accept her dependence on others. She wrote of the horrible institutions for the aged. "There is a connection between any place where humans are helpless and a prison." As she gave up much of what she loved, she asked, "What is it I can still have that I still want?" During this time, many of her friends grew ill and died. She said, "Everyone after seventy-five lives in a de-peopled world." And finally she wrote, "Hope dies last."

## *Loss*

LETTER WRITERS CAN'T WRITE. Handwriting becomes shaky and illegible. Avid readers can't read. Hikers can't hike; climbers can't climb. People no longer can garden, cook, or dance. They stop going to movies or concert halls because the light is low and the footing precarious. As an old man, W. H. Auden introduced his lectures by saying, "If there are any of you at the back who can't hear me, don't raise your hands, because I'm also nearsighted."

People stop being able to buy their own groceries or go to church. I think of Aunt Grace turning to Uncle Otis in his recliner. He'd been a wily storekeeper and salesman, but now he had Alzheimer's disease and Aunt Grace had blood pressure problems. She said, "Otis, did you think it would ever come to this?"

Marathon runners' legs fail them. Bikers give their bikes to their grandchildren. State champion athletes worry about making it to the bathroom. As bodies age, interests that gave joy to a lifetime fall away. Of course, there are a few eighty-year-old marathon runners, and many old people can exercise. Swimming, in particular, is a forgiving sport. The truth is, though, there aren't many athletes who can pursue their sports into old-old age. Exercise provides pleasure, relieves stress, and keeps people centered and optimistic. Without it, many people lose mental acuity and grow depressed and anxious. People feel about their bodies, as Yeats put it, that they are "tied to a dying animal."

Some old people lose their memory of recent events. They spend more time looking for their car keys and reading glasses. They scramble family names and call their daughters by the names of their sisters, their grandsons by the name of their sons. They forget the names of people they met last week. They forget what they did last week. I met an old man at an airport who had worked at Boeing in California for years. He knew everything about the early days of Boeing and about Los Angeles in the 1950s. He told me the names of streets that movie stars lived on, and the menus of the restaurants in Beverly Hills. He remembered going to the garden with his father when he was a boy. His father was tired after his long day's work in the factory. He'd pick them each a warm tomato, and they'd sit on a rock and eat their delicious snack together. However, this same man's recent memory was poor. His wife needed to tell him where they were traveling, who they would be visiting, and over and over again when the plane would be leaving.

There is a paradox of old age and memory. The old forget a great deal, yet they lead lives filled with memories. Everything begins to remind them of something else. Many live increasingly in the past. Ram Dass offered a possible explanation. Before his stroke he was future-oriented, but after his stroke he had little to look forward to except loss and debilitation. He found himself returning in his thoughts to happier times long ago.

When they age, most people experience some loss of sexual interest and/or function. Many experts stress that this loss isn't inevitable or necessary. With creativity and communication, old people can have satisfying sex lives. That is good news for some, but not all. Many people want permission to slow down, especially in this sex-obsessed culture of ours. They are looking for the freedom of not defining relationships sexually or worrying about performance.

I think of a popular joke among the old here in Nebraska. A man finds a frog who says that if she is kissed, she'll turn into a beautiful princess. Instead of kissing the frog, the man puts her in his pocket. The frog croaks, "Don't you want to kiss me and have a beautiful princess?" The man says, "Frankly, at my age, I'd rather have a talking frog."

That doesn't mean that there is not sadness at the loss of sexual interest along the way. I think of Joe, an older client, who deeply mourned the loss of his sexual power. He was balding and getting a pot belly. His flirtations, once generally welcomed, were now perceived as laughable. For Joe, sex wasn't one of myriad pleasures, it was central. He was lost.

Illness affects conversation. The old talk about comas, incontinence, oxygen tanks, chemotherapy, medicare, dialysis, emphysema, and gout. They talk about living wills, funerals, the recently widowed, and the newly dead. They talk about these things because their lives are filled with them. Once, during a long discussion of the health problems of his friends, Uncle Clair caught my eye and said, "The trouble with us is we have lived too long."

When they age, some people become confused or addled, to use an old-fashioned word. They are forgetful and sometimes mildly delusional. Especially if they live in institutions where every day is very much the same, they are likely to lose track of time and of events outside the institution.

I think of my husband's great-aunt Minnie. One day when Jim's father visited her at the rest home, she was upset because she was sure that she would be forced to marry the man across the hall. His family wanted her money. Bernie didn't argue but only said, "The first thing tomorrow I'll go to the courthouse and get a court order and stop it." His kindness and tact calmed her down.

Illness affects moods. Pain, frustration, and a lack of positive ways to cope with stress can lead to irritability. Being nauseated, congested, and/or exhausted makes people crabby and depressed. Paul, a neighbor with chronic back pain, said to me, "You should have known me before I hurt my back. I was a lot of fun." He was right, he wasn't much fun. He always looked tense and tired, and he rarely volunteered conversation. When Paul realized that he had more bad days than good, he lost his optimism. He said sorrowfully, "Nothing is easy. Everything is work. The body is no place to live in."

I think of Lilah, who could always find the negative. If Lilah took a trip to Florida, she would remember the one bad meal or rainy day. If she had a lovely party, she would notice the punch wasn't cold or the clarinet player was flat. Once, while looking at the wedding pictures of a young couple, she said ominously, "They're happy now." Lilah hadn't always been this way. As a younger woman she was reasonably perky and optimistic, but years of congestive heart failure had sapped her energy and optimism.

Illness leads to many vicious circles. People are in pain, so they take drugs, which further incapacitate them and eventually lead to more physical problems and pain. A heavy person can't exercise because of arthritis, so she grows heavier and the arthritis worsens. Illness, physical inactivity, and depression often go together. Drugs counteract one another. Treatment helps one problem but hurts another. Being ill makes one less resilient, which in turn makes one more likely to get ill.

Pain, which makes people needy, also makes many people cranky and drives away potential helpers. A person desperately wants to work, but the job hurts his/her health. A man who has had a heart attack wants to climb one last mountain but is afraid it will kill him. Even tension between couples can worsen as one person feels his disease is exacerbated by stress. Arguments feel like life-and-death matters: "Don't fight with me or you'll make my blood pressure go up."

The negative reactions of ill people are not necessarily personal. It's easier for adult children to be helpful if they don't take these behaviors personally, but rather see them as part of a general reaction to the stresses of being old-old.

The amazing story is how well people adapt to such difficult circumstances. Humans can adjust to anything, and many people rise to the occasion. I think of Aunt Henrietta joking with the hospital staff who helped her after she broke her hip, or of Winnie and Carl. Winnie has diabetes and can no longer walk more than a few feet, and Carl has congestive heart failure. They've made a decision that they will live as always. With a wheelchair in the back of their car, they go to the symphony, to art museums, and to parties. Carl wheels Winnie in, and they have fun. Between gala affairs, much of their lives is suffering, but they always have events to look forward to. Almost no one knows about their pains and prognoses.

There is also the loss of landscape. Old neighbors die or retire to Florida, and condos are built. Corner groceries and cafes are replaced by Quick Stops. Hardware stores disappear, and discount malls spring up. A riverbank where morel mushrooms grew is now owned by a development company. "Keep out" signs are posted. The bakery that sold the crispies a man enjoyed all his life is replaced by a video store. Even the musicians, the movie stars, and the politicians who made up one's public world die. They are replaced by younger people whose names are difficult to remember. Trees are cut down. Rivers change channels.

Home is the repository of memory, and its loss causes a loss of connection to the self. I think of Aunt Betty, who lived on a farm in Idaho that she and my uncle bought during the Depression. At one time they had been surrounded only by fields, but the landscape she knew had vanished. Because her home was near wilderness areas, people were building vacation houses and her town was now a boom town. There were New Age settlers and yuppies among the old farms, and cappuccino cafes and bagel shops among the old-fashioned diners.

When I last visited, I saw a banner advertising a Leo Kottke performance next to the building where Uncle Lloyd had shod horses. Beside the Rexall Drug was a travel agency offering trips to sacred spaces in Malta and "goddess" tours to Ireland with shamanic divination training. As I drove out to the farm, I passed bumper stickers that demonstrated the ideological differences among neighbors. One sticker said, "If God is your copilot, switch seats," and one said, "Puppets for Jesus." Another said, "US Forever, UN Never." And another, "Friends don't let friends vote Republican." Log homes with solar panels sat beside clapboard houses. The old yards bloomed with hollyhocks and daylilies, the new ones sported moonbeam coreopsis, purple coneflowers, or goldstrum. Just to the east of Betty's was a modern home with a *New York Times* mailbox. To the west was the headquarters of Promise of America, an Aryan Nation group.

Betty took me up on Sweitzer Mountain to show me where, sixty-five years before, she and Lloyd had found huckleberries. The road to the mountain used to be a rocky path, but now we drove on blacktop up to a ski resort with lifts and condos for 1,000. There was a fine restaurant that served pesto pasta and scallop salad.

Betty ignored all the new buildings; she wanted to find the old trail. We looked for a long time, but the mountain had been altered for buildings and ski runs. It was beautiful still, with wild strips of berries and flowers and a good view of Lake Pend Oreille. Finally Betty located the trail behind one of the condos, and she insisted we hike it.

As she climbed, Betty breathed hard and got red-faced. She stopped frequently and walked slowly. Her balance was poor, and twice she fell. However, in spite of her slow pace and labored breathing, she was enjoying this walk. She didn't notice the scars the ski lifts and roads had made. She saw this mountain as it was sixty-five years ago. And she saw herself as a young wife and Lloyd as a virile, handsome logger.

She showed me Oregon grapevines and her favorite blue wildflowers. I convinced her to sit by a stream while I went on up to the huckleberry patch. I never found it, but I pretended I had, and she pretended to believe me.

Going down, she held my hand all the way. She stumbled several times, but as we passed the dude ranch she saw kids trying to chase a horse back into a corral. She stopped and told them to get a bag of oats and lure it back in. With some pride, she said to me, "I know how to get a horse in a pen."

Home for my aunt was much more than her house. It was the land, the berries, the horses, and the people she had known all her life. She lost her home by inches: first the landscape, then her mate, and finally her farm. Shortly after my visit, Betty moved into town to a rest home. It had been a hard decision for her and her children, but finally the Idaho winters won. No one wanted her trapped on a farm for weeks at a time with impassable roads and no company.

Because of the importance of home, the decision to move into a new place is often one of the hardest ones associated with this stage of life. We still are learning how to organize rest homes. Too often institutions are about the needs of the institution, not of the patients. I recall visiting an old client in a hospital. Carrie had just suffered a stroke and was weak and anxious. Just as we began our talk, a worker came in to give her occupational therapy. Carrie pleaded, "Couldn't this wait? I'm so tired, and Mary is here." The worker said, "My shift ends in half an hour so we must do it now." I waited for this worker to finish with Carrie. Afterward, Carrie was tired but still wanted to talk. Just as we began again, the respiratory therapist showed up. She also needed to do her job right then so she could leave for the day. I sympathized with these workers' needs, but my client didn't get what she most wanted and needed, and she was the ill person.

There are horror stories. I've seen old people with bedsores, or waiting for bedding changes, baths, or pain medications. Some of the old have no one to feed them and can't feed themselves. Some need physical therapy but cannot get it authorized by their insurance companies. They lie idly when they could be relearning how to walk or use an arm.

As I went down a hall in a new rest home, I saw a care worker hit a woman in a wheelchair. When she saw me observing her, the staff member jumped. Clearly she was unhappy at being discovered, but not at bullying her helpless charge. This same facility didn't allow spouses to share a room, and patients were kept medicated so that they wouldn't make trouble.

Recently I received a letter from a woman who described herself as an elder trapped in a rest home. She wrote, "There are times when I come to my room, lie in the bed, and wish I could just fly out of the window and get away from here." She discussed the problems—understaffing, large staff turnover, and a lack of respect and value for the residents. She said she needed to ring three or four times before her buzzer would be answered. Many times the residents were told lies and promises were broken. She wrote poignantly, "Our esteem, aspirations, and productivity are stolen from us. Instead we live in an abysmal culture for the allotted time."

Our elders need as much control and connection as possible. It's important that they continue to attend their churches, see their friends and families, and visit their favorite stores, parks, and cafes; that they have their own furniture, pictures, and books. They need telephones and newspapers, computers and newsletters, whatever they have always had in their lives to keep them connected to the world.

They need the freedom to make all possible choices about their own lives. In some homes, residents are "managed to death." "Good" clients, that is, the compliant ones, die the fastest. Some rest homes are decorated like day-care centers, and the old are infantilized. In her book *Fountain of Age*, Betty Friedan describes a place where all the work was done for the residents. People were segregated away from the young and spent their days watching TV. Friedan calls such places "playpens for adults."

Thankfully, many homes are better than these. Most care workers are in this field because they like old people and want to help. The problems don't arise from a lack of motivation but from limited funds and inadequate information on how to manage the extraordinarily difficult problems of old-old age. They arise from our lack of collective wisdom about valuing the old.

We need cultural rituals to help families make the move from homes to rest homes. I know a woman who was tricked into entering a rest home. She was taken for a drive and never saw her home again. My client Regina told me about moving her grandmother into a rest home. Regina's grandmother hadn't wanted to leave her home of a lifetime, but her children worried about her. She forgot to flush the toilet, and the place smelled bad. She took all of her pills for the week on Sunday. Sometimes she'd bake a pot pie but forget to take it out of the oven for a few days. Finally, the grandmother caved in to her children's pressure. Regina said, "Mother wanted it to go well, by which she meant that no one would get emotional. I went along because I wanted to give Grandmother permission to cry. I told her it was okay to feel sad. I would have felt sad in her situation."

We need "saying good-bye to neighbors" parties and "saying good-bye to a house and yard" ceremonies. We need "driving to the institution" rituals and "entering the new place" rituals. For example, Regina's grandmother was a piano player. She had always favored happy songs, ragtime music, and fox-trots, and she insisted that when she died she wanted only fast songs played at her funeral. Regina arranged things so that when her grandmother first arrived at the home there was a small electric piano waiting in her room. She asked the staff to gather and listen as her grandmother played "Maple Leaf Rag."

Blessing and welcoming ceremonies to bring happiness, friendship, and good luck seem in order. We need calming rituals that assure the old they are still loved and part of the human community. I think of the Buddhist custom of blessing new homes. Prayers, flowers, readings, music, and hugs all can help ease a person into a new life. Letters of introduction to the staff from friends and family members could help the staff see the new resident as a person. These letters might be part of a ceremony.

Transitions are tough on healthy young people who are going from one good thing to another good thing. It's hard to imagine the stress of going from a beloved home into a setting that we fear and dread. How many times have you heard someone say they would rather die than be in rest home? Rituals and ceremonies could ease the transition and make it feel less like abandonment to the gulag.

All over the country, rest homes are becoming more user friendly. Many now have pets, aviaries, gardening projects, and flexible meal schedules. Many rest homes have day-care programs so that the old and young can help each other. A San Francisco program called On Lok (Cantonese for peaceful, happy abode) offers a medical clinic, comfortable beds, and a beautiful garden for the day treatment of Alzheimer's patients. At night the patients can return to their families. At best, rest homes are a return to communal living. To a generation who grew up in a communal culture, they can be familiar and comforting.

ONE DAY AROUND CHRISTMAS when I was shopping in Walgreen's, I heard an old woman talking to the checker as she bought toilet paper and Band-Aids. She said, "All the people I love most are underground. I just want to be with them. I'm homesick for heaven. Why does God make me stay here alone and suffer?" At a certain time in life, friends begin to peel off. Siblings who visited frequently die or can no longer travel. Supper clubs break up. Social routines that lasted a lifetime are lost. Willa Cather described this feeling as "going to a play after most of the characters had died."

Communities keep people healthy. In 1988, James House of the University of Michigan found that the lack of social relationships constituted a major health risk, rivaling cigarette smoking or high blood pressure. Research on Roseto, a village of Italian immigrants with three-generational households, indicated that people lived longer if they stayed in Roseto than if they moved away. This increase in longevity rates wherever there is community is called the Roseto effect.

In America, people seventy-five or older who live alone have 2.5 times the mortality rate of those with companions. Even people with plants or pets live longer than those with nothing to care for. Research shows that people who talk to one another in doctors' offices while they are waiting are more likely to get better faster. In some rest homes, tapes of loved ones' voices are played to calm down the residents for sleep. Clearly, one way to help old people is to get them around other people.

Maintaining connection is a challenge. Visiting may be a labor of love, but visiting a tennis partner after he has had a debilitating stroke is also a labor. It hurts to see a best friend with a feeding tube and catheter. At a certain point, most of an old person's long-term relationships are buried. As Florene put it, "I wish I could e-mail heaven."

In Tekamah every week, my parents-in-law see the death announcement of another person they have known all their lives. My mother-in-law said, "I never thought I'd have to live my life without some of these people." As I write I think of my father-in-law, who just lost his barber of sixty years. Fred had cut his hair since before Bernie was married. Fifteen years before, Fred retired, but he still came by Bernie's to give him a haircut. Then he grew ill with cancer and Bernie went to Fred's house for a haircut. Two weeks before his death, Fred gave Bernie his last haircut. My father-in-law told me about Fred at breakfast. He was calm and matter-of-fact. Losing his lifelong companions is his regular experience.

If a partner's health suffers, the other partner also is affected. Either they both stop doing certain things or the healthy mate carries on alone. My client Marilyn told me her mother went alone on a cruise to celebrate her fiftieth wedding anniversary. She and her husband had saved and planned for this cruise for years, but now he was unable to walk and in a modified-care unit following surgery. He insisted his wife enjoy the cruise. Marilyn's mother calls her husband to tell him about her cruise. She tries to make it sound as fun as she can so that he can enjoy things vicariously. She calls Marilyn every day to check on her husband and to tell the truth. She says, "There is no lonelier feeling than watching an ocean sunset alone or standing by myself on deck under the stars and hearing the band play a Glenn Miller song."

For many people, the hardest loss is of a mate. Bernie and Phyllis went to grade school together. Otis and Grace married in their early teens and have celebrated their seventieth wedding anniversary. Betty and Lloyd have been married more than sixty years, but now Lloyd has Alzheimer's. Betty recently wrote me, "He can't understand me, and I can't understand him. . . . I can't let him go, and I can't make him stay."

A. D. Hope wrote that when they age, couples "grow closer and closer apart." That may be true, but it's also true that couples share memories and chores. They worry about each other and cheer each other up. They correct for each other's disabilities. The one who walks well pushes the wheelchair. The one who hears well answers the phone. A truism is that with the loss of a spouse, women mourn and men replace. Perhaps for younger people, but almost every old-old person mourns.

Barbara's husband, Dick, has Pick's disease, which is similar to Alzheimer's. Dick requires special care at a rest home near Barbara's condo. She told me they'd had a happy marriage, but she laughed and said, "There were times when it could have been happier." Barbara first noticed Dick was having problems when he failed his driver's-license test. He was upset, but she said, "Don't worry. I'll help you study, and you can take it again." He wouldn't do that, and soon afterwards he gave Barbara the checkbook to manage. For the last two years, he's been on a locked ward. Barbara said, "I never expected we would live apart."

When Barbara drives over to see him, he runs to embrace her. They have a scrapbook that holds all his papers. Many Sundays they take this book to the library and work on it. It is mostly cards and letters from friends and family. Other times Barbara takes him to the synagogue, or down to the university to walk around. At the synagogue he can sing and chant just like always. She brings him to her place and shows him the pictures she has of him. One Sunday recently they spent most of the afternoon watching a squirrel gather nuts for his nest. She has loyal friends who invite them over for pie or cocktails. Her current definition of a friend is someone who treats Dick well.

Barbara said that in the family she is known as "the rock of Gibraltar," but when I visited she was having a bad day. It was icy outside, and she was afraid to drive to Dick's ward with supplies he needed. When she called to explain, the staff was curt with her. She told him that she hoped they wouldn't take their frustration out on Dick, and tears filled her eyes. She said, "I could hear steeliness in the aide's voice when she talked to me. I felt rebuffed."

It's a miracle that people survive the losses of their mates. There are so many widows and widowers, and we tend to underestimate the magnitude of each individual tragedy. In our country we expect people to recover very quickly from grief. People are asked about their losses for a few months and then expected to move on. Even though most people don't recover nearly that quickly, they stop talking about their losses. The rest of us assume they feel better than they really do.

My aunt Margaret educated me about widowhood. She's a good coper, but after the death of her husband of sixty years, she was lost. At the time of Fred's memorial service, she wrote, "As sweetly as an opening bud you came to me. As silently as the setting sun you left. Between, one long and glorious day." Later she wrote this poem.

"To Fred"

*To walk alone, where there is none*
*but memories. To be the one*
*remaining when you are gone.*

*The day you left me, dear,*
*My life was rent in two.*
*Now walking wounded I go along*
*Through life as half.*

*One leg is not enough*
*To keep my balance and to move*
*Along my destined way*
*With strength and dignity.*

*So many things I cannot do*
*With only one small hand.*
*Unfinished tasks reproach me*
*and mock my helplessness.*

*I cannot hear the music clear.*
*Nor see the sunsets glow.*
*My senses dimmed, my mind grew dull*
*When I lost sight of you.*

*But, most of all I lost my heart,*
*not half for you owned all of it.*
*The shell remains, it walks and talks,*
*But joy there is none.*
*How could there be*
*When Love is gone?*

She compared her reaction to Fred's death to a tree that is hit by lightning: At first the tree looks like a goner, but then bark grows over the devastated places. Her books, her church, and her connection to the natural world helped her recover. For a while she craved solitude. She loved to watch the sunsets and think of Fred. Playing in the ocean with her great-grandchildren helped her heal. She quoted Longfellow to express her abating sorrow: "A feeling of sadness and longing,/That is not akin to pain/And resembles sorrow only/As the mist resembles rain."

Many of the widowed stay in relationships after death. If ghosts don't exist literally, they certainly exist metaphorically. The widowed include their mates in their prayers and conversations. Many talk to their mates as they eat their meals or when they visit their graves. They look forward to reunions in heaven. Their partners have died, but the relationships haven't.

## Work

IN MY HOMETOWN there is an old woman who cares for her sixty-year-old ne'er-do-well son, Thom. Well, he isn't a ne'er-do-well exactly, he just never grew up and left home. He doesn't work, and he likes his mother's cooking. Of course, over the years the son has been much criticized by the townspeople for his laziness and dependency. While they have a point, I want to note that his mother is the youngest-looking eighty-five-year-old in town. When I see her at the grocery store, she is bustling around getting fresh peaches for pie—peach is Thom's favorite—or buying big boxes of cereal—which Thom likes to snack on when he watches TV. As a psychologist, I could easily comment on the unhealthy aspects of this family, but what is relevant here is how useful the mother feels and how lucky she is to have a life with a point.

When I was in graduate school, one of my supervisors was Dr. Lana Edwards, a psychologist in her seventies who ran an inpatient unit for schizophrenics. I picture her in group therapy, dressed in her wool suits and therapeutic shoes, with her knitting on her lap, making astute observations and kind remarks to the patients. That was twenty years ago, and last winter I heard that Dr. Edwards is still working on the unit. The person who told me said, "She must be about a hundred and ten by now."

The loss of work has killed many a person. For men who have few interests outside of work, the first few years after retirement are critical. They must find new ways to structure their time, new ways to be respected in their families, and new ways to be useful. Women who are used to second-shift work generally fare better. Many of their jobs stay with them until they die.

Especially as people lose some of their abilities, it's important that they be able to use what remains to help others. Older people often derive great pleasure from being able to drive their friends on errands. Cooking an angel food cake for a grandson, showing a grandnephew how to use a shortwave radio, or helping another resident in a rest home find her way to the dining hall makes people feel useful—that most essential of feelings.

Losing physical beauty is hard for some older women. If a woman has always been stunning, liver spots, extra pounds, and wrinkles can affect core identity issues. Ordinary-looking women are likely to fare better. They have less to mourn—they have identities built on relationships, not complexions. Ann Menebroker wrote, "The way to stay beautiful is to avoid mirrors and look only at those who truly love back."

## The Wedding Anniversary

LAST FALL, I received an invitation to my high school English teacher's fiftieth wedding anniversary. I hadn't seen Ramona Miner in years, but I'd heard that she had leukemia. She'd spent much of the summer in hospitals and had even flown to the Mayo Clinic. No one expected her to live for another anniversary.

I remembered her as an elegant, sophisticated world traveler. In the classroom, she wore cashmere sweaters, silk scarves, and glittery earrings and bracelets. She brought the *New York Times* to class and told us, "I want you to know there is a big world outside of Nebraska." When she recited poems by Whitman, Dickinson, and Blake, she wept at their beauty. She insisted we learn poetry "by heart" so that we would have it with us when we really needed it.

Ramona grew up in our town, but she studied abroad. Much later she came home and married a high school classmate. Mr. Miner was a sweet-natured man who devoted his life to pleasing Ramona. I remember them driving down Main Street on summer nights in their shiny convertible. Mr. Miner kept his arm over his wife's shoulders. Her long blond hair blew in the wind, and she waved her bejeweled arms at everyone. They never had children because, as Mr. Miner put it, "It wouldn't be fair. I could never love a child as much as I love Ramona."

In November I drove home for their anniversary celebration. I sang all the way across the state. Particularly in the 1990s, I like to visit a place where people remember when I needed help tying my shoes. I like people who remember my parents and call me "kiddo."

The first event was a community lunch at the high school in Mrs. Miner's honor. When I arrived, the dining hall was already packed and lively. At the head table sat Mr. and Mrs. Miner, but if I hadn't seen their name tags I wouldn't have recognized them. Mrs. Miner's face was puffy from steroids, and she had dark raccoon circles under her eyes. She was heavy and needed help getting up out of chairs. As always she was beautifully dressed, today in a pale blue silk suit with matching high heels. Her hair was carefully arranged, and her makeup expertly applied. Beside her, Mr. Miner was tired and gray-looking, thin in the face. He wore a blue business suit, now faded and shiny at the knees and elbows. They smiled, and hugged all their friends. When I walked over, Mrs. Miner got tears in her eyes.

Mrs. Miner's old boyfriend Lester from high school was expected. He had left town after graduation and was now a millionaire in Phoenix. People kept whispering the word "millionaire" and looking toward the door. I wondered what Lester would think of Mrs. Miner now. When he'd dated her, she'd been the star of the high school plays, the valedictorian, the breezy blond who dressed like a model. In college, so many guys had wanted to date her that there was talk of having a lottery.

At noon Lester still hadn't arrived. The crowd gave him ten minutes and then went ahead without him. Even a millionaire can't stop Nebraskans from eating lunch. The meal had been prepared by the 4-H students. We all took our trays and went through a long line of casseroles, desserts, and salads. I took some lasagna and a dipperful of chicken and homemade dumplings. I couldn't tell the desserts from the salads. There were a few pasta and lettuce salads, but the rest were made of Jell-O—orange with carrots, lime with walnuts, and cherry with mayo and Cool Whip. The desserts were pudding- and Jell-O-filled tarts, also with Cool Whip.

After lunch, I walked over to the cemetery to look at my family's graves. About an inch of snow covered the ground, and a few flakes were still in the air. It was cold and windy, but I liked it. The walk was filled with memories for me. This park is where I told ghost stories to my friends. This corner is where our dog was hit by a car thirty-five years ago. At the grave-yard, I recognized the names of my baby-sitter's parents and my friends' grandparents.

I walked past one garish grave. It was heart-shaped and said "Together Forever." It had a mailbox with Mickey and Minnie Mouse painted on its side. Lawn ornaments, whirligigs, and plastic flowers covered this couple's plot just as they once had covered their lawn. I snickered at their taste, but I was touched. I wondered where Mrs. Miner's grave would go. As I walked down the hill, I passed an old Chevy. There was a baby asleep in a car seat, young parents, and an old man in a gray jacket. The old man tottered over to a grave and then back to look at the baby. He said to the parents, "They come and they go."

It was snowing hard by the time I went to the party at the Miners' house. Women had come early with hors d'oeuvres—ham salad in cream puffs, gulf shrimp, and spinach dip with rye bread. There were trays of brownies and little pecan pies, and there was a wedding cake just like their original one years ago. The women encouraged one another to eat, a habit that came from a time when food was scarce.

Lester came in with the other men, explaining that his plane had been delayed in Denver. He carried an expensive wool coat and smelled of some exotic aftershave. He carried himself like he knew he was attractive to women. On his arm was a woman in her fifties whom he introduced as Tonya. She was a looker who managed to convey subtly that she was a little above rural Nebraskans. I wanted to shout at her, "If Mrs. Miner weren't sick, she'd be as pretty as you."

At first Lester didn't even recognize Mrs. Miner. His eyes scanned the room for her, and he passed her over. But then a man pointed her out and he said under his breath, "Holy Toledo." He approached her immediately, took her hands in his, and said, "How ya doing, baby doll?" Ramona answered that she was having a wonderful day. She smiled graciously at Tonya and complimented her elegant outfit.

Lester talked golf with the few men who played golf. The other men talked about football games that had been played fifty years earlier. I heard one man say, "The coach should have played you more." His friend replied modestly, "Oh, I don't know about that." Mattie had just retired from her job as city librarian. As she put it, she was "tired and retired." But she missed the people. John, a retired pilot, told Tonya, "The superior pilot uses his superior judgment to avoid having to use his superior skills."

Mr. Miner passed drinks and stoked the fire in the fireplace. Mrs. Miner sat in a big chair and urged people to drink more wine. I wondered if Whitman and Blake were helping her through this gathering. I thought of the courage it must have taken her to be in public knowing she would die soon and looking like she did today. It was a kind of undervalued courage, "grace under fire," to be in pain and fearful and still to laugh and ask about others and even to smile at the arrogant beau in his four-hundred-dollar suit and to not let him know, or anyone else know, that this was a hard day.

## Post-Traumatic Stress Disorder

*My working definition of an optimist is a person who hasn't lived very long.*

—DORIS GRUMBACH

*Each of us will die, naked and alone on some battlefield not of our own choosing.*

—THOMAS CAHILL

In *Reviving Ophelia*, I wrote that one way to think of teenagers is as constantly being on LSD. Similarly, one way to think of the old is as victims of chronic post-traumatic stress disorder. For the most part, they are ordinary healthy people for whom all hell has broken loose.

PTSD refers to a variety of symptoms that people experience after they have undergone extreme stress. There are different kinds of reactions to loss. Some people see danger everywhere. They are jumpy, worried about everything, and easily upset. They may be irritable and find it hard to sleep or concentrate. They often experience depression and nightmares. They may feel survivor guilt or lose their belief in God or whatever else they believed in. They may become chronic pessimists with a sense that life is over for them.

Two widows I saw in therapy had PTSD reactions of very different sorts. Janine suffered the heightened emotionality of a PTSD reaction. Other people, like Wanda, experience an emotional numbing.

Janine and Wanda differ also in the kinds of loss they are experiencing. Janine lost a loving relationship. Her grief, while intense, is clean, relatively uncomplicated by other emotions such as anger at her deceased mate. Wanda had a "can't live with him, can't live without him" marriage, and her grief is messier and more complex. She takes longer to heal.

## JANINE
*"The center of my life wasn't in me or in him. It was between us."*

WHEN I MET JANINE, she'd just lost Arnie, her husband of fifty-two years. Two weeks earlier he had died of a heart attack. When Janine discovered him dead, she went into physical shock. When Janine came to see me, she already had made it through the funeral and the first nights alone, but she still reminded me of a passage from Mark Twain's autobiography. He'd returned from Europe to hear that his daughter had died suddenly. He wrote that he felt as if a lightning bolt passed through his body, and he wondered at his own physical survival.

Janine felt guilty that she had cooked Arnie eggs and sausage, that she hadn't insisted he exercise, that she hadn't saved him, and finally, that she had survived him. She lay awake nights worrying about the health of other family members and friends. She alternated between worrying about her own health and wishing she could get something terminal and put herself out of her misery.

When she forgot Arnie was dead, even for a few moments, she would remember with a jolt. Several times she set the table for two, sat down alone, remembered, and sobbed into her dinner. Arnie had woven himself into the walls of her life, and it was inconceivable that he was gone. Every morning when she awoke the news would re-hit her, hard in the face.

Janine was in a grief hangover, chronically feeling that things were not right. The first time we met she quoted me the lines of a Vern Gosdin country song: "You haven't felt heartbreak until it's written in stone." She wanted to know if I had lost anyone. She said, "If you haven't, you couldn't possibly understand what I am experiencing."

She said that the hardest thing was realizing that the world goes on, that even though her heart was broken, the neighbors still set out bulbs, read the paper, and walked their dogs. The nightly news still came on, children played basketball, and the ice cream truck clanged past.

Even though Janine and Arnie had worked together in their small business, they never fought. Janine said, "What was there to fight about? We saw things eye to eye." Arnie was a joker, easygoing and calm, and Janine missed his perspective. "Just telling him what happened calmed me down." She said, "The center of my life wasn't in me or in him. It was between us."

Now that Arnie was gone, Janine worried about her mental stability. Her children hurt her feelings, and little irritations that Arnie could have joked away grated on her. "Arnie had a better memory than me," she told me. "If I forgot something I'd ask him. He even remembered what movies I liked. Now I have no one to jog my memory of events, no one to ask, 'Now, what year did we do that?'"

She couldn't listen to music or concentrate to read, but she could walk. Every day she walked in a park outside of town. This park had a small stream, where Janine found some peace: "Looking at the water helps me accept Arnie's death."

She liked seeing me and having coffee with her friend Madge. She said, "When I had Arnie I didn't need many other people, but that has changed." The real cure turned out to be something serendipitous. One day, when Janine was alone thumbing through a magazine, the doorbell rang. It was the two-year-old from next door, released from his house by the springtime. Troy invited himself in and toddled around her house looking at stuff and asking questions. She called his mother to ask if he could stay awhile, and two hours later she took him home.

After that, her bell rang daily. She'd answer to see Troy in his training pants and cowboy boots ready for another adventure. She didn't want to fall in love, but she did. Troy was insistent, he made her laugh in spite of herself. As she followed him around, served him cookies, showed him what he could and couldn't touch, she forgot her pain. She told me later, "Troy pulled me back into the world. He helped me see that the best thing is that life goes on."

## WANDA
### *"The year the sky fell down"*

WANDA AND I met in January after the death of her husband from leukemia. Wayne had been a lawyer, and they'd been married thirty-nine years. With the help of Hospice and a good doctor, Wanda had cared for him at home. Also that year she'd lost her mother, father, and her favorite nephew. It was, to quote her, "the year the sky fell down."

Wanda's osteoporosis had worsened recently. Since Wayne died, she'd broken vertebrae twice. Wanda was in constant pain, and her appetite wasn't good. She said, "I thought I would feel better after Wayne's death. We didn't have a great marriage, and I was so homebound during his last year. But I don't feel better, I feel empty."

Wayne and Wanda had a "marry in haste, regret at leisure" kind of marriage. There was no abuse, but they weren't compatible. As Wanda put it, "Wayne gave at the office." He never could find time for a date with Wanda, or a family vacation. Actually, he was very frugal. Whenever Wanda wanted to spend money on herself or the children, he would warn her, "Someday you'll be eating dog food." Wanda had alternated between confrontation and sulking as a way to influence Wayne. Neither had been effective, and eventually they had a marriage of convenience. They lived together politely with almost no interaction but with a mound of unresolved pain between them.

I was relieved that Wanda wasn't sugar-coating her relationship with Wayne. She wasn't experiencing the "dangerous amnesia" of some people who lose their mates. Some partners forget the bad and remember only the good, even if the relationship was mostly bad. Although temporarily comforting, doing so can cause people to fail in new relationships. It also may cause conflict between them and family members with a more realistic view of the past. Even though Wanda experienced few feelings, her thoughts about Wayne were honest. As she said to me, "I'll tell you the pure and simple truth about Wayne, although the truth is rarely pure and never simple."

Since Wayne's death, Wanda woke up every morning asking, "What is the point?" She watched TV or read paperback mysteries. She dropped out of her sewing circle and prayer group and avoided family members. After she'd snapped at her grandchildren, her daughter had told her she "carried a lot of anger," a remark that surprised Wanda, who felt nothing at all.

When I recommended she write her feelings in a journal, Wanda said, "What feelings?" I said that if she gave herself time, feelings would come. Wanda was skeptical—she'd never been an open person—but she agreed to cooperate. She was tired of living in a tapioca-flavored world.

She came in for several months, and over time, Wanda did a most uncharacteristic thing: She discussed feelings. Much to her surprise, when she talked about Wayne, she felt anger, regret, love, and hate. She mourned her parents and her nephew. She cried about her broken health and her physical pain. In one session she worried that her children would think she was a burden. In another she talked about her isolation from everyone but widows. She described a day when she yearned to touch a man's tweed coat and the smell of aftershave lotions had made her ache.

Complicated relationships are the hardest to grieve. People like Wanda, who feel great ambivalence about someone they have lost, have the hardest time moving through the grief process. Only when Wanda allowed herself to share her feelings was she able to move on. Only after she experienced the negative emotions of grief could she begin to have the positive emotions.

Eventually Wanda became a happy person. She learned to drive and to manage her money. She loved the freedom to cook or not to cook, and to buy herself and her grandchildren small gifts. She rejoined her clubs and made a close friend for the first time in her life. She traveled with her daughter's family, and enjoyed them and all the places they visited. She said, "Finally I am having some of those family vacations I always wanted."

A COMMON REACTION to trauma is to tell trauma stories over and over again. I think of Gail, who related everything to her husband's violent death in a train wreck. If someone mentioned the weather, she would say, "Yes, it reminds me of the weather the day Walter died." If someone mentioned going out for pie, she would say "Walter loved chocolate pie." If a friend tried to tell her about a trip to Canada, Gail would say, "Walter wanted to visit Canada, but he was hit by a train."

This need to tell the story isn't about transmitting information, it's therapy. Denial and repression are physically, emotionally, and mentally expensive. Releasing feelings is part of the healing process. Talking through and reliving trauma can eventually put it to rest.

Like other victims of PTSD, the old become obsessed with that which has traumatized them. Anniversaries and holidays can trigger fresh PTSD reactions, as can new traumas. Family members may note depression and irritability or hear the endless stories about health, and not connect them to PTSD.

Many of the old are interested in the health stories of those they don't even know. As I write, I think of Josepha. When I was at her house for lunch, we talked of nothing but health problems. She had bursitis in her left knee and needed Darvocet and cortisone. The cold weather was hard on her, and she'd been in the hospital with pneumonia. She had seen a pulmonary specialist and been on prednisone. As if her own problems weren't enough, she told me this awful story about a woman I didn't know with fluid in her lungs. She kept saying the friend had "stiff lungs."

It was hard to listen while we were eating split pea soup. I was new to my work with the aged and hadn't yet become desensitized to all the health talk. I found it boring and revolting at the same time. Now I would react differently. After I have spent several years with old people, health stories no longer get to me.

At first, all this illness talk baffled me. Don't the old have enough sad stories without telling ones about perfect strangers? Don't they get bored with health problems? But now I understand. The old live in Susan Sontag's "kingdom of the sick." Many become desensitized to discussions of bowels, catheters, and open sores. They will go into extravagant detail about medical procedures. I remember a discussion I had with Gladys when she had pain from gallstones. She told me, "They drained a gallon of urine out of me." My neighbor told me about his sister's knee surgery: "The doctor took out her stitches without even looking. Her leg burst open and is infected."

Illness is the battleground of old age. It is where we all make our last stand. It is the World War, the Great Depression, the Hurricane Hugo. Like all PTSD victims, the old are interested in trauma stories. They talk to work through the trauma. They talk because health issues are the fast-breaking disaster story. As Bettelheim said, "That which cannot be talked about cannot be put to rest."

I have always been interested in disaster stories. The Donner Party, the

Scott expedition to the South Pole, and the sinking of the *Titanic* show humans at their best and worst. Individual disaster stories are instructive, too. When Marie Antoinette, the beautiful, spoiled French queen, was thrown into the Bastille, her hair turned gray overnight. But in the awful last months, starved, mocked, chained to a wall in a dark dungeon, she managed to behave with dignity.

Disaster stories tell us what humans do when they are shoved hard against the wall. Old age is our own personal disaster story, our own worst-case scenario. Each of us will experience our ship going down; we'll experience being lost and alone far from home. From our responses come the best and worst stories.

People suffering from PTSD alternate between being overwhelmed by emotions and feeling nothing at all. Sometimes people who can't express what they feel develop physical problems or bad habits. Some people get stuck in their traumas. I think of my great-granny Lee, who had a pessimistic disposition. As a child I avoided her because she was always critical and complaining. She lived with her daughter, my grandma Glessie, whom she bossed around mercilessly. When she was irritated with Glessie, Great-Granny Lee would throw her food across the room and hurl insults at my gentle grandmother.

I was an adult before I realized how traumatic Great-Granny Lee's life must have been. Her husband had been killed by a runaway buggy. Her son-in-law had gone crazy, and she had developed arthritis so severe that she could not leave the daybed in my grandmother's living room. She was in constant pain and had lost all her money to quacks and snake-oil salesmen. A more resilient person might have handled her tragedies differently. But she was who she was, stunted and soured by the harsh events of her life. When I knew her she had, as Robert Frost said, "nothing to look backward to with pride, and nothing to look forward to with hope."

From the inside, PTSD feels like pain, anger, and shock. From the outside, PTSD looks like anger, apathy, or depression. I think of my friend Jolene, who visits her aunt once a week at the rest home. Aunt Ardith calls the home a snakepit and blames Jolene for her situation. She criticizes Jolene's clothes, weight, and hair, and pouts because Jolene doesn't come more often. She never asks her niece about her life. Jolene hates to go but doesn't feel anyone should have to live without relationships.

Aunt Ardith was never a paragon of good mental health. However, she coped adequately until her husband died and she developed sciatica. Her poor health and her depression sapped all of her energy for life. As Aunt Ardith grew more self-absorbed and negative, fewer friends stopped by and things grew worse. Today she has only Jolene.

Sometimes the old are traumatized in ways no one suspects. A nurse told me about a hearing-impaired client who lived with her middle-aged, mentally disturbed son who bullied and blackmailed her. He wanted money for cocaine, clothes, and cars. Her client had begged the son to let her move into a retirement village, but he refused to consider it. The son kept his mother isolated from her friends. Finally, the woman's doctor suspected abuse and called social services. The woman was rescued from what was essentially a hostage situation. The nurse said, "We all thought she was a little nuts, but now that she is safe and well cared for, she is a lovely, sane person."

Obsessions can be reactions to trauma. We had an older neighbor who just knew that her elm tree was going to fall on her house. She couldn't sleep nights for worry, and she talked about this impending disaster all the time. Eventually she had a beautiful healthy tree cut down because none of us could persuade her that she was safe. Another woman who lost her husband was sure that the neighbors were stealing her vegetables and garden tools. She heard things in the night, and even though the tools were still in her garage in the morning, she told us that whoever stole them returned them before dawn.

Addictions also can be PTSD reactions. Many functional alcoholics become less functional after they have been traumatized. Social drinkers with no one to talk to become alcoholics; teetotalers drink to fall asleep in the first sad months after they lose their mates. Many of the old have no one to monitor their drinking. Maybe they can't do what they used to do, but they can still drink. When her father was dying, Ellen came into therapy. She was the oldest daughter and the only child who lived near her alcoholic parents. Her father had been a prominent physician, and her mother had been a club woman who golfed and played tennis. All their lives they'd been in the martini culture. Now with the stress of Ellen's father's cancer, they both are drinking to kill the pain. Ellen never thought she would have to deal with a drinking problem in her family.

Having PTSD at any age can lead to truncated growth—as if a person needs all his psychic energy just for survival, leaving none for growth. Of course, reactions vary according to the nature of the trauma, the resiliency of the victim, and the quality of the support system. There are surprises. Wimps become strong as steel, and towers of strength grow petulant and helpless. Isolated people and those who "can't catch their breaths" from one trauma to the next are more at risk for self-absorption.

Carl Jung believed that if the old didn't develop inner strength they became defensive, dogmatic, depressed, and cynical. The only true cure for PTSD is inner growth. Treatment involves restoring control and connection in the life of the victim. What is most healing for people is the knowledge that they are still loved and capable of loving. The ability to turn suffering into a gift for others, what Robert Jay Lifton called a "survivor mission," also helps the old heal from loss.

However, until people tell their stories, they may not be interested in helping others or even in other subjects. A grandfather may not listen to an account of his grandson's swim meet, not because he doesn't love his grandson but because he is preoccupied by the traumatic events of the last few months. Aunt Tillie may not ask about her nephew's new job because she is worried about her next doctor's appointment.

Certain people know how to ask questions and to listen calmly, conveying empathy and respect. The old desperately need natural healers in their lives, people who are not in a hurry and who care what they are thinking and feeling.

New interests, new skills, and new relationships also help people move on. The old need root friends from the past, and flowering friends who bring new life. Another way old people can grow is by acquiring some of the skills of a younger generation. A father may learn to hug his adult son and say "I love you." A mother may learn to assert herself and ask for what she needs. Older parents may learn to talk honestly about things they were ashamed to discuss earlier.

From all the loss they experience, the old can become bitter, dull, and self-absorbed. However, the people who don't decline with age become more integrated and individual, more fully human, more uniquely who they are, and more compassionate. They learn, to quote Auden, to "love each other or perish."

Our elders need places where they can be physically well cared for and respected. It's hard to overstate the benefits of physical closeness. Simple, everyday tasks are much easier to handle if family is nearby. Being together makes life easier not only for the older person but also for their younger caregivers. I know a principal in Oregon who built a guest cottage for her parents in her backyard. At first the parents just visited briefly, but as they grew older, their visits lengthened and finally they moved in. There were adjustments to be made on all sides, but in the end everyone was pleased by the situation. My friend could help her parents age. The grandparents were there for their grandchildren's orchestra performances and soccer games, for the holiday meals and sleepovers. And later the children were able to be with their grandparents the last days of their lives.

Some friends of mine built a home for their son and his family next door to his grandmother's apartment so they all could look out for one another. My friends live two blocks away and are delighted with how easy it is to see their son and daughter-in-law, their grandchildren, and their aging parent. The whole family has brunch every Sunday. The son mows his grandmother's yard and helps with small repairs. The grandmother has her great-granddaughters over for tea and stories.

The old also need doctors who are close by, physically and emotionally—doctors who treat them as whole people, not symptom clusters or checkbooks; doctors whom they trust and who truly care about their welfare. They need people who will listen as they talk about physical or emotional pain, and who will advocate for them in our managed-care medical system. Having physicians who knew our elders when they were younger and who know something of their families also helps.

Mental health care needn't involve therapists, but the old must have support. One of the best support groups I know is a group of widowers who meet weekly for breakfast at a local pancake house. Senior centers, church groups, elder hostels, card clubs, and quilting circles all are places where the old can get the support they need to recover from loss.

Stress is cumulative. The old are already coping with so much stress that small stresses can overwhelm them. When a person has just heard that a friend has terminal cancer, an unexpected piece of bad financial news or a fender bender can feel tragic. A client who coped heroically with the loss of her mate fell apart with the stress and bureaucratic hassles of donating her husband's body to science. It's important to put the smaller griefs in the context of the larger ones.

When visiting the old, it's good to ask for updates on their health and that of their friends. If a friend has died, ask about that person. What was their relationship? What were some of their good times together? How did the friend die? The old may need to talk about trauma before they can focus on the present.

Humor helps. One client who had a difficult time getting in to see her doctor finally called and said, "I'll have the hearse deliver me to your office." It's also good to remind the old of what they have accomplished, not what they haven't, to say, "Remember the good moments, not the wasted ones." And, "Learn from your mistakes, don't waste another minute of your life." The saddest thing about old age isn't loss but the failure to grow from experiences.

## THE WILSONS
*"Dad was never much of a nurturer,
and now he wants to be nurtured."*

SUSAN AND JANE came in to talk about their father, Bailey. He was eighty, living alone, irascible, and dying of colon cancer. He wouldn't enter a health-care facility or allow any hired help into his house. The daughters, both working women, had for several months alternated weeks caring for him. Meanwhile, Bailey's health had worsened and his daughters had grown reluctant to be responsible for his care. Susan and Jane were unsure what their next step should be.

We talked first about their lives. Jane was an attorney who practiced in the law firm her father had started. She laughed and said, "I'm the proverbial Snow White. I was a good student and a good daughter. That's what makes this hard for me. I am used to doing what Dad wants. Only now he isn't rational."

Susan said, "I did the unthinkable: I went to art school. I guess I should call myself Rose Red." We all laughed, and Susan continued, "I'm not wild anymore. I'm married and have twins in ninth grade. I taught art until last month, when Dad's health worsened. I've taken a leave of absence and canceled my private students. I don't much like Bailey, but we are connected. I'll do what I can for him, but I'm at my limit."

I asked about other people in Bailey's life. "Bailey's an only child," Jane answered. "He never had friends. Several years ago he left Mother for a younger woman. The woman eventually returned to her first husband. We wish she would have stayed."

Susan added, "Mother lives here in town, and she feels for us. But she wouldn't go near Bailey with a ten-foot pole."

"My children are in college out of state, but my husband helps us." Jane sighed. "Bailey has never liked Don much, but Don isn't doing what he does for Bailey's sake—he's helping me. Bless his heart, he is handling the insurance and bills."

"Don is a saint," Susan said. "I can't believe all he does for Dad. My husband, who Dad also disapproves of, doesn't even pretend to care."

"Dad was never much of a nurturer, and now he wants to be nurtured," Jane said.

"You're too kind," Susan said. "He orders us around like functionaries. Has he ever said 'Thank you' for anything?"

"He doesn't say it, but I can tell he's appreciative."

Susan snorted. "There is another issue that brings us in," she said. "I believe in holistic health and alternative medicine. Jane wants Dad to fly to the Cleveland Clinic."

Until this point in the session, the sisters had been relaxed and warm with each other, but now Susan stiffened and Jane's face reddened. Jane said, "That's not quite it. Dad suggested Cleveland."

"That was two weeks ago. The last few days, he has wanted to die," said Susan. Jane looked at me and threw up her hands. "He tells us different things, and we hear things differently. We both want to respect Dad's wishes, but he is almost beyond the point where he has wishes."

"I talked to him about vitamins and therapeutic touch," Susan said. "I didn't think they would cure him, but they might make his last months more comfortable. He called my ideas 'New Age hooey.'"

I congratulated these two sisters. They were doing many things right—sharing the load, respecting their father's wishes, trying to plan ahead, and communicating about differences. Bailey was heavily medicated and nauseated, but still able to voice opinions. I recommended they sit down with their father and talk several things through: their need for some help from outsiders, various treatment options, and what he wanted to see happen between now and when he died. I mentioned Hospice, but Jane winced and said, "Dad isn't ready for that."

I reminded both women to get out for a date with their husbands, to get plenty of sleep and exercise, and every now and then to give themselves a day off from these problems. "This situation may be tough for a long time," I said. "Be marathon runners. Pace yourselves."

SESSION TWO

Two weeks later the sisters were back, looking older and more tired. Since we'd first met, Bailey had been hospitalized for emergency care. The experience had shaken them up.

Jane shouted, "What has happened to hospitals?"

Neither sister had been in one since they'd had babies years before. They couldn't believe the changes. Bailey's regular doctor was out of town, and the substitute doctor was overworked and harried. The nursing staff was frantic. Bailey had been out of his head and couldn't ask for anything or accurately report on his condition. No staff member ever even called Bailey by name or bothered to introduce him- or herself to the sisters. The sisters couldn't get information. The place smelled bad and looked dirty. Many times they rang Bailey's buzzer for help, and no one responded. As Susan put it, "He could have been Code Blue and no one would have rushed in."

The sisters alternated shifts. One night, when they "slacked off" and went for coffee in the hospital cafeteria, Bailey fell out of bed and got a goose egg on his forehead. Susan said, "We realized that he could die if we weren't there to watch things."

"I actually started telling everyone I was a lawyer, hoping that would scare them into taking better care of Dad," Jane said. "It didn't."

Five days later, Bailey was released to his daughters. Right now the hospital offered follow-up care, but that would end in a few days. Don was arranging for home health care and looking into assisted-living facilities. However, all the good places were full, and no one even pretended to be eager to take on a cantankerous dying man.

"Bailey is breaking my heart," Jane said. "Twice he has called out 'Kevorkian, Kevorkian.'" She stopped talking to compose herself, then continued, "He alternates between being confused and being upset. He doesn't want to go back into a hospital. He doesn't want me to leave him, and he yells at the visiting nurses."

Susan added, "He is like a sick baby, a miserable authoritarian baby."

I asked how the sisters were getting along together.

"Actually, better. Misery loves company." Susan laughed. "Who else but Jane really cares what Bailey's temperature was last night, or whether the home health aide smoked cigarettes on the job?"

"We aren't debating treatment anymore," Jane said. "We can't face another hospital."

"The problem is that we won't be able to manage much longer," said Susan. "I'm thinking Hospice."

Jane agreed that it was time. I recommended they call a woman I know, a clinical nurse specialist. I said I thought she could help Bailey make some good decisions. I again congratulated them for their good care of their father. Jane nodded tiredly. Susan said half in jest, "If he doesn't die soon I'm going to kill him."

## SESSION THREE (TWO MONTHS LATER)

This session ended up being our last one. The sisters came in mainly to thank me for introducing them and their dad to Karen, the nurse specialist and advocate for the elderly.

When they came into the office, they were laughing. They looked calmer and more rested. Susan had been able to attend her twins' orchestra concert and resume teaching some art lessons. Jane and her husband had gone out to dinner on Saturday night. Mainly, though, they were more relaxed because Bailey was less cranky and frightened. They both considered Karen a miracle worker.

They had interviewed Karen together. Both sisters liked her frankness. Susan said, "I liked her philosophy of minimal intervention. She believes that doctors shouldn't suck the old into treatments. Eighty-year-old bodies don't do well with pills or surgery."

Jane liked her honesty about prognosis. She quoted Karen as saying, "After a health crisis, a fifty-year-old walks back. A seventy-year-old crawls back, and a eighty-year-old often doesn't make it."

When her clients go to the hospital, Karen goes with them as their advocate. She makes sure paperwork is in order. She asks the doctors questions. Many of the old are not assertive with medical staff or are too ill to ask questions. Karen makes sure that their wishes about life support and other heroic measures are carried out.

"When we introduced her to Dad, he was pretty resistant," Jane said. "But Karen was an expert at listening. She could hear his pain and fear. Even in his deteriorated state, Dad figured out he could trust this woman."

Susan said, "Karen was strong-willed and outspoken, and she respected that in Bailey."

The first time, Karen and Bailey just got acquainted, but when she left, Karen said, "When I come back we'll talk about your death." That honest talk on the second visit helped them all. Karen set guidelines. She wouldn't do anything illegal or unethical, and she wouldn't allow her clients to be unsafe or in pain. But within those constraints, she would try to do whatever Bailey wanted.

Susan said, "She told us an interesting thing. Movies suggest that when people are dying they want to travel all over the world or have one last great adventure. But Karen said that is almost never the case. What the old generally want is to see their families and preserve their routines. They want to live as they always have lived."

Jane said, "Karen worked with Dad's medications and finally got them adjusted so that he wasn't in pain and was more alert than he'd been in months. We'd thought his confusion was related to his health, but mostly it was the medicine."

"I was happy she recommended massage and some herbal medications," Susan said. "She treated the whole person."

"Bailey and Karen talked things over," Jane continued. "He asked for certain things. He wanted my kids to come home from college for a visit. He wanted to stay at home, and he wanted Hospice. They agreed he would call Karen instead of 911 in a medical emergency. She would help carry out his wishes."

"Since then everything has been better," Susan said. "We're still in a marathon, but we're no longer hitting the wall. Dad is more comfortable. He actually has had a little energy to give to his family." She paused and choked up at that statement. "He held my hand last night and actually forgave me for art school."

"That was big of him," Jane said. They laughed at this absurdity.

I was no longer needed. Karen had helped this family. So often the interventions the old receive are about technology, medications, and money. They are serviced by strangers, and just when they most need respect and affection, they are anonymous, helpless patients in institutional settings.

Near the end, what the old need most is a good intuitive listener who will help them think clearly and make good decisions. And often they need help implementing those decisions in our modern health-care system. Karen's is a new profession but one that will grow as more of us age. Jane and Susan already proselytize about her services in our city. She helped their family keep the peace, even reconcile, and she is helping their father die with dignity.

## CRYSTAL
*"Music connects to the heart."*

I INTERVIEWED CRYSTAL, a music therapist at the Manor, a local nursing home. We met for coffee, and Crystal told me about the residents. Before they came to the home, many had owned houses, traveled, and had interesting, productive lives. Now they were in the home because of health problems. Crystal said that at first, living at the Manor requires a big adjustment. Institutions take away control and spontaneity. Everything is scheduled. There are lots of rules and new faces. She believes that music takes the edge off the pain and gives a voice to the individual.

Crystal has a music cart that she pushes from room to room. Many of the old people living there have always wanted to play instruments but never had a chance, so she gives them that chance. If someone is too ill to play, Crystal will ask him or her to choose a song. She schedules her work so that she is never in a hurry.

The main thing the residents want is her time. Often people pull out scrapbooks with old pictures of their parents and families. Crystal asks questions like "What did you get in trouble for?" or "How did you meet your spouse?" She tries to focus on good times and accomplishments. Wedding-day stories tend to be funny and happy. Sometimes she holds the residents' hands. One old man said to her, "You are my best friend."

Just that morning, Crystal had attended the funeral of a resident. This woman rarely left her room and her piano, but the other residents gathered outside her room to listen to her concerts. She composed songs and practiced all the time. Crystal encouraged this woman to share her music with small groups and she printed up a book of the woman's songs.

"Music connects to the heart," Crystal said. One man who had had a stroke cries every time he hears music. Even patients with dementia and Alzheimer's will tap their fingers and toes to a good rhythm.

Crystal gave the Manor credit for doing its best to keep people connected to those they love. They have "couples dinners," with candles and flowers. The couples are encouraged to dress up and get their pictures taken, a favorite activity. Many adult children and grandchildren are involved in loving ways with the residents. They come for daily visits, take the residents out for dinner or drives, and attend their performances.

Crystal noted that the people at the Manor take care of one another. They worry if their friends are not eating. Residents speak up for one another, visit the shut-ins, and send cards. They make sure Crystal plays every person's favorite song. Crystal said a few residents always want to be the star, to answer all the questions, and to select every song. She laughed. "They don't know how to play well with others. They aren't very popular."

Crystal said the residents' main goals are to stay in good health and to see their families. These elders help her keep things in perspective. None of them has money, but the ones who are happy have people they love. One ninety-year-old woman has a best friend from second grade who visits regularly. Crystal hopes she can be like her favorite residents when she is old—good-natured and good-hearted, not a complainer.

Crystal isn't a mental-health professional, but she gives the gifts of touch and laughter. She doesn't give much advice, just listens to the sad stories and then encourages people to enjoy good memories.

THE TOUGHNESS OF the old-old developmental stage is hard to overstate. Old-old people are in their Arctic winter and experience what the Eskimos call *perlerorneq,* or feeling the weight of life. They often are scared, lonely, and losing all that is most precious. They react in the same ways as other survivors of extreme stress.

I encourage the adult children to keep the big picture in mind: that these are the people on your boat; these are the people with whom you are granted the privilege of traveling across the ocean of life. All you have is each other. It is not just a burden but also a joy to help those we love. It is our chance to stay connected, to return love, and to grow ourselves. Of course there are times when helping is not convenient or easy. There are unpleasant and painful times. But few people regret their choice to help. We care for the old because it is good for them, and for us.

# CHAPTER 7

# The Weariest River

From too much love of living,
From hope and fear set free,
We thank with brief thanksgiving
Whatever gods may be
That no life lives forever;
That dead men rise up never;
That even the weariest river
Winds somewhere safe to sea.

—ALGERNON CHARLES SWINBURNE,
"The Garden of Proserpine"

THIS CHAPTER ON DEATH HAS MORE POETRY THAN DO MOST chapters—partly because death is so big that it's best handled by metaphor. Poets write more eloquently than do social scientists. Also there is a great gap between the language of science and the language of human experience. This gap reflects a larger problem, which is the great split in our culture between hearts and minds, souls and bodies. The language of subjective personal experience is radically different from the technical or objective descriptions of those events. Our dualistic language system makes writing about death hard. After all, death is a very unified experience. The body and soul, the heart and mind, and the subject and object all are transformed. When we talk about death without some recognition of this unity, we sound empty-headed.

In most places and times, death has been visible, acknowledged, and heavily ritualized. Until recently, most people died at home. Children saw death—often the deaths of their grandparents and even parents. Families washed the bodies and prepared them for burial. Neighbors came by and sat all night with the body. Death was a community event. Now, for the first time in the history of the world, people die in hospitals and extended-care facilities, often far from family and surrounded by machines and strangers.

In the last century and early 1900s, death was a familiar experience to everyone. While the omnipresence of death produced a certain morbidity, it also inspired people to come to terms with it. Death could not be ignored as it can be today. The verses below from Abe Lincoln's favorite poem, "Mortality," capture how death was viewed in a certain place and time.

> *Oh, why should the spirit of mortal be proud?*
> *Like a swift-fleeting meteor, a fast-flying cloud,*
> *A flash of the lightning, a break of the wave,*
> *He passes from life to his rest in the grave. . . .*
>
> *So the multitude goes—like the flower or the weed*
> *That withers away to let others succeed;*
> *So the multitude comes—even those we behold,*
> *To repeat every tale that has often been told.*
>
> *For we are the same that our fathers have been;*
> *We see the same sights that our fathers have seen;*
> *We drink the same stream, we feel the same sun,*
> *And run the same course that our fathers have run.*

*The thoughts we are thinking, our fathers would think;*
*From the death we are shrinking, our fathers would shrink;*
*To the life we are clinging, they also would cling—*
*But it speeds from us all like a bird on the wing. . . .*

*'Tis the wink of an eye—'tis the draught of a breath—*
*From the blossom of health to the paleness of death,*
*From the gilded saloon to the bier and the shroud*
*Oh, why should the spirit of mortal be proud?*

—WILLIAM KNOX

Last words of the famous and infamous often were recorded. William Saroyan's father said to his wife, "Tahooki, don't beat the kids." O. Henry said, "Turn up the lights, I don't want to go home in the dark." Anna Pavlova said, "Get my swan costume ready." A few days before his death, Henry David Thoreau was asked by his friend Parker Pillsbury, "You seem so near the brink of the dark river that I wonder how the opposite shore may appear to you." Thoreau answered, "One world at a time."

Last words carry weight. At the end, a surprising number of people say "I love you" or "Thank you." Often last words are interpreted metaphorically. For example, I have a friend whose mother's last words to her were, "What size are you?" My friend sees that as a statement about what was important to her mother. My grandfather's last words were, "That was a great dinner," a typical statement for my grandfather, who was an appreciator of food and family.

Final requests have great power. Some requests may be healing. An injunction from grandfather to love one another may help a troubled family settle down. A mother may encourage her son to marry his common-law wife or reconcile with a child. A father may ask his daughter to quit drinking or go back to school. Others may put the survivors in a bind. A dying elder might say, "My last request is that you become a Christian." Or a husband might say, "Promise me you will never remarry." A good response to the latter requests is to say simply, "I promise I will remember what you requested."

My friend Joseph made requests of all his friends. He was a socialist in Vienna when the Nazis arrived. His parents died of poverty, and many of his socialist and Jewish friends were killed. Joseph was sent to the camps. After the war, he came to this country to study. The war years burned into him a commitment to social justice. When Joseph was dying, he was calm and open about his death. Joseph's main concern was for the social causes that he had championed. He asked each of his friends to take one of them on for him, to write the letters he would have written, to find the money and sit on the committees.

Studs Terkel said, "The reason I don't regret dying is that I have had a really good time." Many of the old are not so lucky. They feel despair as they look back on bad choices, wasted time, or missed opportunities to be kind. Many people feel they could have been much more than they ended up being. "The saddest words of tongue or pen are these four words: it might have been." As W. S. Maugham said, "All my life I have believed in later. But there is no later now."

People often say they wish they could erase parts of their lives—harsh words spoken, days spent in self-pity, moments being crabby when they could have been laughing, or family meals spent feuding. People regret, as Ferlinghetti put it, "picking their noses when they could have been dancing."

As Greg Brown sings, "One wrong turn is all it takes." People make mistakes that have lifelong consequences. They may devote their lives to shallow pursuits and only at the end discover love or beauty. Sometimes as people are dying they speak about the piano lessons they never took, the summer vacation they never quite had time for, or the years they were too busy for their children. These regrets must be voiced and acknowledged.

When asked what he would change about his life, Aldous Huxley said,

"I would have been kinder to people." Most people wish they had done more for others. Especially as death approaches, people want to be remembered as good people. All of us want to do something noble before we die. It is a way to wrest some kind of victory from the defeat of death.

Often people debate the advantages of slow versus sudden death. Having had two parents die slowly and painfully, I am a fan of sudden death or at least rapid declines. No one wants months of expensive medical procedures and weeks of miserable hospital time. As Shelby Foote put it, "I never was one who couldn't stand to leave the party." Sometimes people suffer way too much. As Daniel Pinkwater said of his mother's death, "We wouldn't let a dog suffer that much."

As with all endings, death matters enormously. How a death occurs becomes metaphorical. When a gentle person dies gently, that says something. When a gentle person dies in anguish, that too speaks to the human condition. Most people want the same things. They want to die at home with loved ones nearby and without too much pain or indignity. Many people want one last chance to discuss their lives.

I visited Steve, a widower, at a nearby hospital. His daughter lived far away and had children in school. She would come weekends, but she asked if I could visit her father on Wednesdays. At first I went out of a sense of duty and obligation to my friend. But soon I looked forward to those visits. Steve was a World War II veteran, like my own father had been. And perhaps because we were strangers, he found it easy to talk to me.

Steve joked about the hospital's "dishwater coffee," so I brought him good strong coffee. Along with the coffee I brought a weather report. I listened as he reviewed his life during the Depression and the war.

For the first time in his life, he talked about the battles and the killing. We talked about his marriage and children. The more I listened to Steve, the more I understood what a complicated life he had had. Tolstoy said that the life of an ordinary man, if accurately captured, would be the best and most complex piece of literature ever written. Steve and many of the other people I interviewed made me think of Tolstoy's point.

My friend eventually moved into a nearby hotel to be closer to her father. However, I continued to visit Steve, as much for myself as for him. Over the several months I visited him at the VA hospital, he weakened. Our conversations grew shorter. He asked me to make arrangements to buy his grandchildren a computer. He told me to periodically remind his daughter not to work too hard and not to take herself so seriously.

The last weeks were especially hard on Steve. He was heavily medicated with painkillers and often confused. Sometimes he thought I was his sister and he would hug me fiercely. His eyes were sunken and dull with tiredness. His hands were cold, and he could no longer drink the coffee I brought him. He said, "You drink it for me." I knew he was close to the end when he stopped asking for my weather reports.

The last time I visited, Steve talked as though he were in a foreign country trying to get home from the war. He directed the nurses as if they were his troops, telling them to take cover and keep their heads down. His fingers plucked the sheet and moved restlessly across the cloth. His eyes scanned the room in jumpy movements as he searched for lost soldiers.

He taught me about dying. Until that last visit he joked and smiled. He complained little and appreciated much. No matter how weak he was, he never failed to thank me for coming. Even in a hospital bed, he found small things to enjoy. He managed to tell his daughter he loved her, a new behavior for him.

He arranged everything so that he would be a minimum of bother. His will was in order, and his funeral planned and paid for. He even managed to die on a three-day weekend so that he didn't disrupt his family's schedules. I wasn't with him when he died, but my friend told me he died with courage and dignity. His last words to her were, "You can never know how much I love your family."

The Japanese have a word that captures the intensity of feeling two strong emotions at the same time. *Wabi-sabi* means experiencing beauty and sadness. We need such a word in the English language. The word would describe that mixture of happiness and sadness when we drive away from a wonderful reunion, loved and loving and empty and alone all at the same moment. It's the feeling we have when we listen to good jazz or classical music or read a poem that connects us to another person's soul but also reminds us of the tragedy of all our lives. Our closest English words are *bittersweet* and *poignancy,* but they don't capture the power of these feelings and their importance. *Bittersweet* and *poignant* generally are used to describe something small.

My friend Pam heard the word *thusness* used to describe a *wabi-sabi* feeling. A sense of the thusness of life comes to all of us, but most often to the old. Awareness of life's ephemeral nature often produces deep love. As Abraham Maslow put it after the death of a loved one, "I am stabbed by the beauty of flowers and babies." Approaching death makes life a limited commodity, and scarcity confers value. There is a tremendous sweetness in the evanescent. Many of the old feel, as Hortense Calisher wrote, that "beauty bombards us from wherever it can."

> *I wished for death often*
> *but now that I am at its door*
> *I have changed my mind about the world.*
> *It should go on; it is beautiful,*
> *even as a dream filled with water and seed,*
> *plants and animals, others like myself,*
> *ships and buildings and messages*
> *filling the air—a beauty,*
> *if I have ever seen one.*
> *In the next world, should I remember*
> *this one, I will praise it*
> *above everything.*

—DAVID IGNATOW,
"Above Everything"

## ALMA *(age 86)*
### *"The redbird in the garden"*

A PROFESSOR WROTE me about a remarkable woman who cared for her profoundly retarded daughter. The professor said, "I despise the role of caregiver, but I respect this woman tremendously. Seeing Alma makes me question much of what I have learned about happiness." She didn't want Alma's story to go untold.

Alma had been homebound for the last sixty-six years. She cared for her daughter, Violet, who was not toilet trained, couldn't speak or walk, and who communicated in shrieks and grunts. Violet couldn't watch TV because she was afraid of the flickering images. Mostly Violet perched atop her bed listening to country music and playing with a small rope tied to the bed. Since Alma's husband had died twenty-five years before, Alma and Violet were alone except for their dog, Sadie.

The professor said that Alma was a keen observer who was starved for knowledge of the external world. Her diminishing eyesight and hearing made it hard for her to stay connected to others. Once, when the professor had taken Alma to an outdoor tea, she found her staring at a flower. Alma said, "My eyes are failing me. I am trying to memorize this flower so that when I go blind I can enjoy it all over again."

I first interviewed Alma in January, in her small house in a quiet neighborhood. She was dressed in a faded housedress and had unruly iron-gray hair. She was short and round and reminded me of Peter Ostrushko's line about Ukrainian women, who are "built low to the ground for picking potatoes."

The house was cheery and tidy, with candles everywhere. When I sat down, a mechanical parrot startled me by calling out, "Polly want a cracker." Alma laughed heartily at my jump. Alma had china redbirds and a porcelain Siamese cat with blue jewel eyes. Small reproductions of landscapes covered the walls. As I looked at her biggest seascape, I remembered a man who said he had never left his hometown but traveled all over the world via *National Geographic*.

At first Sadie barked at me, but soon the black Lab was wagging her tail and licking my hand. Alma told me that when Sadie's owner moved, he brought Sadie and his six-year-old daughter to Alma's back door. He said, "Here's your new dog." Alma didn't want to upset the little girl, so she took Sadie, thinking she would find her a home. But Sadie quickly fit right into the family and now she was Alma's great joy.

Alma excused herself to get batteries for her hearing aid. She had many health problems, including diabetes. She needed to get to the eye doctor, but her senior companion, who ordinarily would take her, had been sick herself. I offered to take her, but she didn't want to be a nuisance. Many people wanted to help Alma. I remembered a line from Raymond Carver: "She liked people, and they liked her back."

Violet was sleeping. Alma and I settled down in the living room. I asked her to talk about herself, and she protested that she wasn't interesting. I understood how she could think that. In this country we think of interesting people as adventurers and celebrities, as Harrison Fords who leap from tall buildings and save lives, or as supermodels who travel to the Riviera with rich companions. But I coaxed her and soon she was remembering events from long ago.

Alma was born at home in 1910. She was the third of nine girls. The night she was born, Halley's Comet was so terribly bright that her mother joked that she felt like she was delivering the Christ child. Alma and her siblings had heard that if you were born under Halley's Comet you would die when the comet returned. But Alma told me with a laugh, "I asked my doctor if I was likely to live through that year, and he said I couldn't be killed with an ax."

Her father had a good job for the railroad, but he lost it and became a day laborer. They moved around, and Alma's education had lots of interruptions. She missed many days of school and couldn't get the basics down. Alma said, "I was sharp, but my grades weren't good."

Alma's family was always hungry. They ate everything, and no one ever complained about a dish. "Mom really knew how to stretch food," Alma said. Because their houses were always small, they played outside in the summer. In the winter the oldest sister would light the lamp and read to them. Alma loved the book *Girl of the Limberlost*. They cried at the descriptions of poverty. "We didn't realize we were poorer than the sad people in the books," Alma explained.

Alma had a girlfriend who said that Alma "never had enough brains to get mad." Alma described herself as a happy child, "happy with nothing." When she was young, she figured out that she needed to please others to get her needs met. That strategy had worked for her all her life.

Alma quit high school when her books were stolen and she couldn't afford new ones. She met her husband, Jake, at a friend's birthday party. After one hour, he was ready to get married. She laughed. "I didn't feel that way. He wasn't good-looking." But during the deepest part of the Depression, they got married in a very simple ceremony. Alma said, "Even rich people couldn't afford weddings that year." They were young when they married, but Alma had always been "old-headed," by which she meant responsible and mature.

Alma never regretted her marriage. Jake was a draftsman who worked for the same man all his life. Her happiest memory was working together to fix up their house. They were in card clubs, and they danced at the Pla-Mor Ballroom. After five years they had their only child, Violet. Alma was the first in her family to have a baby at a hospital. A railroad doctor, who'd been drinking, was called in at midnight. He ordered an injection to slow the delivery down, and then he disappeared. He came back eight hours later and gave Alma a drug to start the labor again. Alma had horrible pains. She was hemorrhaging terribly, and was torn up inside and out. When Violet was born, Alma knew right away that her baby wasn't normal.

Alma said, "I have given up my freedom for Violet." Alma and Jake couldn't take Violet many places, and they could afford a sitter only once a month. When she was younger and stronger, Alma used to drive and take

Violet places with her, but years before, she'd had a car wreck. Violet wasn't badly hurt, but Alma broke seven ribs and was hospitalized for a month. She said, "I was in so much pain I wanted to die. But I had to live to take care of Violet."

While Jake was alive, life was pretty good. He was funny and loved company. Sometimes for the whole summer they cared for nieces and nephews. Alma missed the kids, who had grown up and moved away. And she missed many of her siblings and old friends who had died. Jake and Alma had a big celebration for their fortieth wedding anniversary. People came from eight states, and they had a program at the church and a wedding cake. She said the anniversary party was something she needed. It was the happiest day of her life.

Two years later, Jake died. He was in his big chair watching "The Honeymooners" when he had a heart attack. Alma called 911 and followed the ambulance to the hospital. That night Jake's heart stopped twelve times, then he was gone. The suddenness of it was hard. Alma and Violet had depended on him as their connection to the outside world. She cried every day for a year.

Alma believed that she would see Jake in heaven and that Violet would go there too some day. I said, "If you're not there yet, Jake can take care of her." Alma corrected me: "I like to think she will no longer need care, that she will be able to care for herself in heaven."

Alma believed that things turned out in ways that allowed her to cope. She told me about the first Christmas after Jake's death. The family always came to their place for dinner. On Christmas morning she was really blue. She missed Jake's help with the dinner and their holiday routines. She cooked alone and then took some trash out before the guests arrived. As she walked toward the trash can a bright red bird, not a cardinal and unlike any bird she had ever seen, flew onto the trash can. He sat two feet from her, looked her in the eyes, and sang her a lovely song, a song like she imagined a tropical songbird might sing. She cried all through the song but it comforted her immensely. She is sure that Jake sent that bird to cheer her up.

After that song, Alma realized that she must move on. This is a typical Alma story. She reminds me of St. Theresa, who could weep over the gift of a sardine. She could find comfort and hope in the smallest mercies.

When Violet awoke, Alma asked if I would like to meet her. We walked back to the bedroom that Alma, her husband, and Violet had always shared. There were three single beds lined up, as Alma said, "like they were the three bears." Violet sat perched on the bed in a bright yellow sweat suit, looking like a giant canary. Her gray hair was neatly combed, but she had only two teeth. She had saggy breasts and lots of wrinkles. Violet was playing with her little rope, and she didn't smile.

Alma patted her and introduced us. Violet's eyes were piercing but she gave no acknowledgment that she heard her mother. Alma rubbed her head and spoke to her fondly. Alma showed me where Sadie slept and noted that the three of them were still like the three bears. She said, "When we tuck in at night, we are very cozy."

Alma said that Violet was "artistic," but she meant autistic. Violet was sixty-four, and Alma fed, bathed, and dressed her. Since Alma had turned eighty, she'd had help from "home health." Now Violet moved only from the dining room table to the bath to the bed. She preferred to be alone. She was disturbed by humans or even by birds flying outside.

We returned to the living room. I was amazed by how happy Alma was. She believed that most people are as happy as they make up their minds to be. Something interesting always happened. She laughed. "One day it's chickens, and the next day it's feathers." She counted her blessings every day. I asked her what she was grateful for the day I visited. She said, "Well, for your company. And this morning I was thinking of my mother. It's below zero outside, and she used to chop firewood to heat our little house and to cook. There would be ice on the well when she went out to pump water. I am glad I don't have to pump water or build a fire to cook."

Alma worried about her health. She gave herself two shots of insulin a day and avoided sweets. She smiled and told me, "That is easy to do, I never go out." She wanted to live as long as she could to be of use to Violet. She felt lucky financially. Her husband hadn't left her much, but when Jake's boss died, he had left her money.

Alma spoke with no self-pity. She was one of those people that Reynolds Price described as "having the ability to get up each morning and take what comes." Over the years, the hardest thing for Alma was missing the weddings, the funerals, and the celebrations of her friends and family. But she knew that she was essential to another human being.

This story has another chapter. A few months after my visit, Violet died in her sleep and Alma sold her house and moved into an assisted-living facility. I visited her apartment on what Alma called the "garden level" of the Kelly Center. Alma looked healthier than the last time I'd seen her. Her place was small but bright and clean, with furniture from her home, including her painting of the sea. Alma told me about the center's many activities and the three "relaxed" meals every day. She said, "We aren't supposed to worry about time. We're to visit."

After eighty years of cooking she was happy not to cook. She said that toward the end of Violet's life, she hadn't fixed balanced meals. She'd make one big pot of something and eat it for a week. At the Kelly Center she'd gained weight. She knew she should ask for smaller servings, but every day she decided she would "get on the freckle tomorrow."

Alma spoke about exercise classes, current-events meetings, the read-aloud club, and "goody" bingo. She loved Cornhusker game days, when everyone wore red and sang the Nebraska fight song at meals. Recently she'd bought apple cider and doughnuts and had several residents in for a pinochle party. Alma's eyes sparkled like a child's when she talked about parties and costumes. This afternoon she would paint a face on one of the small plastic pumpkins they used to decorate the tables.

Alma, who had always served others, was now being served. A librarian brought her large-print Louis L'Amour books, and a driver chauffeured her to the grocery store or Target. There was a nurse to check on her health, and a doctor to fit her hearing aids. Staff cleaned her apartment and brought her fresh towels, "all you could possibly want." She winked at me. "I don't object."

After Violet's death, one of the home-health nurses persuaded Alma to take a trip. Alma pulled out her new scrapbook of her trip to Iowa. They had visited the Little Brown Church in the Vale. She laughed and said, "We sat in the pews and sang the song three times." She had pictures of the church and a copy of the hymn. We looked through the scrapbook at post-cards of Iowa and at placemats from the restaurants where she'd eaten. The last thing she and the nurse did was stop at a casino. Alma had never seen one. She put a nickel in a one-armed bandit and won fourteen dollars. She had her picture taken gambling. She laughed and said she later found out that it was illegal. I am reasonably sure that was the first time Alma had ever broken a law.

This coming weekend, someone was taking her to Colorado to visit her sister, whom she hadn't seen for twenty years. I marveled at the number of young people who love Alma. I was not the only person to find joy in her presence. Her secret is an open heart, an easy laugh, and her appreciation of moments. Alma makes the world seem fresh to jaded eyes. She puts things into perspective and reminds us all to be grateful.

I wondered what Alma would do without daily work. But Alma had done nothing but work her whole life, and she loved receiving the petting she'd always given others. Alma told me that at first she felt guilty about liking the home so much. She thought, *Did Violet have to die and Sadie go to a new home for me to be happy?* But everyone told her, "You are eighty-eight, you have cared for Violet for sixty-four years. It's your turn to enjoy your-self." She smiled softly and said, "So that's what I am trying to do."

As I listened to her talk, I thought that our psychological theories don't fit the Almas of this world. I wondered how she had managed to feel joyful about a life of sacrifice. Alma was raised in a time when women were trained to serve others, but still, many well-trained women are filled with anger. One difference between Alma and many others is that Violet needed Alma. Women are most resentful when they do for others that which those

others could do for themselves, and when the served person isn't suffi-
ciently appreciative of their sacrifice or is even damaged by their help.
None of this applied to Violet and Alma.

Alma had a truncated life in some ways, but she'd accepted her fate and
found inner peace. She'd played a bad hand of cards extremely well, and
she knew it. There was honor in that. Willa Cather said there are two reasons for living: to make use of the tools one has been given and to love
someone. Alma has accomplished both of these.

As I left her in the hall filled with her new friends, Alma whispered that
her niece had figured out her money. With the sale of her house, her savings, and her husband's pension, Alma could live here until she was ninety-
nine years old, eleven more years. She laughed. "Then I'll go back to that
casino and earn me some more money."

*And, did you get what you wanted from this life, even so?*
*I did*
*And what did you want?*
*To call myself beloved, to feel myself beloved on this earth.*

—RAYMOND CARVER,
"Late Fragment"

Acceptance is the last great gift of old age. At the end, if people are
lucky and wise, they see their lives as a whole and feel satisfied. They don't
romanticize the past or gloss over their mistakes and misfortunes, but they
also feel they have had great moments. They can look back with pride on
their work and their relationships.

Even with death at the door, good copers keep coping. As Pearl S. Buck
wrote, "One faces the future with one's past." There are surprises, but generally people take all their strengths, skills, and attitudes into the new country of old-old age. As Eleanor Roosevelt put it when she was asked about
the afterlife, "Whatever it is, I daresay I shall be able to cope with it."

Worriers stay worried. Happy people stay pretty happy. Researchers have postulated a set point of happiness that accounts for about 80 percent of people's reported happiness. They reported that after a diagnosis of cancer or winning the *Reader's Digest* sweepstakes, people's level of happiness will temporarily go down or up, but then it will rapidly return to a set point.

The year after my grandmother was widowed, she contracted leukemia. She had daughters who came to care for her. When she was feeling strong enough, they played cards and listened to music. Her friends dropped by on a regular schedule. My mother helped her control her pain so that she could die at home. Even though she was dying, she had a good last year. I remember the tenderness in her eyes, the look that said how glorious children are, and flowers and sunsets. When I complimented her on how well she handled things, she said, "What choices do I have? I am dying anyway. I might as well do it with dignity."

Most people handle death surprisingly well. As an old friend, Ray Barger, said, "Nobody lives forever." Emotionally sturdy people can handle anything, even their own death and the deaths of their loved ones. Often people who are dying have their most heroic moments. It's important not to spare people the experience of their death. Suffering allows people an opportunity to deepen their characters and behave with great courage. Marcel Proust wrote, "Happiness is good for the body, but it is grief which develops strengths of mind," and Bob Dylan said, "Behind every beautiful thing, there's been some kind of pain."

As many of the old are in physical decline, they experience great psychological growth. There is an amazing calculus. Anyone who isn't an idiot becomes a philosopher. With a failing body and a life filled with losses, a person can't help but think of the meaning of life. As there is more to accept, there is more capacity to accept. Aunt Henrietta said, "Every goodbye is a lesson in loss." As life gets harder, many of the old greatly appreciate what is left that is good. As bodies become frail and vulnerable, souls often grow strong and resilient.

Old age can be about finding the redbird singing on Christmas morning in the snowy garden. It can be answering the phone, "Kelly's mule barn," when you're having trouble breathing. With all the sadness comes growth in compassion, understanding, and wisdom. Much of what the old learn doesn't show up on an IQ test. They become more complicated, deeper, broader, and more who they are. By suffering, the old learn to endure; in sorrow they find wisdom.

> *Some time when the river is ice ask me*
> *mistakes I have made. Ask me whether*
> *what I have done is my life. Others*
> *have come in their slow way into*
> *my thought, and some have tried to help*
> *or to hurt: ask me what difference*
> *their strongest love or hate has made.*
>
> *I will listen to what you say.*
> *You and I can turn and look*
> *at the silent river and wait. We know*
> *the current is there, hidden; and there*
> *are comings and goings from miles away*
> *that hold the stillness exactly before us.*
> *What the river says, that is what I say.*

—WILLIAM STAFFORD,
"Ask Me"

Religion helps people with the great sorrows of life. Christianity, for example, teaches that death is only a passage into eternal life. While people may fear the actual dying process, there is nothing to fear beyond. Faith also connects people to something larger and more important than themselves, and puts suffering in a context. It gives people hope for the future. Faith and prayer can be great comforts. As people approach death, many read their Bibles, their Torahs, their Koran, or other religious texts.

A doctor I know reads his dying patients Walt Whitman's poetry. He realizes that the language of science is no balm to the dying. Many of the issues toward the end are spiritual, not medical. He says that Whitman heals wounded spirits and helps people see death as part of something beautiful and natural. As poet Walter McDonald wrote, "The earth turns green again, no matter what."

The natural world offers the dying great comfort. On their deathbeds, many people remember beautiful places they have been. They talk about trees, rivers, mountains, lakes, and seashores. They enjoy birds, flowers, butterflies, and stars. As people approach death, they find joy in connecting with that which came before and which will remain after their own short lives. Likewise, a forest, a kitten, or a blue sky is an antidote to the sickroom world of syringes, pill bottles, and monitoring machines. It is an oasis of sensual pleasure and solace in a world of pain and sorrow.

My friend Laura was far away in Scotland when her grandfather died in Oklahoma. She had her own memorial ceremony beside the sea. As she watched the water and thought of her grandfather, she noticed whales spouting in the bay. Her grandfather had always loved whales, and she felt this visit from whales was a gift from him.

When I have lost people, I've found consolation in connecting their memories to things I regularly experience. My father and I had many happy times fishing together, and when I catch a big fish I hold it up to the sky for him to see. I connect Jim's grandmother with the Pleiades, the Seven Sisters, because she was from a family with seven daughters. My mother I associate with sunsets because we often walked together that time of day. Sunsets also connect me to my grandmother, who walked with my mother at dusk on her ranch in Colorado. When I experience these natural phenomena I feel close to people I love.

Many people find great reassurance in the thought they will be reunited with their kin on the other side of the river. The traditional song "Going Home" has the lines:

*It's not far, just close by, through an open door, work all done, care laid by, blind to fear no more.*

*Mother's there, expecting me, Father's waiting too. Lots of folks are gathered there, all the friends I knew. I'm gonna meet the friends I knew. I'm goin' home.*

Or as Ralph Stanley sang in "I'll Not Be a Stranger":

*I'll not be a stranger when I get to that city, I'm acquainted with folks over there. There'll be friends there to greet me, there'll be loved ones to meet me, at the gate of that city four square.*

Many people associate heaven with healing and being whole. The sick will be well, the poor will be rich, the unhappy happy, and the lonely with their families and friends. At my mother's funeral, Uncle Fred recalled how many nights they all had sat up talking. He said, "I hope we'll sit up all night talking in heaven."

Poets write about death, but even if we aren't poets, we need metaphors to help us understand the great unknowable experience. Townes Van Zandt sang of death as "tyin' on my flyin' shoes." For Robert Frost, death was the snowy woods.

*Now it is autumn and the falling fruit*
*And the long journey towards oblivion. . . .*

*And it's time to go, to bid farewell*
*to one's own self, and find an exit*
*from the fallen self. . . .*

*Oh build your ship of death, your little ark*
*and furnish it with food, with little cakes, and wine*
*for the dark flight down oblivion. . . .*

—D. H. Lawrence,
"The Ship of Death"

*Let the light of late afternoon*
*shine through chinks in the barn, moving*
*up the bales as the sun moves down.*

*Let the cricket take up chafing*
*as a woman takes up her needles*
*and her yarn. Let evening come.*

*Let dew collect on the hoe abandoned*
*in long grass. Let the stars appear*
*and the moon disclose her silver horn.*

*Let the fox go back to its sandy den.*
*Let the wind die down. Let the shed*
*go black inside. Let evening come.*

*To the bottle in the ditch, to the scoop*
*in the oats, to the air in the lung*
*let evening come.*

*Let it come, as it will, and don't*
*be afraid. God does not leave us*
*comfortless, so let evening come.*

—Jane Kenyon,
"Let Evening Come"

*The most beautiful Americans I've been around are people who are almost dead. They're not busy being lost in their identities—rich, poor, fat, smart, needy, Buddhist, the adult child of an alcoholic. Those things aren't too important when you're dying and you're whittled down to an essential level of being."*

—DALE BORGLUM

Parents aging can be both a horrible and a wonderful experience. It can be the most growth-promoting time in the history of the family. Many people say, "I know this sounds strange, but that last year was the best year of my parents' lives. I was my best. They were their best. Our relationships were the closest and strongest ever," or, "The pain and suffering were terrible. However, we all learned from it. I wouldn't have wanted things to be different."

Crises are crucibles that bring out the best and the worst in families. They often expose the wimps and scoundrels, and they allow the strong and the good to be heroes. In a best-case scenario, they build and strengthen family feeling and allow everyone to be courageous. People act together to do the right thing, and the family is changed by the power of that experience.

Humans are wired so that we grow to love what we care for and hate what we abuse and ignore. What is loved reveals its loveliness. We mend what we value, and we value what we mend.

The best moments, the most honest and love-filled moments with family often are connected to caring and saying good-bye. After a death in the family, all people have is how they behaved during the good-byes. Members always ask, "Did we do the right things? Did we do all we could?" There is great satisfaction in being able to say yes; great sorrow in saying no.

What is true for families is true also for couples. Often couples have their best moments near the end of their lives. Partners get their chance to be truly kind. They ask for and receive great gifts from each other. Old couples support each other. Men who never cooked learn so that they can prepare meals for their ill wives. For the first time, some husbands become nurturers and social planners. Wives learn to manage the car, the yard, and the money, and they nurse their husbands. Feeble women somehow are able to help husbands twice their size in and out of beds and bathtubs. Couples figure out ways to pass the time and keep up each other's spirits. Otis helps Grace in the garden. Grace cuts Otis's toenails and makes his favorite kind of cobbler. Clair makes Agnes milkshakes to hide the taste of her medicines. Henrietta holds Max's hand at the Oldefield Opry. Often the love couples show each other is the best love they ever have experienced.

When my cousin Abby was dying, her husband was beside her at the hospital from early morning until ten at night. When the hospital doors opened, he was there with a newspaper and a Thermos of coffee. When his wife felt well enough, they talked or he read aloud to her. At the end he just sat quietly by the bed, holding her hand. When I visited, he quoted a verse from "To a Waterfowl": "All day thy wings have fanned,/At that far height, the cold thin atmosphere,/Yet stoop not, weary, to the welcome land,/Though the dark night is near." He reminded me of a Canada goose, a bird known for its constancy. When one goose is dying, its partner stays by its side. It is fine goose behavior, and fine human behavior as well.

## DEAN AND JANICE (*ages 75 and 71*)
*"I am grateful for every day that we have together."*

DEAN AND JANICE were old family friends whom I hadn't visited in years. However, when I heard that Dean had emphysema and was homebound, I scheduled a visit. Janice met me at the door with a hug. She was trim, and brisk in her movements. I could still see the Janice I had known well—the gardener and traveler who liked a house full of kids and company. But she looked like she'd had a hard year. Her hair was gray, and she had worry lines around her eyes. As we walked to Dean's room, I asked how she was doing. "I get a little tired; Dean is up a lot in the night. But Hospice is coming now, and that helps. I am grateful for every day that we have together."

Dean lay on a daybed in their living room. He had been a man who hadn't liked movies or church because he had to sit too long indoors. From my childhood, I remembered people asking Dean, "Don't you ever sit still?"

Today he was propped up against a wall of pillows awaiting my visit. Beside him was a table with a computer, pills, Kleenex, and lotion. He looked like himself with his white bushy eyebrows and wild white hair, except he was thin and had supplemental oxygen. He took my hand and smiled.

I asked how he was feeling. He answered honestly and in some detail. He wasn't in pain, just tired. He could walk only a few steps without resting, and he no longer climbed stairs. There were days he couldn't get enough oxygen, and that was scary. He'd lost peripheral vision but still could use his computer and watch videos. He said he was learning patience, a virtue he'd never before possessed.

"I got old, but Jan stayed young," Dean said. "We have a date every night to watch sports on television. She fixes us Cokes, and we cheer our favorite teams on."

Janice had planned carefully. The room was filled with things that gave Dean some control and connection. His telephone and personal planner were close at hand. On a table by the daybed were letters, newspapers, and bird-identification books. Dean's bed looked out on bird and squirrel feeders and a birdbath.

He commented ironically on his view of the finches and sparrows: "Just when I slow down enough to get interested in birds, my eyes are so damn bad, I can hardly see them." We laughed, and he continued. "We've got it all wrong in this culture. The young should identify birds. They've got the eyes and ears for it. The old should go to rock concerts. We can hear that music and see the light shows just fine."

We laughed some more, but Dean leaned back tiredly against his pillow. Janice adjusted his blankets and said, "Dean can't keep food down. That worries me the most. Hospice said that it's time to consider a feeding tube, but he's not sure he'll do that. Dean has one bedsore that won't heal. The doctor is watching it."

She sighed and looked wanly at Dean. "I make you sound like a mess."

They laughed, and she continued in a lighter tone. "Really, it's not all bad. Dean and I have had some very good times. We've talked over everything and looked at all our photo albums. We have our son over one night a week, and our daughter on another. We've had plenty of time with our grandchildren. Parker comes for lunch on Tuesdays. Carolyn mows the lawn and watches sports on Thursdays. Since Dean's illness has slowed us down, we have time for everyone."

Dean said, "I can still eat my favorite foods, chocolate ice cream and scrambled eggs. Janice knows just how I like my eggs. The computer is a godsend. I'm e-mailing all my cousins and old fraternity brothers."

We talked about Dean's life. As people approach the end, they like to review their lives. They want to talk about the good and bad times, the victories and great sadnesses. Dean was no exception.

While we all have lives shaped by accidents, Dean's life was particularly so. His parents had died in the influenza epidemic of 1918. During the war, Dean missed a train and fell asleep on a bench at the Kansas City station. When he woke up, Janice was sitting nearby and offered him fruit and coffee. Later he got a job as an engineer because just as he walked in the door of the plant, another engineer announced he was quitting. Dean's daughter was born on his mother's birthday and had her name. Lily looked very much like her grandmother, whom she'd never met. When we talked about these events, Dean cried a little, something I had never seen him do before. He wasn't embarrassed, though, and merely said, "Now that I'm old, I cry more."

We talked about Janice and Dean's friendship with my parents. Dean and my father had been fishing buddies. Janice and my mother had waterskied together. We laughed at images of the two women learning to water-ski in our town sandpit. He recalled how generous my father had been.

Except for his parents' early deaths, Dean had experienced a lucky life. But his luck was running out. Even as we spoke he began wheezing, and Janice reattached the oxygen tube. She asked if he could swallow a pill, and he said hoarsely, "Later."

We waited a few minutes while Dean concentrated on breathing. Then he wanted to talk about his children. His main regret was that his kids didn't get along better. Lily was a vegetarian, a Unitarian, and a liberal. Rob was a Republican Christian who liked to hunt. They had always been competitive and intolerant of each other. Both had stored up hurts and by now they barely spoke.

Dean said, "I'm proud of our kids. They get on great with us, but not so well with each other. Now that we're getting old, I hope they'll pull together. When we're gone, they'll need each other."

Janice said, "Dean plans to talk to them about this soon."

He laughed. "Yeah, they need one last lecture from their old man."

We had tea and watched the squirrels and birds. While Dean looked up a finch in Peterson's bird guide, Janice put on some classical music. She dug out pictures of my folks, and we looked at all of us when we were younger and mostly out of doors. I stayed until Dean fell asleep.

I next saw Janice at Dean's funeral two months later. She was composed that day and looked less exhausted than when last we'd met. She said that Dean had died at home, which is what he'd wanted. Hospice had been wonderful. His last weeks were tough, but he'd managed to stay mentally clear. He'd e-mailed his friends good-bye.

I asked if he managed to deliver his last lecture to the kids. Janice smiled. "The day before he died, he had us all hold hands in a circle around his bed. He made us promise to stay together and look out for one another. Rob and Lily both promised. It wasn't a lecture, but I think it will do the trick. The kids have helped each other through this. Their children were pallbearers. I think Dean will get his last wish."

Families that work together through the death of one member experience many rewards. The adult children have the opportunity to say thank you and to repay parents for their help. The parents have the opportunity to receive gratitude and to rest like trees in winter. It is their last chance to help their children grow. Often parents feel great pride in how their children respond to the challenges of this time.

Adult children are strengthened by the difficulty of this stage, and they will need that strength later for their own old age. They also learn by observation how to handle illness and good-byes. Caring for my mother while she died, I observed how well she handled pain. She loved visitors because they got her mind off her problems. She was hungry for jokes and news of the weather outside. I saw the joy that cards and letters gave her.

I watched my mother smile when she heard violin music or remembered a summer vacation. I saw how much difference a kind nurse or a respectful doctor made in her days. I learned about patience in the face of enormous frustration. I learned about the importance of small, temporary victories—of wresting moments of victory from the great jaws of defeat. I made notes to myself that I'll pull out and read when my time comes.

During this process, things happen in families that have never happened before. Dad hugs his sons, or Mother tells about her miscarriage. A suicide or jail sentence is discussed. Parents who were nicknamed the "Bickersons" are suddenly gentle with each other. In the cauldron of loss, new aspects of character unfurl. This last stage gives parents and children opportunities to know each other in new ways.

Caring for parents often means that children have more time with their grandparents and even great-grandparents, which is good for children at any age but especially important for teenagers. Grandparents tend to be wiser and kinder than adolescent peers. They offer children different lessons and perspectives. They are less busy than parents. As one woman put it, "My parents were always telling me to hurry up, and my grandparents always told me to slow down."

Even in the worst of families, healing and reconciliation are possible.

People have one last chance to work through relationships, to understand, and to forgive. A client of mine had a horrible family history. As a boy, Scott had been neglected, abused, and finally abandoned by an alcoholic mother. He graduated from high school while in foster care, and worked his way through college. He made a good life for himself that didn't include his absent mother. When she was dying, his mother contacted him for the first time in thirty years. In one of our sessions, he debated whether to drive the six hours to see her. I encouraged it.

The next week he cried as he described the reunion. His mother was weak and battle-scarred. She wanted to explain and to apologize. He listened greedily to her stories. He accepted her apology and was with her when she died. Her last words to him were a blessing. She said, "I want you to be happy when I am gone." This meeting helped Scott forgive and move on. He is less haunted now by memories of the past. He said, "A bad life was redeemed by a good death."

How we deal with parents will influence the way we grow and develop in our life stages. This time is a developmental stage for us as well as for them. Our actions will determine our future lives. Will we be nurturing or distant, responsible or hedonistic? The choices we make don't have to do just with parents but with us. Everyone gets a chance to "grow their souls," as psychologist Frank Pittman puts it.

My client Robert stayed away from his parents. They had expected all their sons to become doctors. Robert had been the bad son, the child who wouldn't do as they wanted. His older brother had been their favorite, a graduate of Columbia Medical School, a researcher, and a big money-maker who had given them something to brag about. Robert was a carpenter, which in this family was tantamount to being a bum.

After the father's death, the mother was old and ill. The doctor brother paid for expensive home health care but was too busy to visit. When he did come over, he was bossy and rushed, too stressed with his own life to notice his mother's loneliness. When Robert came, he stayed a long time. He and his mother played Trivial Pursuit and looked though old photo books.

They watched old movies together, and he cut her hair and nails. Now Robert is loved for his devotion—something that was always there but undervalued in other times.

Helping parents through these hard times is one of our best chances to grow up. We are no longer helpless children; we can become truly helpful. If we say no to this challenge, a part of us stays forever young and helpless. Our own growth is truncated. The stories below are of two very different kinds of families. One is a pretty normal family, with some children closer than others to their parents. The other is a less common story of an estranged father and son. In both stories, the good-bye to a father was a transforming experience.

## THE MOTT FAMILY
*"What could Dad possibly
have done to deserve this?"*

EARLY IN DECEMBER, Betsy came in to talk about the holidays. She had her usual case of seasonal affective disorder, but mostly she was stressed at the thought of Christmas dinner. The family had experienced a terrible year. Last April her dad had a debilitating stroke. He'd been playing Scrabble when he complained of a headache and slumped over in his chair. Betsy said, "I know why they call it a stroke. In one second our lives changed totally and forever. The stroke left him crippled and aphasic. He stopped being an auctioneer, and Mom had to quit her job to care for him."

The year had been filled with hard lessons. "We learned who our friends were," Betsy said. "Some of Dad's old buddies dropped out of his life. Other people came by daily and brought vegetables from their gardens or videos to watch with the folks. I learned what my brothers were like in a pinch."

Here Betsy paused and inhaled sharply. "My dad wasn't perfect. He was a fifties dad—he worked too much, he was strict, and he wasn't good at showing affection. I was his little sweetheart, but he was hard on my brothers."

I asked how her brothers were dealing with her father. "That brings us back to Christmas. Wendell, my oldest brother, will come for dinner. But he's spending Christmas Eve at the casinos. He calls Dad once a month, but mostly he is too busy to help. I am angry at him for his selfishness, but he is a prince compared to Stanley.

"Stanley left home after high school and never returned. He's totally cut off from the folks. He thought that Dad loved me the most and Mom loved Wendell. There was a fight about an old car, and that's all he needed to write our family off." Betsy stopped and swallowed hard. "He won't be home for Christmas. I hate him for how he is hurting the folks."

Betsy told me sad stories about the year. Her father had lost his sense of time and could be very impatient. If she or her mother was even a few minutes late, he'd be worried she had been hurt. Once he nagged Betsy to bring him some turkey she was frying, wailing that he was hungry and insisting that it was done. Finally in exasperation, Betsy gave him the turkey, which was still raw inside. She said, "He ate the bloody turkey rather than admit he was wrong."

Her father was on a blood-thinning medication, and when he fell down the front steps, he almost bled to death. Another time he'd been arrested for drunk and disorderly behavior. His speech was slurred, and he was reeling down a street shouting because he was lost and upset. He couldn't explain that he was a stroke victim and so he was taken to jail.

The family had been traumatized once by the stroke and a second time by the medical system, with its financial and bureaucratic demands. Betsy had driven her folks to the hospital and doctors' appointments. She'd helped with the complicated insurance forms and endless, incomprehensible bills. She'd worked under the guidance of a speech therapist to help her father relearn to speak.

Of her dad's hospital time, Betsy said tersely, "It's a great life if you don't weaken." She told of a nurse who called her dad "honey" and treated him like a baby because he couldn't speak clearly. Betsy finally shouted at her, "You're talking to my father. He's an auctioneer, not a toddler."

Helping her folks was a full-time job, especially without the support of her brothers. Betsy had children at home and a husband running for state senate. She said, "I want to be the kind of person who helps my parents. I need to see myself as a good daughter." Wendell was never there when needed. Betsy said bitterly, "His assumption was that I would do anything that wasn't convenient for him."

When Stanley called her every now and then to check in, she wanted to yell at him, "Why have you abandoned our parents? What could Dad have possibly done to deserve this?"

Now with her dad demoralized and helpless, she hated facing the holidays. I encouraged her to ask her brothers for help. She couldn't control what they did, but she could at least let them know what she needed. We talked about how she could make things nice for her parents and her children. I advised her to enjoy what she could at the holidays. This might be her dad's last Christmas.

## SESSION TWO

I next saw Betsy in early summer. Her father had died in May. At Christmas, Betsy had made her father's favorite candies, peanut brittle and divinity, and cut down a big tree for her parents' celebration. She and Wendell had hosted an open house for her parents' friends. Fellow auctioneers, relatives, and old farmers had come from around the county. Betsy and her mother had sung carols to the assembled friends, something that made her dad proud of "his girls."

Betsy said, "I'm glad we had Christmas because the spring was hard." Her father had several more strokes before he died, each one taking away a little more of his life. By the end, he was almost blind, barely able to speak, and unable to walk. Betsy said, "The last few weeks, when he did speak, he said, 'Please, kill me.'"

The best thing that happened that spring was that Wendell came around. The Christmas party changed him. After that his priorities were different. Suddenly he had time to visit his dad twice a week and to call his folks daily. He offered to help Betsy with the chauffeuring and the medical arrangements. Betsy's mother especially valued Wendell's help. He had a way of joking with her that always could make her smile and forget her problems, at least for a few minutes. Betsy also stopped resenting Wendell and began to regard him as a genuine resource.

The hardest thing was that Stanley never returned to the fold. "Toward the end, Dad had a desperate desire to see Stanley," Betsy said. "When the phone rang, he'd call out, 'Stanley, Stanley, Stanley.' He never gave up. He'd watch for Stanley at the door to his room; he'd listen for Stanley's voice and look disappointed when another day passed without his son. At first we lied to him. We said Stanley was out of the country. But by the end, he knew that Stanley chose not to visit him."

Betsy started to cry. "Nothing had broken Dad's spirit, not even all the strokes, but that broke him. I'll never forgive Stanley for what he did." She looked at me wide-eyed with disbelief. "There is no one I wouldn't visit when they were dying. I'd visit Hitler on his deathbed if he wanted me."

She cried for a long while. I asked about the end.

"Mom, Wendell, and I were there. That last week Dad was in an ICU, we camped in the waiting room. We were there for the hard decisions and for when they turned off the machines and his heart stopped beating." She cried some more. I breathed deeply and waited.

Finally I said, "The sad thing is Stanley will never be able to say good-bye. He passed on his last chance to grow up, to let go of the past, and to forgive. Now he will always have to hate his father in order to justify his bad behavior at the end. He will always be the black sheep, locked in a role he could have jettisoned. He will have to remember every bad thing that he can to keep his hate alive. He won't be able to afford to calm down."

Betsy said, "I know I should pity him, and I will someday. Now I am still too hurt and angry. I still can see my father crippled and weak, calling out his name."

In the end we talked about what went right. She and Wendell had grown through this experience. They felt closer to each other and to their parents. Betsy had been able to be the caring, mature daughter she wanted to be. Wendell had become a deeper and kinder person. He no longer organized his life around casino gambling. She and Wendell were able to say good-bye as loving adults who had forgiven an imperfect father. Betsy had the sense of a job well done. Her husband had supported her and her folks and still managed to win his race. She laughed. "I'm not sure whether that's good news or bad news. Politics isn't for the faint of heart."

She had taught her children the meaning of family. They had shared many sad and happy times with their grandfather. No matter how discouraged her father was, he always liked to see her kids. She knew her mother felt supported and her father felt loved by her. When she kissed her father good-bye for the last time, she had felt no guilt, only good, clean sorrow.

## JEFF AND HARRY
*"Dad is bitter and clingy. He has learned
nothing from his long wasted life. But he has
an emotional power over me that I detest."*

JEFF, A MUCH-RESPECTED painter in our town, came in to talk about his relationship with his father, Harry, who was dying of emphysema in Alabama. Harry had been a gambler and a womanizer. As Jeff put it, "He had every vice known to man. The only thing he didn't do to me and my sister was sexually abuse us, and for that we are grateful."

Because of Harry's behavior, Jeff's family had been poor, shunned by neighbors, and generally miserable. Harry had been one of those petty dictators who kept everyone in the family scared and quiet. In the 1950s in Alabama, women stayed with their men, so his mother stayed. But his parents barely spoke to each other. Jeff's mom clerked at the five and dime, and unless Harry took her money for his own uses, she bought the groceries. When Jeff was in high school, Harry left with a woman he'd met at the bar. Two years later, Jeff's mother died of breast cancer.

Jeff remembered wondering if his dad's stupidity in human relationships was genetic and if he would grow up to be mean and racist like Harry. However, it turned out just the opposite. Jeff had supported his mother financially and emotionally through her cancer and death. He was so determined not to be Harry that he became a sensitive, frugal, and hard-working person. As Jeff put it, "The endless paradox with my old man is that his bad behavior made me a good man."

We talked about Harry's health and living situation. Jeff said, "I feel guilty because I am not with him, and guilty because I don't like him."

He couldn't ask his sister for help. The last time she saw Harry, she'd become physically ill. She'd told Jeff, "I will do anything for you except be involved with Harry."

In his twenties, Jeff had cut his dad out of his life. "But then," he reflected ruefully, "his second wife followed my lead. I felt like he needed someone, so I let him back in." Jeff was left with this broke and irascible old man. He said angrily, "Dad robbed me of my childhood, and now he is trying to rob me of a happy adulthood."

At forty, Jeff was married to a woman he'd met in Chicago at art school. Laura taught him to swim and ride a bike. He said, "I had no model for how to be a good partner, but I have learned from Laura." He showed me her picture and said, "In my teens, I had given up hope I could ever have a normal life. Now I am happy. I am living a life I couldn't even have dreamed of having."

But Harry wouldn't go away. Every day he wrote Jeff long letters complaining about the staff and the food at the rest home and begging for more money. Even at Twin Oaks he gambled and smoked. Several times a week he called and rambled on and on. He sulked that Jeff and Laura didn't visit him. Laura, who usually liked everyone, couldn't stand Harry, who had bossed her around once too often. Even though they were none too wealthy, she agreed to send him a monthly check, but when the phone rang, she'd look imploringly at Jeff and say, "It might be your father. You'd better get it."

Jeff said, "I hate Father's Day. It takes me hours to find a card. All the cards have sentiments that don't fit—'Dad, you're a pal,' or 'I've always been able to count on you,' or 'You taught me how to be a man,' or 'Let's go hunting.' They don't have any 'Dad, you were a mean-spirited snake who scared the hell out of us and broke our mother's heart' cards." He laughed. "I guess those aren't in big demand."

If Jeff's feelings had been 100-percent negative, things would have been easier. But nothing was simple.

Jeff sighed and looked out the window. "Dad is bitter and clingy. He has learned nothing from his long wasted life. But he has an emotional power over me that I detest." Jeff felt guilt that he rarely visited, that he didn't read the letters, and finally that he wanted his dad to die. Many people had advised Jeff to run from Harry. Even Laura had said, "You owe him nothing." However, Jeff was here because he wasn't a runner. He needed the sense that what could be done was being done.

I gave Jeff his first assignments. I said, "Write down what you envision as the best-case scenario between you two. What can you reasonably expect to give and get under optimal circumstances?"

## SESSION TWO

Jeff was back in two weeks, considerably more cheerful. He'd won a national award for a painting, and he and Laura had been rock climbing. His dad hadn't called in six days, and already Jeff looked more relaxed. Even his breathing seemed slower and deeper.

Jeff pulled out a piece of paper and said, "It helped to write down what I wanted." He read that he would give his father a monthly check and visit twice a year. Laura and he were buying a machine to screen calls. Henceforth, he would talk to Harry only once a week.

Jeff didn't expect apologies or enormous changes at the last minute.

The less he expected, the more grateful he would feel if something good happened between them. He knew they would never have a serious talk, but he thought he might enjoy sharing news about his art or his hobbies with his father. He thought that now and then he might have a nice moment with his dad, maybe talking about sports or playing cards.

He didn't love his father. Jeff said, "If I didn't feel guilt and anger toward Harry, I don't know what I would feel. Harry was a rat. People don't always get what they deserve."

I told him about Harlow's monkey experiments. Harlow found that baby monkeys need a parent so badly that they will bond with a metal pole or a towel. I described the heartbreaking pictures of baby monkeys clinging to inanimate objects, and I said that sometimes people are in the same predicament. They need a parent and they get a metal post or a towel.

Jeff sighed and said, "I do what I do grudgingly. I take much better care of Dad than he ever took of me."

I asked if Jeff had found any men who helped him along the way. He answered, "I didn't have a good father, but I had a good teacher." He told me about an art teacher from the art institute. This man had taken him under his wing and taught him about drawing, but more important, taught him about relationships—that men could nurture one another and tell their heart's truth. Jeff was still in contact with his teacher, who now lived in a retirement community in Arkansas.

Our time was up. I encouraged Jeff to work toward his best-case scenario and keep having a good time with those he loved. He left optimistic, although his last words were, "Things seem to be going too well."

SESSION THREE

Jeff came in discouraged. Harry had been rehospitalized with pneumonia, and Jeff would fly down tomorrow. He'd miss an art opening and a spring weekend with Laura. If Harry had been grateful, the trip would be bearable, but instead Harry had been mad that Jeff wasn't coming sooner and staying longer. Plus, as usual, Harry needed money. He'd gambled away most of his last check and was strapped for cash just when he was too sick to maneuver.

We talked about how to handle Harry's request for money, and Jeff decided he wouldn't give him more than the usual amount. After all, his dad was safe and well cared for. Sick as he was, Harry still wanted money to buy cigarettes, alcohol, and Lotto tickets. Jeff laughed. "I have to admire the old man's consistency. He will be who he is until the end."

Still, Jeff hated to be around Harry and the staff. He said, "Harry doesn't see himself as a good person, so he has nothing to lose by being a jerk." On the other hand, Jeff wanted to be a good person, which put him at a tremendous disadvantage when dealing with his father. He said, "People like Harry who don't fight fair can generally win when they deal with someone who is civilized and reasonable."

He clenched his fists. "I hate to give Harry my attention instead of Laura. Sometimes I have nightmares that somehow he'll suck me back into all the pain. That I'll lose Laura over this." He started to cry.

I waited a while, then said, "You are strong, and Harry is weak. He doesn't have the power he once had over your life. You must remember that. He cannot rob you of your adult life."

"A friend said maybe Harry would surprise me," Jeff said. "But Harry won't ever surprise me by acting heroic."

Jeff blew his nose and wiped his eyes. He said, "It is hard to believe my good luck will last."

I smiled. "Your life now is solid. A few days with Harry won't destroy it."

Jeff decided that while he was in Alabama, he'd take care of himself. He would take time to call Laura daily and to eat some barbecue. He'd come home as soon as possible. "It's better for him this way," Jeff said wryly. "If I stayed longer, I'd probably murder him."

"Try to find something to enjoy each day you are there," I suggested.

Jeff asked, "Shall I bring you back some barbecue sauce?"

SESSION FOUR (SIX WEEKS LATER)

Jeff stayed in Alabama a week. Harry had died three days after he arrived. He'd made the funeral arrangements, and Laura and Jeff's sister had flown down for the event. Jeff said, "With the nursing-home director and the funeral attendant, that made five of us. Harry didn't leave behind a lot of friends." He chuckled when he recalled how hard it was for the funeral attendant to say anything good about this old man he had never known.

Jeff was glad he'd gone down for Harry's last days. He had found an eighty-year-old man who weighed less than 110 pounds, lying in an intensive care unit. Harry didn't look powerful, he looked pathetic. It erased some of the pictures Jeff had in his head of his father as a dictator and a bully. His dad had remained feisty. At one point Harry said he was afraid he'd die in his sleep. Jeff had said somewhat stupidly, "That wouldn't be so bad, would it?" and Harry had replied archly, "Depends who we're talking about."

Jeff laughed as he recalled Harry's words. "I felt compassion for him, and I like feeling compassion instead of anger."

He also felt something else new for Harry: He felt curious. He wanted to know what Harry thought about his life. Jeff asked him about heaven, and Harry said, "I don't figure I'll make the cut. I wouldn't want to go any place a bunch of sanctimonious stuffed shirts were going anyway." Jeff smiled. "Harry stayed in character to the end."

"I asked him how he felt about my birth, and he said he wished he'd been there. He admitted that he hadn't been a good father." Jeff smiled wryly and said, "He didn't say much, but that little bit helped."

They had spent plenty of time together, maybe the most time of their entire relationship. Jeff had even sketched Harry, who had been too weak to complain much. Before he got too ill, they'd watched baseball on TV and played some poker. He chuckled. "I tried to let him win a few games, but he caught me cheating. Even mostly dead, he's a hell of a lot sharper at cards than I am."

Jeff said, "The thing that worked on this visit was that I let go of any fantasies that I could get love or truth from Harry. Maybe I could make him comfortable. Maybe we could have a few laughs."

He looked out my window. "I stopped feeling guilty about Harry's situation. He was the architect of his own life. I wasn't responsible for his behavior. I was a little kid when he went off the track. He has reaped what he sowed. I wouldn't want his life, but he chose it. It wasn't my job to protect him from his choices."

Jeff continued. "Harry was on a respirator toward the end, and we couldn't talk much. I did hold his hand." He stopped talking for a moment, and I saw tears in his eyes. I waited, and soon he said, "Damn. I hadn't planned on crying for the old man.

"When Harry died, I realized that I would never know my father. I have questions about his life and mine that will never be answered. He couldn't tell me who he was because he couldn't face who he was."

He sighed. "Still, I'm glad I was there. I feel I did the right thing."

Jeff looked sad as he said this, and I sat with him for a while.

He continued. "Most of what I needed from Harry he could not deliver. But I can get it from other people. Laura and my art teacher, my friends. "

I asked softly, "What did you get from Harry?"

Jeff thought awhile. "Harry was like that father in the country song who named his son Sue so that he would grow up a fighter. By being such a derelict, Harry gave me the chance to grow up self-sufficient. For that I owe him."

We talked a little longer, about his plans to go camping with Laura and about his next art show. Really he didn't need any more sessions. He had come in for help dealing with a difficult situation that had disappeared with Harry's death. Because of the way he handled the death, there were no ghosts haunting him as he went on with his life.

THE DEATH OF A PARENT offers the last chance for a relationship to heal, or if it can't heal, at least move toward healing. But many adults miss that chance to work things out with their parents. They may have reasons for not being with a dying parent, but in the end, what is more important than saying good-bye?

In this last part of our century we are isolated from our old-old and dying relatives. Many cultures integrate death into the life cycle much better than we Americans do. In Vietnam, before the old die, they invite all their friends and family to visit them. They set aside a week or two to reminisce, to tell their true feelings, to try to understand their enemies, to forgive, and to say good-bye. The Japanese have Obon, the Buddhist festival of the dead. In mid-August, the living and dead reunite. Everyone returns home to eat and visit with their departed relatives. In Mexico, images of death are everywhere. Death is smiling, riding in carts, and dancing. Death is a part of everyday life, much discussed and even joked about by children and adults.

In America we tend to deny and repress death. We all need opportunities for recognition and catharsis. We need more markers, rituals, and rites of passage for the old and the dying. We need traditions that help families deal with death, not just at the funeral but for months and even years before and after.

In the absence of good cultural rituals, we can invent new ones. My client Terry, who was dying of brain cancer, had a memorial service before his death. He wanted a ceremony while he was still alive to let people know they were appreciated. At this service his friends and family talked about him, and he talked about them. His favorite music was played, and afterward everyone dined on a beautiful cake he had ordered.

Scott, whose friends were scattered all over the country, had a slumber party before he died. He invited his closest friends for a weekend. He was weak and couldn't leave his home. Before the event, he almost died, but he hung on, and as his friends arrived, he rallied. We spent the weekend at his home, playing cards and listening to our favorite "Big Chill" music from the sixties. We brought in Chinese takeout and told jokes and old stories. It was a very good time. Three days after we all went home, our friend slipped into a coma and died. My friends and I still talk about what a good weekend it was.

I encourage families to celebrate decade birthdays with family reunions, tributes, poems, and songs in honor of the birthday person. Along with all the celebrating, having a day of discussion about what the next ten years might reasonably bring and how events ideally will be handled is good. Families need structures for talking about the past and the future. Planning for death should be like planning for college, something that happens routinely after research, thought, and discussion.

Adult children and their parents should have a certain day, perhaps every year for the old-old, when they discuss the future. This talk can include health updates, financial and housing plans, discussions of new needs and new anxieties. These talks will help everyone be calm and prepared when crises occur.

Many people have written about death and dying. In *Dying Well*, Ira Byock says that the end of life allows people to achieve certain landmarks such as the completion of worldly affairs, closure on relationships, and acceptance of the finality of life. The Hospice movement has a well-developed philosophy about death. Hospice teaches that a pain-free and conscious death around loving people can be a person's last opportunity to find meaning. Hospice workers have found five common tasks for the dying. They must say, "I forgive you," "Please, forgive me," "Thank you," "I love you," and "Good-bye."

We baby boomers are good at getting our needs met. I predict that as we move into the next century we will have more planners, such as clinical nurse specialists, who help us with old-old age and death. Our institutions may be better prepared for our generation than they have been for our parents'. Our culture may have more rituals and more respect for the old. Housing choices may be better, and the old may not be so isolated from mainstream culture. We may have the road maps we need to navigate our way home.

Our parents' generation is giving us one last gift: the time and experience with their aging and dying. They can help us test different ways of handling those last, hard years. They can help us think things through, design better rituals and institutions and better cultural and familial attitudes. They are our teachers, even to the end, and for this we owe them an enormous debt of gratitude.

*Part Three*

# Moving
# Toward
# Wholeness

CHAPTER 8

# Let a Thousand
# Old Flowers Bloom:
# Resiliency

*We cannot help the birds of sadness flying over our heads,
but we need not let them build nests in our hair.*

—CHINESE SAYING, QUOTED BY HELEN NEARING
IN *Loving and Leaving the Good Life*

*You have set the powers of the four quarters of the earth to
cross each other. You have made me cross the good road and the
road of difficulties, and where they cross, the place is holy.*

—BLACK ELK

THIS CHAPTER IS ABOUT PEOPLE WHO ARE RESILIENT IN THE
face of adversity. They are, to use psychologist Lois Murphy's term, "good
copers." They have learned about psychological survival from their long
and complicated lives. The resilient old carry on in spite of losses. They
tend to be practical, sensible, and well organized. All have interests and
relationships that sustain them. They aren't bitter or sulky, and, in fact, they
all are appreciators, grateful for a fresh muffin, a phone call from a friend,
or a good sunset. They discover pleasure in small moments. As much is

taken away, that which remains grows more precious. The resilient old have discovered independently the same truths—that acceptance is the key to serenity, and gratitude is the key to happiness.

Good copers keep busy, focus on interests, and take things one day at a time. They are not worriers or overburdened with angst. They have mostly happy memories and thoughts, and balance their sorrows with humor. I have never laughed more than I once laughed with Jim's grandmother at a wedding. We sat toward the back of the church and joked until tears ran down our faces. Resilient old people remember funny stories from seventy years ago. They have colorful language. When I asked Uncle Clair if he still went to Denver, he replied, "I didn't lose anything in Denver so I don't need to go back." My old neighbor was once "so broke he couldn't pay attention." My friend Ray Barger spoke of a man "who wasn't crazy but would do until crazy gets here." My friend Jim Peterson quoted an old buddy as saying, "He's so cheap he wouldn't pay a nickel to watch an ant eat a bale of hay."

The resilient old have reasonable expectations. They have learned to tolerate frustrations and limitations. Virginia Galligher, age 106, said, "I was always satisfied with whatever we had. It pleased me, I liked it, and I never thought we should have something better."

The resilient old assume responsibility for their own choices. For the most part, they see their lives as something they have constructed. They are not self-pitiers or -blamers. Most are hard workers with a tremendous sense of pride and accomplishment. But they have played hard, too, and many tell stories of trips, parties, dances, and other kinds of fun. Relationships have held their lives in place. All the good copers had long histories of stable relationships with people of all ages. As a group they were tolerant and warm-hearted. They didn't get worked up about other people's behaviors. They believed that most people did the best they could. They minded their own business, and they didn't have lots of expectations for how others would behave.

By the time people are old-old they all have seen great suffering. The resilient old have chosen to respond with compassion rather than anger and despair. As Rabbi Abraham Joshua Heschel said, "When I was young, I used to admire intelligent people. Now I admire kind people." Henry James wrote, "Three things in human life are important. The first is to be kind. The second is to be kind. And the third is to be kind."

All lives are ultimately tragedies. Not only does nobody get out of this place alive, but nobody gets out without loss and despair. As Willa Cather said, "Hardship is the only thing that brings out the good in most people." Resilient old people have used their hardships to grow souls. Their lives have taught them who they truly are.

The resilient old people I interviewed had strong spiritual beliefs. They believed in something larger and more transcendent than their own egos. Cather wrote in *My Antonia*, "That is happiness; to be dissolved into something complete and great." Those words are written on her tombstone.

As people age, time, not money, becomes real wealth. As I age, all my decisions are about time. When I turned fifty, I invented a mnemonic device to help me make good decisions about time. I needed five things in my life: respect, relationships, results, relaxation, and realization. Since then, I have tried to use the Five R's to budget my time. When I have choices to make, I ask, "Will this project bring me what I want? Will this decision make me more relaxed or respected? Will it bring results in the culture or for those I love?" If the answer is no, I try to turn down activities and projects. I try to make every minute matter. There is time for only the Five R's.

The Five R's are best conceptualized as a circle, not a tower. I don't think of them in terms of priorities, but rather as all important, but in moderation and balance. Contrast is critical. After working for results, it's gratifying to feel respected. After relationship time, it's important to have time alone for self-realization. All five are necessary for a good life, and none is more essential than the others. Even relaxation is important, both so that work can be done and so that relationships can be maintained.

Relaxation is about bonding. Couples don't stay together because they figure out who does the dishes and writes the checks. They stay together because they have fun. As Margaret Mead pointed out long ago, mothers don't care for their babies because the babies cry, they care for them because they laugh and smile. Also, with relaxation comes gratitude. Relaxation brings laughter and a sense of perspective.

Thinking about resilient old people, I realized that my mnemonic device could be used to describe their needs as well as my own. We humans actually have a fairly small and elemental set of needs. Our surface structures are very different, but we all have the same deep structure. We want to be loved, respected, and useful. We want to have fun, and we want to develop our talents. The resilient old have relationships, ways to be useful in their communities, ways to relax, ways to develop their potential, and ways to feel respected.

This chapter gives examples of old people who are meeting these needs. My aunts Grace and Henrietta are good at relaxing and relationships. Jane organizes her life around her work. Sarah is much respected for her energy and her intelligence. Effie is a seeker, a person who organizes her life around growth. However, all the stories are about people who balanced these Five R's. They are the good copers, the resilient old.

## Relaxation

MY AUNT GRACE married Otis when they were young and times were hard. Over the years they moved frequently and raised three children. Many relatives lived with them during the Depression and the early days of their marriage. Grace fixed up her houses so that they were pretty and comfortable. She fed the multitudes with berry cobblers, fried bluegill, chicken and dumplings, and crisp salads of poke greens and homemade dressings. She sewed, gardened, fished, and ran a general store. When her life slowed down a little, she paid two dollars a lesson and learned to paint.

Currently Grace and Otis have fallen on a new kind of hard times. Grace has had a stroke, and Otis has Alzheimer's disease. They cope using the skills that got them through the Depression. They keep busy and spend time with family and outdoors. They face the future honestly, but calmly.

Grace has a hard time in the mornings now, but by afternoon she feels better. That's when she does her quilting or baking or tends to her birds. On summer afternoons she and Otis work in their garden. Grace gives the orders, and Otis carries them out. Just off the kitchen in her bird room, Grace raises canaries, parakeets, and other songbirds to sell. She likes to buy old-fashioned cages at garage sales. About these birds, she says, "I love what I love."

Her voice is filled with honey. The vowel sound "ah" precedes every verb, and the verbs end with "in," not "ing," as in "We were a-goin, or a-comin to town." When we last talked, she told me about her train ride through the Rockies. Grace and Otis liked to "ride the rails." About twice a year they board Amtrak and tour the western half of the country. They talk to people on the trains and walk in the cities. They like the views and the train meals. When they are in Los Angeles, they sit in the studio audience of "The Price Is Right." They are Bob Barker fans.

RELAXING IS ESPECIALLY IMPORTANT for people who are coping with loss. When Doris was undergoing chemotherapy and radiation treatments for her cancer, she borrowed money to buy a hot tub. She'd wanted a hot tub all her life but never could quite afford it. Now the idea of being physically comfortable had tremendous appeal. She told me, "I could make it through those awful days with the oncologist if I could go home and soak in my hot tub. I'd think of it all day long. At night under the stars, I could find a little hope."

Partly to offset the loss of physical powers, the old need sensory experiences that are pleasing. It's important for them to have comfortable chairs, sunny spots in which to sit, fireplaces, and rooms with good views. They like lotions, good drinks, and soft fabrics. It is hard to overstate the importance of delicious food. When my mother was dying, she grew weary of hospital fare. She asked for grapes and for Braunschweiger. These foods were too much for her easily upset stomach, but she nibbled a little. Mainly, though, the smells and sights of these foods made her happy.

## Knights of Columbus Bingo

JIM AND I ARRIVED early for Monday-night bingo, but the place was already packed. We were greeted by several older men who gave us dobbers and paper sheets for the first bingo games. On a little stage up front, a man selected the numbers from a rolling canister and called them out. Behind him, these same numbers flashed on a board.

Most of the players were older than seventy. They were eating hot dogs, drinking coffee, and lining up their cards. There were widows, mother-daughter pairs, couples, and grandparents with grandchildren. The men wore seed caps and had the turkey necks and thin arms of old farmers. Most of the women wore sweat suits or jeans and T-shirts.

When we sat down at a long table, Marie and Howard introduced themselves and eagerly instructed us on the rules for blackout and double bingo. We had only two cards, a piddly number compared to Bertie, who sat beside me with twenty. She chain-smoked and worked like a maniac during the games to keep up. Bertie had bad teeth and looked like she'd had a life of grinding poverty, but tonight she was having a ball.

We played straight bingo, double bingo, blackout, Mutt and Jeff bingo, bowtie bingo, and razzle-dazzle bingo. Marie and Howard bought popcorn and giant Cokes. They knew most of the other players and visited between the games and the drawings for free turkeys. Bingo reminded me of small-town life, with lots of jokes and banter and talk of food, weather, and people. Nothing profound happened, but everyone, including Jim and me, had fun.

Music is the miracle drug for the old. To quote Chekhov, "Music unlocks the frozen rivers of the heart." At my son's wedding dance, Aunt Grace requested her favorite song, "Lara's Theme," from *Dr. Zhivago*, which begins "Somewhere, my love . . ." When she was younger, Grace had a music box that played that song, and it always made her cry. I watched her face as the song played. She was seeing people and hearing voices of people long gone.

Mark Twain said, "The older I get the more clearly I remember things that never happened." The old love to tell stories, to recall things that happened and never happened. Memory can be jogged by songs, books, and pictures. The old like to talk details. My older relatives will visit for hours, talking about: When was it you bought that green sofa? How many miles did you put on the Studebaker? What summer did you drive your kids to Yellowstone? Is that fence we built together still standing? How much did Lloyd sell that last hundred acres for? What year was the wheat hailed out?

When people are in pain or dying, having beautiful memories of the past can help. Once, when Jim's mother was ill, Jim helped her imagine her favorite beach on Sanibel Island—to envision the sky and the anhingas, to hear the waves crash, and to smell the tropical salty air. As Phyllis lay in her hospital bed, having one more IV inserted, mentally she walked the beach looking for shells.

When my mother was dying, I pretended we were camping in the wilderness. She was born in Colorado and had always loved the mountains. Her bed was a sleeping bag. The oxygen bubbling was a mountain stream. The hospital sounds in the hall were pine branches in the wind. It helped her sleep.

## Relationships

### HENRIETTA AND MAX
*"She's up on the roof flying a kite."*

MY AUNT AND UNCLE have been married for more than fifty years and still are lovebirds; physically affectionate and absorbed in each other. They live in a double-wide trailer on Highway 13 in Missouri. Like every other place they have lived, this place is neat, homey, and utterly unpretentious.

In his seventies, Max is still handsome and sharp as a tack. He's a joker. The last time I called and asked for Henri, he said, "She's up on the roof flying a kite." He sets his answering machine to say, "We're out on the porch watching the wind blow. When it stops blowing, we'll come in and answer the phone."

Henrietta has soft southern speech and a hearty laugh. She hasn't had an easy life. She was born after her father moved into a mental institution, and grew up with a succession of stepfathers. She saw them come and go. Henri laughed. "Mama could get along with anyone except her husbands. We had money when she was married, and we were broke when she wasn't."

Of her childhood, Henri said, "I was happy. We always had good food." However, I think she's forgotten some of the hard times. Family stories hint at dire poverty. Her brother, my father, drank the water the cabbage was boiled in and was once so hungry that he mistook dishwater for cabbage water. He drank it down and enjoyed it. Henrietta told of living on a small farm near Petelo. One cold winter my father fed them by catching wild game. He built a little trap that he carried into the woods, where he would hide and watch it all day. At dusk, Henri would stand in the window and wait for him to return. If he had something in his hand, she'd be happy. She laughed and said, "Otherwise, it was gloomy."

Henrietta said, "Mama could dress anything—possum, squirrel, or rabbit—anything. We were crazy about rabbit." She remembered putting playing cards in the bottom of her shoes to fill the holes. She worried about what she would do when she ran out of cards. But she said, "I never felt poor in my heart."

Henri has always been rich in relationships. She was loved and petted by her mama. For a while, Henri lived with Grace and Otis. My father, Frank, slept on the kitchen floor, and Henri slept in Grace and Otis's bedroom with their children. When they finally got a radio, she and Grace sang all the Hit Parade songs. They loved Al Jolson and Will Rogers. Friends came over on Saturday nights and listened to the Grand Ole Opry. They rarely had money for movies, but they did see *Gone With the Wind*. Mostly they played pitch and rook and swam in the creeks.

Max grew up a mile from her, and she'd known him all her life. They dated for three years before they married. Henri said, "Max was the best thing that ever happened to me." He wanted her to have whatever she wanted. Henri smiled at me and said, "Nobody but Mama ever loved me like Max."

As a young couple, Henri was a stay-at-home mother with two sons, and Max moved from job to job. They didn't save much money. Henri laughed and confessed, "We enjoyed life too much." Max's brother Preston asked him to sell meat for the Welsh Packing Company. From his first paycheck Max was the top salesman. Once Preston was overstocked on lard, and he told Max to push it. Max sold so much that by the afternoon, Preston called him and said, "Stop, don't sell anymore." Once Max's delivery truck was loaded so full it wouldn't move. "Max could sell three tons of wieners in two days," Henri bragged.

Max made good money at Welsh's, but he was driving 1,000 miles a week and had several fender benders. Henri wanted him off the road. So Max bought the Sears store in Ava. These were their happiest and most prosperous years. The Sears store went from almost nothing to half a million dollars a year in sales. Max was the reason. Every customer would come in and ask, "Where's Max?" People trusted him to tell the truth. One time a woman in the store called Max a liar. He said, "If you'd been a man, you wouldn't call me a liar but once."

Henri told of the store in Ava being robbed. Max was home with hay fever, and the store was being minded by two women, one a blond and one a brunette. A robber came in and held them up at gunpoint. They were tied up and left on the floor while the robber emptied the cash register. After the robber left, they called the police and Max. When Max got to the store, the brunette was pale as a ghost and the blond was pink as a cooked lobster. After that, Max always joked about how people turn different colors when they are stressed out. A few weeks later, a teacher in Ava had her students write an essay about a political figure of the day entitled "Who was Bert Lance?" None of the kids knew who he was, and all their dopey answers were read aloud on Johnny Carson. One kid wrote, "He's the guy who robbed the Sears store at Ava." Henri laughed until she cried when she told me this story.

Max has had a heart attack, and Henri has been hurt in a car accident. She has trouble leaving her trailer. They mostly stay home and their family comes to them. On Saturday nights, though, they drive down to the Old-field Opry with Aunt Grace and Uncle Otis. The Opry was organized by a group of musicians, including their son Steve, who have been friends since childhood. It's free, and donations go to needy members of the community.

Henri's family is very close. If Max is away, he calls home every few hours to say "I love you." Both sons and their families live nearby, and Paul often comes over for lunch. Steve calls almost daily and drops in twice a week. Both sons are like Henrietta, "gifted at loving." Henri said of Steve, "He never gets enough sleep. He is always busy helping people." Everyone in the family comes for dinner on Sundays and holidays. Henri said to me, "Family is all we have." She always ends her calls by saying, "There aren't any words to say how we feel about you."

*Each time of life has its own kind of love.*

—TOLSTOY,
*Family Happiness*

Family and friends are the true riches. Especially for women who have lost their husbands, female friendships are strong during the last years of life. In the Midwest we have villages filled with resilient widows who have formed their own social groups. They meet at cafes or in church study groups, book clubs, and quilting circles. They know one another's cholesterol levels, histories, and great-grandchildren.

In *Crossing to Safety*, Wallace Stegner wrote that what he looked back

on with joy wasn't his work, his books gettting published, or his professional recognition but rather his friends. As he aged, friendship was what
sustained him and gave him happy memories. What was true for him is true
for most of the old.

People need new relationships and old ones. Margaret Mead said that
the deepest human need is to have someone who cares if we come home at
night. This need for connection is so strong that the old are vulnerable to
scam artists, telemarketers, and the shopping channel. I know old people
who order jewelry and dishes just so they will have twenty seconds of conversation with the on-air salesman.

The old need conversation, touch, children, and pets. I recall an old
attorney at a Masonic meeting. As he accepted a sixty-year attendance
award, he thanked the middle-aged couple who had brought him to the ceremony. He spoke of their care for him and of how much he liked their children and their home. This family clearly was responsible for this man's
happiness, and they knew it. They smiled proudly.

A lesbian couple, friends of a lifetime, were separated by work and
family responsibilities. Now in their seventies, they can live together for the
first time. They take long walks, trips to Cape Cod and the mountains, and
they attend concerts and ballets. Arlene has Parkinson's disease, and
Dolores suffers from systemic lupus, but they are a fun-loving pair. Whenever I see them they are holding hands.

The need for physical affection never ends. Even before birth, touch is
important. Local twins, put in separate cribs at birth, had "failure to thrive"
symptoms at the hospital. When their doctors placed them in the same crib,
they quieted down and gained weight. The older sibling put his arm around
the younger one. Touch is important at the end of life as well. Healing takes
place only with the laying on of hands. I remember my friend John holding
his mother's hand as they walked into a concert on a university campus. She
had recently lost her mate. Her son's hand in hers seemed very important to
her.

Pets are a great source of affection, and they buffer stress. Joseph

Struckus found that nursing-home residents with visits from pets were less depressed, anxious, and confused than those who saw no pets. Judith Siegal found that pet owners made significantly fewer trips to doctors. Animals help humans communicate with one another, teach us how to relax, and meet our needs for touch and warmth. They also give people unconditional positive regard as well as a reason to get out of bed in the morning.

A neighbor, Constance, had a long-term intimate in her dachshund, Cookie. Cookie had her favorite meals, her special walks and toys. Whenever I saw Constance I asked about Cookie, and I would hear her proud stories. When Cookie died, Constance had her cremated and made plans for the two of them to be buried together. Cookie's ashes are now on her fireplace mantle along with many fine pictures of Cookie.

I know an old man who lives to care for his black Lab, Shadow. He bought her as a puppy when he lost his wife fifteen years before. His days are organized around caring for Shadow, and he spends a good share of his meager food allowance on her favorite dog food. Hugh keeps his children and grandchildren posted on Shadow's health and activities. Shadow adores Hugh and never leaves his side. They sleep and eat together. They worry over any change in the other's routines. They are a couple, as loving as any other happy couple I know.

## Results

> *The greatest good fortune for the old is to have projects, to have days filled with useful and interesting work, to never be bored.*

—HELEN NEARING

Americans have odd attitudes toward work. We are socialized to believe that endless luxury and leisure are what will make us happy, but it is not true. Endless leisure leads to apathy and despair. What feels good to most people is being useful. What gives life meaning is its effects on other people. Rest feels good only if it is in contrast to work. What makes life enjoyable is pacing. A work/rest cycle is stimulating. Rest all the time grows wearisome, as many people discover when they retire.

Forced retirement can have a devastating effect on the old. When men who have had no activities outside of work retire, they have nothing useful to do. If they have had few relationships outside of work, when they lose their jobs, they lose their friends. They may drive their mates crazy. As one wife said to me, "I told my husband, 'You don't have to work, but you have to get out of the house. I can't take you here from morning until night.'"

I met a cab driver who had plenty of money but couldn't take staying home. He liked meeting people and being out on the streets. Once I stayed in a Best Western hotel where an old man worked in the breakfast area. He made homemade waffles for guests, poured their fruit juice and milk. He could have retired but he wanted to work. He needed a raison d'être. My son Zeke went to an old barber who was having chest pains. Zeke offered to cancel his haircut and drive him to a hospital, but the barber insisted on working. As he cut Zeke's hair, the old man had two more painful spasms. When Zeke drove him home afterward, the barber said he wanted to keep working until he dropped. "It's what I've done my whole life."

The elderly who loved their work have the hardest time letting go. I think of a popular novelist from Minnesota who kept writing well into his eighties. Fred Manfred was used to the writing life and a mentor to many young writers. He shared his experience, his skills, and his connections. He sponsored readings at his home, Roundwind, a house built of stones he gathered from nearby fields.

My friend Katherine told me that her dad, a seventy-five-year-old attorney, wouldn't retire. For several years he ignored the hints his coworkers kept dropping. Finally in despair they planned a big retirement party for him. He went to his retirement party and had a great time. He danced with all the women and accepted his award, but Monday morning he was back at his desk as if nothing had happened.

People who no longer work at paid jobs still can work. AmeriCorps has a special Senior Corps that offers useful work to volunteers. Many of the old find great joy in teaching the skills they know. Our neighbor's father keeps busy fixing up her house and washing her cars, caring for her children and working in her garden. When Uncle Fred retired, he built houses for his relatives. He never visited relatives without repairing whatever needed fixing in their homes. Uncle Clair grows vegetables for his many old friends who no longer can garden.

It is good for the old to teach what they know. They have skills and experiences that most younger people don't have. The old know how to entertain children without TV sets and Nintendo games. Many are good storytellers. Often they know other languages, customs, cooking, and music. They know about history and the natural world.

One of my friends has her mother living in her home. She asked her mother to teach her children about the olden days. At first her mother protested, "Why would they be interested in that?" But my friend insisted. She pointed out that her mother was the last person her children would know who could explain how kerosene lamps worked, or how to hitch horses to a sled, or what happened at a barn dance on the prairie. And in fact, my friend's children were enthralled by these stories.

Many of the old write autobiographies. Younger relatives often encourage the old to tape oral histories. I encourage an interview format. My experience is that many older people are uncomfortable talking to themselves on a tape. It's better to be there and ask questions. Maps, pictures, food, and objects often stimulate the memory.

Lucky people continue to accomplish and be productive. An old musician on NPR said, "Music is my lifelong mistress, and I'll never let her go." Many musicians, such as Claude Williams, Benny Waters, and Jane Jarvis, manage to keep working into their eighties and nineties. Freud said that happiness is love and work. When either of these disappears, one's life is much diminished.

# JANE JARVIS *(age 81)*
*"Music was a natural part of me,*
*like my nose. My core identity*
*was as a musician."*

I INTERVIEWED JANE JARVIS when she came to Lincoln to play a concert. Jane was five feet tall with a big smile and lively blue eyes. The day we met she wore pink hoop earrings and carried a piano-shaped purse with her name on it. She talked easily about her life.

Jane was born in Vincennes, Indiana. She said, "In the city you must take on armor to survive, but that wasn't true in Vincennes. Many gentle and kind things happened in that place." Her parents were scholars whose home looked like a public library. Her father wrote poetry that Jane said was as good as John Greenleaf Whittier's. He loved to sing, but he had a terrible voice. Once the neighbors wrote him a letter asking him to sing inside. He played the violin, too, but gave it up when he realized that his imperfect playing bothered Jane. Her mother was a schoolteacher who painted equally well with either hand. Jane said of her, "She wasn't an important painter, but whatever she did was beautiful."

Her parents had lost an earlier baby, and Jane grew up an only child. Jane said her parents were ahead of the times. When she was in the womb, her father read her all of Shakespeare and her mother took her to museums and classical music concerts. Her parents wanted her to be exposed to beauty from conception on. When she was just a toddler, her parents taught her the genus names of all the plants in southern Indiana. Jane recalled her folks fondly: "They never denied me an adventure."

Jane continued. "Music was a natural part of me, like my nose. My core identity was as a musician." She called her musicality a gift. "All I had to do was push it along." All of her life, whenever Jane needed a place to hide or rest, music had offered her that safe, cherished place. She said, "I feel badly for people who have no art in their lives. I don't know how they cope."

By the time she was four, Jane had taught herself to play piano. Her parents knew she was a prodigy, but they wanted her settled in school before she had to deal with her talent. When Jane was eight, her parents took her to a teacher at the university. From the start her teacher found it impossible to keep Jane in new sheet music. She said, "Jane drinks music like a sponge drinks water."

This teacher gave Jane a sense of the importance of music. She taught Jane that practicing was an honor and privilege. Her teacher taught her to pay attention to every little detail. Jane could practice only when she was clean and neat. She should approach the piano always as if she were giving a performance. When I said that this teacher reminded me of Rilke's line "Genius is the capacity for taking infinite pains," Jane laughed and responded, "Yes, exactly."

After less than a year of lessons, Jane performed in front of a large crowd. The teacher told Jane that if she put her cold hands in warm water it would help her relax and play well. She said, "All the great musicans do this." Her mother said, "After you take your bow, look at the audience and say to yourself, 'There is no one out there who can do this as well as I.'"

When Jane was eleven, she auditioned for a children's talent show. Radio was very new. Hundreds of local acts showed up. One mother had a daughter who tap-danced, and she had brought a board for the daughter to use. Another mother had a daughter who twirled the baton. Jane laughed at the memories of girls tapping and twirling batons on radio.

While Jane was waiting for the accompanist to arrive so that auditions could begin, she saw some black men practicing a new kind of music in the next room. She asked to play along. They asked her what songs she did, and she answered, "Let's play what you just played. I loved it." At first they were kind to her; then, after she played, they invited her to join their group. Jane loved jazz from that day on. "Jazz is emotional music," she explained. "Fundamentally, jazz musicians are emotional people. When the music works, the connections are magic."

When Jane returned to the talent show, the accompanist still hadn't arrived and Jane volunteered to play for the others. For her selection she played "Nola," which she described as "a cheesy song but very big at the time." She won the contest and got a full-time job at the station for twenty-five dollars a week during the Depression. She rearranged her school schedule so she could work. Just before Jane's show, Doc Sunshine had a motivational program. She met George Jessel, who was nicknamed the "Toastmaster General of the United States." She loved the station and worked for a year, "until the child-labor people caught up" with her.

Until her parents' death when Jane was thirteen, she had a lovely childhood. One night her parents left for a meeting, and Jane invited students over to practice at their apartment. When a policeman came to the door two hours later, Jane thought she was in trouble because of the loud music. The policeman told all the other kids to leave, then he brought in Jane's schoolteacher. Weeping, she told Jane that her parents had been hit by a train and were hurt. That night Jane went to sleep hoping they weren't in any pain. The next morning her uncle arrived and blurted out, "Your parents are dead."

Jane went into shock. At the time, she didn't cry, and she even fell asleep at their funeral. I told Jane that I know that this kind of sleep is a sign of extreme stress. I have seen clients fall asleep when they talk about their toughest issues and experiences. Jane was emotionally numbed for years. She developed a lifelong habit during this time. If anything was too painful, she didn't see it or think about it. She "pulled down the shade."

Until she graduated from high school, Jane moved from relative to relative. Times were hard. "Our little family had always been different from the big family," she told me. "No one was clamoring for me." She also had the stress of a lawsuit against Pennsylvania Railroad. The suit went on for years, and eventually Jane received $2,000 for the deaths of her parents. When she was young, Jane missed her father the most, but as she has grown older, she misses her mother more.

Jane married three times. Her first husband, whom she married right after high school, was wealthy and good-looking. Jane laughed. "All my husbands were good-looking. However, I wouldn't have married them if my dad had been alive." In that first marriage, Jane had a daughter who died. She pulled down the shade. After all these years, if she thinks of her daughter or her parents, she feels an electric jolt shoot through her.

Jane's second husband was a musician, not as good a musician as she was, and that caused problems. Also, he saw other women. Jane laughed again. "To show you how well my shade worked—I cannot remember his name." Her last husband was a doctor, and they had a son and a daughter before the divorce. Jane said, "I could be a good friend to men, but not a wife."

She played at WTMJ and for the Milwaukee Braves. But in 1962, she moved alone to New York City. Right away she got two jobs—one playing for the Mets and one at Muzak. Jane traveled all over the world and produced 300 recordings and composed 500 songs. She produced Dick Hyman's recordings and was in a Woody Allen movie. She played with Lionel Hampton, Clark Terry, and Grady Tate. In 1992 she wrote a musical.

Jane was always choosy about relationships. She wanted to associate with high-caliber people. There were certain kinds of lives she didn't want. Jane could have been richer and more famous, but she didn't use sex to make deals. Partly to avoid being propositioned, Jane always befriended the wives of musicians she played with.

Jane now lives in New York City and Florida. Her son is a musician in New York City. Most of the time, he calls her Mom, but when they discuss music, he calls her Jane. Her daughter Jeanne and her grandchildren live in Florida. Jane misses life on the road with other musicians. Her work life has always been her social life, but now many of her jazz friends are infirm or dead.

Jane toured Japan this fall with the Statesmen of Jazz, and she has recorded two new CDs. She stays busy with concerts and workshops in many places, including New York City. She has no agent and doesn't like the business side of performing. She is lucky that she has some financial security. As she said, "That old hound dog necessity isn't barking at my door. I can do what I want."

Jane is a nominal Catholic who said, "I embrace all religions. The prayers of the Muslims are good prayers, and so are those of the Presbyterians. I can drop into any place of worship anywhere in the world and feel at home." I quoted Willa Cather to her: "The prayers of all good people are good."

Jane smiled. "She said it better in one sentence than I did in three."

She believes that God gave her talent. Otherwise, she asked, "How do you understand a life like mine?"

The night after our interview I went to hear Jane play with Benny Waters at the Zoo Bar. Jane arrived early to check out the grand piano and practice with the sidemen hired from Kansas City. She wore a sparkly blue pantsuit, and her thick silver hair shone in the bar light. As she moved around the stage, her hair flew behind her like a young girl's.

Benny Waters first recorded in 1925. Benny was now the only living musician from King Oliver's band. He was in the pit of the Apollo theater the night Ella Fitzgerald auditioned, and he taught Duke Ellington harmony at the New England Academy of Music. He'd lived in Paris for forty years, but when he got old he moved back to a walk-up apartment in Queens. He'd just played three nights at Birdland. His music was young and eternal, but Benny was ninety-five, as old as jazz itself, and blind and going deaf.

Jane began the set with "I've Got You Under My Skin." Then she played "Midnight Sun," "Snapper," and "Stella by Starlight." The jazz was melodic, accessible, and emotional, and Jane played it with unmatchable style and joy. When she performed "I Remember April," her playing shimmered with color, texture, and musical jokes. The song had a satin surface, but underneath was pain and yearning. In this song I could hear her parents' and her daughter's deaths, her divorces, and her struggle for success.

She introduced Benny as a true statesman of jazz and as "a gas to play with." Wearing a blue suit, a beret, and a medal, and led by his manager, Benny hobbled onto the stage and eased into a chair. As he fumbled with his microphone stand and knocked over a glass, Benny looked fragile. Watching him get situated, I wondered if he was being exploited, but I soon abandoned that idea. When the music started, he looked younger and stronger. He played his courtly, smoldering music with authority. He had a strong husky voice that was soothing and exciting at the same time.

Benny called Jane "babydoll" and the other musicians "cats." He said, "Good evening, ladies and gents. My first song will be 'Exactly Like Me' which is exactly like you." He grinned, exposing a mouth filled with gold teeth. The crowd laughed and applauded. His music was deep, resonant, and happy. His next song was "Autumn Leaves," a bossa nova in A minor. Later he sang "Hurry on Down to My House" and "Cool Water." He laughed and said, "Next set it will be 'Blue Waters.'" It was a standard blues progression jam that he gave a new name every night. When Benny announced "All of Me," he warned, "I don't want to kill nobody, but it's gonna be rapido." Jane was on her home court, but the younger cats had to work to keep up with him.

At break, Jane shook hands, signed CDs, and connected easily with everyone. She was a pro at handling the crowd. But after a while Jane hunted down Benny's manager and said, "Let's get going." He said, "You get a half hour break." Jane said firmly, "I don't want a long break, I want to play. That's what I'm here for."

## Respect

RESILIENT PEOPLE FEEL RESPECTED. The last thing they are willing to lose is their dignity. On a cultural level, respect means turning the elderly into elders. We need media that portrays the old as worthy of our time. We need fewer ageist jokes and plots. We need cultural stories that point us back to older people as a source of joy and wisdom, for their sakes and for ours. On an individual level, respect means giving the old time and attention. It means not trying to control the conversation and not being patronizing. It means waiting patiently, since many old people think carefully before they talk, and then they speak slowly.

When I think of respect for elders, I think of John Harms, who, at ninety-two, lived in a little house on the Oklahoma campus where he had taught much of his adult life. He was a minister who had attended the first World Council of Churches in Amsterdam in 1948. As an old man he wrote on his computer six hours a day. He still traveled abroad with church work, made speeches, and ministered to his campus congregation. He biked and hiked all over the place, but his main interest was his family. He was writing a book on the history of his family. Every year he organized a big family meeting. These meetings lasted more than a week and were both social and educational. There were seminars on topics such as positive parenting and wellness, business meetings that encourage frugality and prudent investments, and, of course, social times. He published a family newsletter between yearly meetings.

I was a friend of one of John's granddaughters who helped plan the programs and organize the meetings. Families from all over the country attended. My friend joked about her grandfather's agenda, but she respected him as well. He was a powerful presence in the family, much loved and honored. The family gathered yearly to hear John's ideas and enjoy one another's company. John managed to keep an enormous scattered family connected physically and emotionally. The ties that bound this family were respect for their patriarch.

## SALLY GORDON  (age 90)
*"I'm not quite ready
to come home."*

I PICKED SALLY up in the lobby of the Cornhusker Hotel. Sally was tall and thin, with exquisite bearing and elaborate makeup. She'd been at a lun-

cheon and was dressed to the nines in a black suit and fancy hat. Under
ordinary conditions, she would have walked home, but today she wore
three-inch heels and could use a ride.

We drove to her small house near the capitol building. The rooms were
filled with plants, books, and oil paintings. She had a Star of David in her
living room, and a basket of knitting beside her chair. As Sally said later,
"The carpets need replacing and the furniture is falling apart. But the
important thing is I'm not falling apart."

She brought me a Diet Coke and a napkin and said, "No charge for a
refill." A local reporter once wrote that "if Sally were a season, she'd be
spring." She talked eagerly about her life. Her memory was excellent, especially for dates and funny stories.

Sally was born Sarah in 1909 in Chicago. She was born with a caul, and
the midwife said Sally would be special. Her parents were Russian immigrants, and her older brother had been born in Russia. Sally remembered
being interested in a green plant that grew out of the sidewalk, the only
plant she'd ever seen. In those days if children had any money, they bought
pickles, sweet corn, or coconut from vendors on the streets. Sally laughed
and said kids wanted food, not drugs, in her childhood.

Later Sally's family moved to Fort Collins, Colorado. While she was
in high school, she won twenty-two awards for her typing, spelling, and
rapid calculations, and a state championship in shorthand. Because of her
excellent secretarial skills, Sally found work easily after high school. She
married young, and she and her husband, Merle, moved to Lincoln in 1940.
Merle worked at an auto-parts store and later ran a combination pawn shop
and jewelry store. In the summer, Sally and Merle played tennis every
morning before work. They had three daughters and a son. Sally said that
her husband was a good man. She recalled that after the kids were grown,
he said to her, "Doll, isn't this wonderful? Aren't you glad we stuck it
out?"

Since 1959, Sally has worked for three governors. Through her work,

Sally met Charlton Heston when he was a Democrat, and Robert Kennedy when he attended a picnic in honor of JFK. She met Lady Bird Johnson, who, Sally said, was charming and much prettier than her pictures suggested. And she said that LBJ looked her right in the eyes and made her feel like she was the only one. Once she was sitting beside Hubert Humphrey at dinner when her earring fell into his drink. He said gallantly, "That's the best thing that ever happened to that drink."

Until the late 1960s, Sally's life was good. But then her mother died a slow and painful death from complications from arthritis. Meanwhile her brother was dying of a brain tumor, and her son, Jim, was wounded in Vietnam. For a week they didn't even know if he was alive. Finally she and her husband received a call that he was hospitalized in Japan. After he returned to this country, he was in rehabilitation for seventeen months and six days. Two years after their son was injured, Merle died. Almost thirty years later, Sally still dreams about him.

Sally has his picture in her room. Every night she kisses the picture good night and then holds a conversation with Merle before falling asleep. She tells him, "Honey, I love you and I miss you, but I'm not quite ready to come home."

Just after her husband's death, Sally began work at the local university. The work saved her. She gave hugs to the students who needed them, but Sally needed them, too. Her one regret from that era is that she turned down a chance to travel to Europe with the students and now she may never go.

Her son is her only child in town. Her daughters, Connie, Sandy, and Janet, want her to visit, but she doesn't like to be away from home too often or too long. Sally keeps in touch with her seven granddaughters and three great-grandchildren, though. Many of her old friends are dead. Sally said life is like a game of dodgeball. In random fashion, people are hit out of the game, one by one, and then your time comes.

Sally has many young friends, including interns who work for the legislature, and neighbors. She attends dances in Antelope Park. She still has three jobs—as a tour guide for the governor's mansion, as a volunteer at the senior center, and as sergeant at arms at the Nebraska state legislature. This job requires her to keep our senators in order when the legislature is in session. She said of her job, "One word from me and the senators do just as they please."

When she is home, Sally plays violin and sings to herself. Just like every other older person I met, she sometimes has trouble sleeping. But if she's up in the middle of the night, she watches old movies. She hasn't owned a car in thirty years, and she walks everywhere. The past summer she walked five miles across town to our big shopping center, Gateway. She grew tired and lay down to rest in the green grass and later awoke surrounded by a rescue squad. Now she walks long distances only in cooler weather. People wave to her and call out, "I like your hat."

Sally bakes her own bread and makes soups. She makes muffins filled with dates, nuts, dried apricots, raisins, apples, and other surprising things. These muffins are very like Sally, unique and wholesome. Every week she makes them differently. Here is the recipe she made up and changes every time she bakes.

### SALLY'S SURPRISE MUFFINS

*2 APPLES, GRATED*

*JUICE AND GRATED RIND OF 1 ORANGE*

*2 SMALL RIPE BANANAS, MASHED*

*1 CUP RAISINS*

*12 DRIED APRICOTS, CUT IN SMALL PIECES*

*½ CUP PECANS*

*1 CUP ZUCCHINI, GRATED*

*5 TABLESPOONS OATMEAL, ANY KIND*

*6 TABLESPOONS FLOUR, ANY KIND*

1 TABLESPOON WHEAT GERM

1 TABLESPOON OAT BRAN

⅛ TEASPOON EACH ALLSPICE, APPLE PIE SEASONING,
    CINNAMON, CLOVES, GINGER, MACE, NUTMEG,
    PUMPKIN PIE SPICE

4 TABLESPOONS WHITE SUGAR

3 TABLESPOONS BROWN SUGAR

1 EGG

1 TABLESPOON BAKING POWDER

SUBSTITUTE OTHER FRUITS, FLOURS, AND LIQUIDS WHEN YOU FEEL LIKE IT. BLEND EVERYTHING TOGETHER AND, IF IT'S TOO THICK, ADD A LITTLE COLD COFFEE. BAKE IN GREASED MUFFIN TINS FOR 20 TO 25 MINUTES AT 350°.

In her late fifties, Sally began her modeling career. She showed me a picture of herself at fifty-six, in a sleeveless formal with long gloves. At age ninety, she is still modeling and doing TV commercials. In our cold, icy winters she walks to work. She said to me, "At my age, if I let down, it's all over."

She writes limericks and poems: "Life goes by at an amazing pace. That's why they call it the human race."

Last week she attended three concerts and two art openings. She knows some of the elderly drink, but, Sally said, "I get high when I gargle." She still gets asked out on dates but she isn't interested. She said that she would be hard to live with by now. She's set in her ways. She laughed about a friend who told her that going out on a date was like "going out on maneuvers." She asked me, "Who needs it?"

Sally is more tolerant of people now than she used to be. She prays and reads her Bible daily. Her belief has gotten stronger as she has gotten older. She thinks that the world is too wonderful to be an accident. Her four rules for life are: Count your blessings, observe the Golden Rule, have a sense of humor, and keep busy.

Sally feels that conversational skills have declined. People are more machine-oriented. She also thinks people are ruder and humor is more off-color and less funny. Phone skills have deteriorated too, especially those of businesspeople. People are overscheduled and don't have time for one another the way they used to.

She feels that prejudice is a constant. Racism is just below the surface. She used to sulk when she heard an anti-Semitic remark, but now she corrects it. She tells people, "There are good Jews and bad Jews. You paint us all with the same brush."

Sally thinks that popular psychology has changed the culture. People talk more about feelings and underlying motives. They are much more suspicious and pick everything apart. She pointed out that now, if you ask people, "How are you?" they might say, "What do you mean by that?"

Sally had cancer surgery in 1965, but now she is in excellent health. She wants to die before she loses her functioning. She wants no machines, rest homes, or heroics. Her feeling is, "If I can't walk, I might as well die." But she hopes to live into the next century. She laughed. "I have a certificate of deposit due in 2002."

Like most healthy old people, Sally has few regrets. She likes young people and believes that when older people are with the young, they are less likely to be gloomy. She has her faith, and says, "I have a hot line to God." She has her memories but doesn't dwell on the past. "Life is good. I have reached the point when I can say no. I do what I like, and I like what I do."

## *Realization*

*We have a thrifty God who lets nothing that is good within us go to waste.*

—SISTER WENDY BECKETT

*Do you not see how necessary a world of pain and troubles is to school an intelligence and make it a soul?*

—JOHN KEATS

Constantly confronted with loss and suffering, the old think about the meaning of life. As people age they understand that there will be nobody like them ever again. This realization brings both sorrow and self-acceptance. Approaching death helps people see what is important. What is unimportant recedes into shadow. The old need wisdom, philosophy, poetry, and a sense of being connected to something meaningful. Their lives become more sacred, as I define the word. To me, sacred is that which moves toward wholeness. Resilience means growing from experience and becoming more who one truly is.

The last goal of the aged is realization, or the growing of a soul. Soul, in the context I use it, is synonymous with character. It is the governor of the system, the beliefs that motivate and explain every action. A soul is that which endures, that which gives meaning. When I write about soul, I think of Effie, who is a lifelong learner. Her whole life has been about growing a soul.

## EFFIE BROWN *(age 86)*
*"I believe in being fully present.*
*I no longer waste time."*

EFFIE REMEMBERS THE PRAIRIE being plowed and said to me, "People didn't know what they were losing." As a child, she had a hearty life, walking everywhere and herding cattle on foot. Her mother prepared four or five meals a day, and no one worried about weight. She and her siblings read *Little Women*, *Five Little Peppers*, and *Treasure Island*, and they made up games based on the books. Effie remembers many happy times, but she also remembers neighbor children who died from influenza. Her family had boils and chilblains from the cold.

Effie was "born interested." In 1935, at the height of the Depression, she got a scholarship to go to college in Chicago. She studied languages and participated in the cultural life of the city. During those hard years, she saw the bodies of starvation and suicide victims floating in Lake Michigan. Later, she moved to New York City and became a translator. In 1941 she met Hal, who had gotten his education at UCLA, "the university on the corner of Lexington Avenue." They married and worked for the Red Cross. I met Effie when I was teaching at the Omega Institute. She'd come from her apartment in Manhattan, near Central Park. She was in her eighties but still very much a young-old woman. She introduced herself as an "old lefty" and told me stories of her civil-rights work in the fifties and sixties. She'd traveled around the world, and now she helped refugees learn English. Effie never missed a poetry reading or a chance to go to the opera. She was an Elderhostel regular and an active Unitarian. "Unitarians don't have answers," she told me proudly. "We have freedom." She was a storehouse of Unitarian jokes. Question: "How do you tell a Unitarian?" Answer, "They'd rather go to a lecture on heaven than to heaven." Question: "Why can't Unitarians sing hymns?" Answer: "They read ahead to make sure they agree with the words."

Effie was brutally honest. When she met me, she said, "You look better than your photo, which is so squinty and unattractive." She had an acerbic wit and didn't tolerate fools gladly. Of one acquaintance, she remarked that he'd had an interesting life but wasn't an interesting person. Referring to another student, she quoted Dr. Johnson: "He was like a mackerel in moonlight—capable of stinking and shining at the same time." Once she admonished me when I was obsessing about some minor situation: "Don't pole-vault over horse turds."

Effie had high expectations for herself as well. She did yoga at the lake at sunrise and ate only healthy vegetarian fare. Effie regularly examined her life to make sure she was using her time well and being of service. She quoted a line from the Talmud: "It is not incumbent on thee to finish the work, but neither art thou permitted to desist from it altogether." She told me, "I believe in being fully present. I no longer waste time. I want every moment of time spent walking, studying, or being helpful."

She quoted Andrew Carnegie, who said, "The man who dies rich dies disgraced." She gave away her money and explained that the central question of her life is, "Is the world a better place because I have lived?"

At Omega, I spent all the time I could with Effie. She and I shared a fascination with the Roosevelts. She'd brought along Doris Kearns Goodwin's book on them, and we visited Hyde Park. As we walked around the grounds, Effie said, "You get to an age where everything that goes on is interesting." She added ruefully, "Just as I get old, I am figuring everything out."

We talked about Hal's death in 1996 after fifty-five years of marriage. She had a year when it seemed as if time had stopped. She couldn't read, listen to music, or even see her friends. Every day she walked around the reservoir in Central Park, but otherwise she sat in her apartment staring into space. She said, "I had a bad case of survivor guilt. Why did I get to go on living when my Hal, who was as worthy of life as me, who loved life as much as me, was in the ground?"

But time passed, and Effie was too mentally healthy to stay isolated. There were children who needed tutoring, and refugees who needed clothes and food. She started to study again. Even though she was in her eighties, she was asked on dates. At first she had no interest. She was determined never to remarry and didn't even want to think about intimacy. Losing Hal had hurt so much that she was determined never to experience that much pain again.

About six months after we met, Effie's life took a surprising turn. She began dating a retired journalist named Chuck. He is a Unitarian her age, a nurturing man with a great sense of humor. They enjoy the same activities and were amazed at the parallels in their backgrounds. They were, as Effie puts it, "rocked in the same cradle."

My next letter from her announced their wedding. "I would never marry for companionship. I have plenty of company, and I like solitude. I find something to enjoy in every day," Effie wrote. "But I am in love. I am optimistic about our marriage. We have over a hundred years of marital experience between us. "

I sensed a new sweetness in her personality. Effie's acerbic wit was less tart, and she seemed less judgmental and more relaxed. She reported that sometimes she let herself sleep in until 7:00. She wrote, "Life goes on, and I've decided that as long as I am living I might as well live."

# CHAPTER 9

# We Grow Our Souls Together: Grandparents

I wasn't there when your body, signaling, woke you,
When you sat, moving yourself to the edge, and stood
And knew July by its heat and wondered what time it was
And steadied yourself, sat down, and called for my mother.

When she came, her impatience visible in the air around her
Because it was hot, and something in the pot needed stirring
When she helped you into the slip worn thin by your patience
When she asked which dress you wanted to wear

And when you pulled on the stockings yourself, and the garters
And stepped into your shoes and looked down and knew
And did not tell my mother you knew
When you asked her please would she comb your hair

When you sat down to the meal with my mother and father
And my father asked would you like some of this and some of this
When you lifted the glass and gazed through the water's prism
When you drank, swallow by swallow all of the water

*And opened the napkin but did not pick up the fork*
*When you folded the napkin and pushed back the plate,*
*Pushed back the chair and stood with no help from anyone*
*and turned saying nothing and walked out of the room*

*When they called you When you did not answer*
*When you shut the door and looked at your face in the mirror*
*Your face that face of longstanding, that trustworthy sister*
*When you took this face in your hands to bid it good-bye*

*And when you said to them I want to lie down now*
*When they laid you down and covered you with a sheet*
*And you said go now, go eat and they did*
*Because they had worked and were hungry and this*
*had happened before*

*When you lay back in it to let it have you*
*Knowing what you had waited for patiently and impatiently*
*What you had longed and hoped for and had abandoned*
*longing and hoping for*
*And prayed for and not received was finally here*

*When you lay back in it to let it have you*
*When you heard for the last time the clink of silver*
*And let go the sheet, let go light on earth*
*When your breath ceased to be a thing that belonged to you*

*I wasn't there*
*Forgive me*
*I wasn't there.*

—MARILYN KRYSL,
"Grandmother"

MARGARET MEAD RECOGNIZED THE UNIVERSAL VALUE OF GRAND-parents. She noted that grandchildren and grandparents were close partly because "they were united against a common enemy—the parents." They were "partners in crime."

Parents and grandparents have very different roles. Parents have the job of socializing children and of raising them to be emotionally sturdy, responsible, and independent people. Grandparents mostly have the job of loving children for who they are at the moment.

Grandparents are often very different as grandparents than they were as parents. By the time they have grandchildren, people often have less responsibility and less to prove. They have a rather different set of priorities than they had as young adults. Parents often marvel at what patient grandparents their parents turned out to be. The improvements are related to developmental stages.

The feelings between grandparents and grandchildren are sometimes labeled sentimental. One writing professor told his students the first day of class, "Nobody wants to read a story about your grandfather's death." Grandparents sometimes feel that it's not socially appropriate to talk about their grandchildren. However, they can't help themselves. Recently I ran into a friend who said, "Forgive me for burdening you with pictures of my grandsons." Then he laughed. "But you know how it is."

The grandparent/grandchild relationship is almost totally ignored by popular media. Rarely is this relationship the plot of any movie, song, or TV show. When is the last time you heard a popular song about grandparents? Are there any? There are more movies about Martians and serial killers than there are about grandparents.

In contrast, some cultures consider nothing more interesting than the relationships between the old and the young. *Grandfather* and *grandmother* are words of great respect. Children learn from the old and share that learning. In our culture, this story of love and respect between generations doesn't mesh with the prevailing discourse. The big American story is about newness, youth, beauty. For the most part, grandparents are not about power, fame, money, or sex, but rather about love—perhaps the purest and the least exploitable love—that humans can feel for one another.

Even though cultural scripts don't encourage close relationships across three generations, family after family, child after child discovers their great value. A recent Gallup poll showed that what the majority of children reported to be their happiest memory wasn't a trip to Disneyland or the day they got a computer but rather the time they spent with their grandparents. I remember a little girl I saw in an airport who was running up the jetway, shrieking, "Grandma, Grandma." Her voice contained all the intensity and fierceness of acknowledged need.

*Heidi* is the archetypal story of a little girl, alone in the world, saved by the love and wisdom of her grandfather. The old often save the young. I spoke with a reporter whose family had moved onto a block filled with old people. At first her children were disappointed that no other children lived nearby. But this reporter baked banana bread for all the neighbors and had her children deliver bread and visit. Soon the children had all these new friends. They now visit with their many buddies after school, sharing food, stories, and projects. The reporter said, "My children have never been less lonely."

One of my graduate students was assigned to do therapy at a rest home. At first she didn't think she was getting anywhere. She had learned to consider therapy as setting goals and achieving objectives. The old people wouldn't stick with her program—they just wanted to talk. However, over time, the staff told her that her clients were perking up. All of the student's clients had gifts for her—smiles, hugs, and little jokes. Some made her pots in their ceramics classes. Others walked her to her car at the end of the day. As she listened to their stories and held their hands, her time at the rest home became her favorite time.

A neighbor recently told me that he must go to church. He is ill and has trouble walking and sitting, but he toughs it out. The reason is Michael, a three-year-old boy who waits for his arrival every Sunday. They'd met two years before, when my neighbor "adopted Michael for a month." He said,

"When Michael sees me, he runs up behind me and embraces my knees. He calls me Grandpa."

Neighbors recently invited their maternal grandmother to move into their home filled with teenagers. The mother said that at first she had been worried it would create more work and tension. However, the opposite had occurred. Grandmother was home when the kids came from school, and she helped with homework, supervision, and meals. Most important, though, she loved the children, and they knew it. All of a sudden the children had another caring adult in their lives, one with time and energy for them.

Given a chance, the old love the young and vice versa. I think of my aunt Margaret splashing in the Pacific surf with her great-granddaughter, who squealed joyfully in her company. I think of my friend Bonnie who had her teenage daughter help a neighborhood woman three afternoons a week during the summer of her eighth-grade year. When she realized that while she was at work, her daughter was watching TV nonstop, Bonnie made the decision to connect her daughter to her neighbor. That summer the girl learned to sew and garden. She stayed out of trouble and stopped begging for money and junk food.

Parenthetically, because the relationships between grandparents and grandchildren tend to be warm and accepting, sometimes adult grandchildren can say things to their grandparents that their sons or daughters can't say. Sometimes grandchildren are the best people to talk to grandfather about his driving, or to grandmother about durable power of attorney. In some cases, the grandparents are more trusting of the grandchildren and much more eager to please them.

There are dozens of good ways to connect the generations. Simple family customs can be important. I know a grandmother who plays piano duets with her grandchildren. My sister-in-law asked her grandmother to help her cut and freeze corn. As they worked, Pam taped her stories and laughter. Our family had a long tradition of dinner at this grandmother's house. When "Mamoo" was too weak to do most of the work, we still went there. We carried all the food in and helped her with the dishes and table. Mamoo hosted this important family event until she died.

One little girl told me proudly that she attended her grandfather's support group for colostomy patients. The beaming grandfather put his hand on her shoulder and said, "She is the star of the group."

My friend Helen has a mother-in-law with severe osteoarthritis. Helen videotapes her children playing in the rain or gathering hailstones with the clouds rolling in. (The grandmother especially loves storms.) Helen also records family dinners, piano recitals, and wild birds at their feeders, and sends these tapes regularly to her homebound mother-in-law.

Recently I ran into a professor whom I respected for his skepticism and hard-headed mental clarity. On the street, he pulled out pictures of his grandkids. Herb said, "Whatever you have heard and expected about being a grandparent, it is even better than that." He talked for fifteen minutes about these kids. He told me what he most liked was that he can really enjoy them. "When I had my own kids I was always exhausted, overworked, worried about money and stupid things like tenure. I had papers to grade," he said. "This time around I am present."

New grandchildren are beautiful, fresh-faced, and loving. They haven't had time to develop severe flaws or to let anyone down. They haven't failed classes, committed crimes, borrowed money they didn't repay, or become surly and unreadable adolescents. Grandparents see joy and renewal in grandchildren.

A friend of mine recently talked to me about a visit with her mother and her grandson. She said, "Brandon is growing up, and my mother is growing down." This was true literally and figuratively. The world was opening to Brandon and closing to her mother. One was learning new skills daily while the other confronted new limitations daily. Just as her mother's losses caused sorrow, her son's growth brought comfort to my friend.

Babies give hope at the time of a death. A widow told me, "Holidays are good again because of my granddaughters." Just last night I dropped a pie by the home of a friend whose mother had died. The living room was filled with family—a diverse lot of people, many far from home, all of them sad. But there was a baby, a blond, blue-eyed toddler who occupied the center area of the living room. He played peekaboo, built a tower of alphabet blocks, and snuggled into the waiting arms of adults in the room. All of us kept our eyes on Calvin. He was hope on that dark night.

There are great nicknames between grandparents and grandkids— partly because kids can't talk very well when they first call out for their grandparents. My husband called his grandfather "Wawa" and his grandmother "Mamoo." But there is more to it than that. Who but a grandchild could call Jim's dignified attorney grandfather "Wawa"? These names stick around long after kids can talk. These nicknames are important because they give grandparents a new status at a time when their social power is declining. They signal the power and uniqueness of this relationship.

My grandmother called me Bright Eyes because I could see to read her recipe or thread a needle. I remember my pride in being useful and my love of the name. Thirty years after my grandmother has died, I remember that name whenever I thread a needle or read small print for an older person.

## CONRAD LEACH

PAT MET ME at a coffeehouse on a cold winter night. Pat described her grandfather Conrad as tall and lanky with pearly white hair that grew curly and long. He wore Western clothes—long-sleeved shirts, boot-cut pants, and a cowboy hat. He always said "Yes, sir" and "No, sir." She thought he was beautiful.

Conrad was born in 1901 in Big Horn, Wyoming. He grew up in a world of people he knew and loved, and he died without ever hearing the word "psychotherapy." Conrad traveled across the country in a covered wagon as a baby, then he grew up on a farm. As a boy, Conrad walked into town for dances, and, walking home, he watched for falling stars. Once, after an ice-skating party, he stood so close to a fire that his pants began to burn.

Conrad went to school until eighth grade, then worked for the rest of his life. In 1926, he married a schoolteacher. After Conrad's marriage, he had two prosperous years followed by a life of hard times. There were ten kids; Pat's dad was the oldest. One of Conrad's children died as an infant, and on his fortieth wedding anniversary, Conrad cried when the baby was mentioned.

After his kids were grown, Conrad and his wife lived on an experimental farm near North Platte. It was a three-story place, with the top two floors serving as dormitories. The bathrooms had several toilets and showers. There was a great rope swing in the front yard. Threshers, researchers, friends, and family all spent summers there. There were big communal meals and outdoor games under the stars. Pat recalled this farm as if it were Camelot.

After Pat started school, she would often spend a week or more with her grandparents. Time moved slowly. In the morning they would walk to the store to buy milk, then they would go to the park. Every afternoon they sat on the porch until the mail came. After supper they might drive to the ball games or town band concerts. They sat in their car and honked if the home team scored or if they liked a song. Before bed, they had Coke floats.

When her grandmother got sick, Pat cooked and cared for her. Pat cried telling me how that summer, for the only time in his life, her grandfather would get down on his knees to pray. After her grandmother died, Pat lived the next several summers with Conrad. They often visited the graveyard with flowers. Relatives came and went all summer long. Her mom coached her to keep macaroni and cheese handy so that no matter what the meal was, she could stretch it.

The only people Conrad criticized were people who beat their kids or wives, or who didn't treat their animals well. Conrad had pictures of all his horses and liked to tell stories about them. When he stopped using horses, he stopped enjoying farming. Conrad loved the rodeo, and whenever he attended, he would yell out greetings to all the horses as if they were old friends.

Pat described Conrad as comfortable in his own skin. After his wife died, he ate Sara Lee pound cake for breakfast. He sent out many birthday cards, always signing "Many happy returns." When Pat was there, they played horseshoes, Connect Four, Rack-O, dominoes, and yard darts. They'd drive around and visit family. He would get tears in his eyes when he said good-bye to people.

He and Pat took road trips to see relatives in Denver. They had a blast. He noticed everything. He even enjoyed the odometer turning over. He called fresh haystacks "wheat bread" and old haystacks "rye bread." He loved hot beef sandwiches. He also knew all the old hymns and would sing the bass parts.

Pat's brother once asked Conrad if he had any regrets. He had only one. When he was young and had a big family to support, he had driven to a farm to apply for a job. He passed a guy walking and decided not to pick him up because the guy was probably going to apply for the same job. Now he regretted that.

Conrad died in 1993 with less than $500 in the bank. He was buried on a windy day in late January. The church was filled with people Conrad had helped. Conrad was Pat's connection to a simpler, slower, and more communal culture. His love for her and his calmness helped make her a calm, confident person. Thanks to her grandparents, Pat is rooted in a family and in a place. She's grounded in the ways people who were lucky enough to grow up near grandparents can be grounded. Calmness and security, a safe place to be a child.

MOST GRANDCHILDREN RECEIVE a feeling of security and continuity from grandparents. Grandchildren speak of a certain quality of attention that they don't get from busy, harried parents. Most grandchildren speak lovingly of certain rituals and routines— cookies before bed, dominoes after dinner, walks to the post office or the south pond. Grandparents make small acts ceremonial. Almost any repeated events with grandparents become rituals.

Many adults feel that their grandparents' farm, hometown, apartment, or cabin by the lake is their hallowed place. Many adults hate to see the old places sold because they associate them with beloved grandparents. Because the ghosts of grandparents live in those places, debates about which grandchild buys the grandparents' summer cabin can be acrimonious. Grandparental property is often sacred ground. If you doubt this, ask people you know to tell you where their grandparents lived, and then listen to their voice tones and watch their eyes.

People also remember the food. I am not sure it is possible to talk about grandmothers without discussing food. Grown men wax eloquent on Grandmother's baked beans or homemade noodles. Over time, Grandmother's cooking becomes a metaphor for grandmother's love. Meals at Grandmother's house are communion.

In *The Heart Can Be Filled Anywhere on Earth*, Bill Holm writes that from his grandmother he learned "the interior confidence that the universe itself is a safe house for us. That if we don't close ourselves away through fear, the currents of simple love, kindness and civility will find us out, feed us cookies and tuck us in." He also wrote of her, "In her world, no child was a stranger. Those were two mutually contradictory states of being." These sentiments about grandmothers are almost universal.

A teacher told me that she can tell which kids in her classes have relationships with grandparents or other older people. They are quieter, calmer, and more trusting. A woman I know who had a chaotic family with troubled parents said, "My grandparents gave me a childhood." My husband said, "My grandparents gave me this deep sense that things will turn out all right in the end."

Grandparents grew up in a slower world, and they slow down as they age. They are the only adults in America who have plenty of time for children—time to sit on the porch and watch a bird build a nest or a squirrel gather acorns; time to read stories or help with stamp collections or a ham radio. They can attend ball games, school plays, and recitals.

Children expect lots of stimulation from TV, radio, Nintendo, VCRs, and computers. Older people played as children in barns and on hay bales. What seems natural to a child of the 1990s looks frenetic to an older person. Sometimes the old teach the young the joys of slowing down. At first children have trouble with the change in time zone, but eventually they love it.

My friend Jerry's grandparents gave him a strong sense of place. They lived in Kentucky in a house Big Daddy had built in the 1920s. The house had a covered wraparound porch where the family played Scrabble at night under a yellow porch light. Jerry said that everything else in his life was changing but that the porch was always the same. Even the furniture never changed.

The house was a good place for children. The lot was the size of a city block and had chickens, grapevines, a garden, apple trees, and old buildings that had sunk into ruins. There was a pump that didn't work except as a home for wasps, and an abandoned garage that smelled of rotting wood and Coleman fuel for fishing lanterns. Jerry remembered looking through his grandparents' stuff or watching "Lawrence Welk" or "Password."

Jerry's family visited Kentucky every summer. They lived in a northern city, and the drive south was really a trip between two cultures. On the way down they would have a manners refresher course. The children were to push in their chairs after meals and say "Yes, ma'am" and "No, sir."

Big Daddy was six feet two inches tall, and fat. He wore a porkpie hat and hiked his pants up high. The kids had contests to see who could reach around him. Once Jerry went along with Big Daddy and his friends on an overnight fishing trip. They drank beer, smoked cigars, and told stories and jokes that women couldn't hear. Jerry's dad was squeamish about language, but not Big Daddy. He once described someone as "so clumsy he couldn't stick his thumb up his butt with both hands."

Jerry remembered Ninnie's biscuits rolled out with a pop bottle and cut with an empty baking-soda can. She fixed fried chicken, ham, hush puppies, redeye gravy, fried apples, and tomatoes. They had grape juice concentrate from their own grapes. Every morning his grandmother would mix Jerry a little glass for breakfast. He called it "Ninnie juice."

When Jerry was a freshman in college, his grandfather died at home. Jerry still keeps Big Daddy's camp cook set and old radio. He is now on his way to visit Ninnie, who is senile. Jerry's mother warned him that she might not know him this time. He said, "That doesn't matter. She will know that somebody who loves her is visiting."

Jerry told me, "My grandparents' town was the closest thing I had to a hometown. It wasn't really mine, but I adopted it." And about his grandparents, Jerry said, "I don't often talk about these people. And yet there was no one more important in my life."

GRANDPARENTS TEACH THE IMPORTANCE of living in moments. Old people understand that we all get a finite number of harvest moons, sunsets, and walks by the sea. Knowing the number of each of these events would create unbearable poignancy, but it would force us to pay attention. If we knew a harvest moon would be our second to last, we would look closely. If we knew a trip to the sea would be our fourth to last, we would linger a bit longer.

My husband had a grandfather with plenty of time. Jim was named for his grandfather James, who died in a nursing home when my husband was eight. Jim said, "I got a basic sense of optimism and trust in the world from him."

James married late in life. His fiancée felt she needed to stay at home and care for her ill mother. Only after this mother died did they marry. They had two sons, Bernie and Emmet, and they took in Aunt Louise, who had rheumatoid arthritis. As Louise grew more crippled, Jim's grandmother slept downstairs and attended to her during the night. James shared a bed with his sons and told them stories as they fell asleep.

By the time his sons had children, James was seventy-three and very eager for a grandson. After Jim's birth, James walked all over town telling everyone the news. He and his wife always wanted to baby-sit. Their house was only a block away, and Jim walked over every day. Great-aunt Louise was there, too, wheelchair-bound and sipping Alka-Seltzer through a straw.

Jim loved to eat with his grandparents. His favorite dishes were navy beans with ketchup and potatoes fried black and crunchy. His grandfather would peel an apple with a pocket knife and give him a piece. Jim explored the house and played with old keys. As an adult, Jim saves keys for his grandchildren-to-be.

Jim's grandfather would pick up Jim in his '38 Buick and drive them downtown to the cafe. Jim would get to switch on the ignition. Whenever James drove this car back into the garage, he would say, "Whoa, Nellie." When Jim learned to talk, he would say "Whoa" with him.

Their days were all about process, not outcome. They would sit on the bench in front of the Burt County State Bank, and Jim would listen to his grandfather talk to "an aggregate of old guys." They joked with Jim a little but mostly talked among themselves. Jim remembers being bored but wanting to stick with his granddad. He'd play with rocks in the street. Later at the cafe, Jim would eat a dish of vanilla ice cream while his grandfather drank strong black coffee.

When Jim was young, his grandparents once gave him a Christmas gift he didn't like. He said so adamantly and wouldn't play with the gift. His parents tried to intervene, but Jim wouldn't settle down or apologize. To this day Jim remembers with sadness how he hurt his grandparents.

*We'd slip us on around the corner in our old brown '38;*
*We'd find four farmers on a smooth worn bench*
*In the shadow of the Burt County State.*
*Then it's "Whoa, Nellie," and a slap on the knee and a*
*    great big how-do-you-do;*
*Just six good friends and an old elm tree with nothing much to do.*

*CHORUS*

> *Whaddaya know, Joe? I don't know nothing, nothing I'd say for free.*
> *I'm up to no good and about five feet nine with a banjo on my knee.*

> *Well, time stood still on that old bank clock, and it had since '53,*
> *But I ain't in no hurry to get there, and it'll be soon enough for me.*
> *We took our sweet time with the time on our hands, and we said*
>      *it was a dirty shame*
> *That we didn't grow different, just older, and things ain't quite the*
>      *same.*

*CHORUS*

> *Well, I'd listen real hard and I'd laugh along, though I never*
>      *did understand,*
> *But I sure felt something special looking up at that old man.*
> *Well, he went to sleep in his dinner, and I cried the whole day long,*
> *But there's times I know he's sitting here just singing that same*
>      *old song.*

*CHORUS*

> —JIM PIPHER,
> "Whaddaya Know, Joe?"

## Unconditional Positive Regard

MOST GRANDPARENTS LOVE their grandchildren totally for who they are, not what they do. Grandparents' faces light up at the mention of their grandkids, and their breathing changes as they tell their stories. Their voices fill with energy as they make the report.

Grandparents often find the smallest aspects of their grandchildren's behavior important or adorable. One friend of mine actually said that her grandson was cute when he had temper tantrums. We all need at least one person who is absolutely crazy about us and thinks we are splendid.

The main job for grandparents is to love the kids. But they often help parents keep things in perspective. A grandmother can remind the distraught mother of a teenager, "You were difficult, too." A grandfather can tell his son, "You didn't like to go to bed either."

Internalized grandparental love gives the self a solidity. Children know when they are loved, and they bask in that love and return it. As a psychology teacher of undergraduates, I read many papers about grandparents. To many of my students, grandparents equaled love and security. Particularly if the students came from troubled homes—and who doesn't in the 1990s?—the grandparents often represent ritual, continuity, and serenity.

The grandparent/grandchild relationship may be the purest relationship that we humans have. Hardened adults soften at the mention of their bubby or nana. Adults who are surly and withdrawn with all other adults will cut their grandparents some slack. Many adults feel that the saddest moment of their lives was the day a particular grandparent died.

A psychologist I know had an abusive, alcoholic father. Patrick learned to seek solace a block away at his mother's parents' house. His grandfather was a carpenter, always working in his shop. When he was troubled, Patrick could go to him. One day Patrick's dad came home drunk and gave Patrick hell for no reason. Finally Patrick was able to escape, and he ran to his grandfather's shop. He grabbed a board and started pounding nails into it as fast and hard as he could. His grandfather just watched him do it and said nothing. Later, Patrick realized he had grabbed a beautiful and expensive piece of wood, one his grandfather had been saving for a special project. He began to cry and apologized to his grandfather. The grandfather only patted him on the head and said, "You sure put a lot of nails in that board."

THE OMAHA TRIBE believes that "when we lose an older person, we lose our history. They teach us our songs, keep our language." Grandparents are the family historians. If they live to be great-grandparents, and if they knew their own great-grandparents, they will have known seven generations of family. They are the keepers of the collective memories and the repositories of stories, the connecting tissue between generations. This sense of a family to which one belongs is crucial for identity. Families are built by memories, and the more memories, the more depth and richness in the family.

Reunions often are a source of family stories. Friends told me of attending a funeral in the deep South. They got to spend a few days with their relatives. Their children heard hours of stories, especially about racism and about the heroism of their own relatives. Their great-aunt had been the first black person to vote in her county; their great-uncle had desegregated the fire department. My friends said, "We will send them back every year for more stories."

My daughter Sara met an old puppet maker while in Thailand. He was sad because now children go to malls and movies, and puppet shows are not so well attended. He told Sara, "We taught children the stories of our culture in these shows. Where will they learn what to believe in?"

As Studs Terkel said, "Our whole country has Alzheimer's." We are losing our cultural memory. We have short attention spans and live in the eternal "now" of advertising. Time is about nanoseconds, not decades. Grandparents can help. In addition to transmitting hundred-year-old family stories, they can make history personal by telling the stories that connect the family to the culture. These may be about the Depression, the Dustbowl, the war, or about immigration and homesteading. They can give us some perspective on our modern times.

My grandmother Glessie lived in a world of outdoor privies, mules, and influenza and cholera epidemics. She ran a boardinghouse for railroad workers and later sold Avon door to door in the Ozark Mountains. She remembered old Civil War veterans with their amputated legs and damaged faces. She remembered when the first car came to Christian County, when the Civilian Conservation Corps planted the pines in the Mark Twain

National Forest, and when the road to Sparta was paved. Thanks to her stories, I know people from early in the century. I know about my relatives five generations back.

## Wisdom and Moral Values

THERE IS AN EARTHINESS to the wisdom of grandparents. Once on a hiking trail, I heard a grandmother tell her tired grandkids, "It doesn't matter how far it is to the trailhead, you've got to do it." I've heard my friend Paulette warn her grandson when he is dawdling, "You don't want me on your tail." When a grandchild complained that the Nebraska landscape was boring, the grandfather said, "Come back with a better pair of eyes." Many people recall colorful sayings from grandparents, such as, "a day late and a dollar short," or, "as worthless as tits on a boar."

Author Molly Davis wrote about her eighty-one-year-old father who was viciously assaulted in a parking garage by a teenager. He was beaten with a blunt object and robbed of three dollars. Several bones in his face were shattered, and an eye was damaged. Molly wrote me, "My father would have given him money and taken him to a cash machine for more, but the attacker never asked. How much richer his attacker would have been if he'd had a conversation with my father."

One of the things we can learn from older people is to deal gently and justly with others. My father-in-law, Bernie, has been a great teacher. When Bernie was a boy, his father was a rural mail carrier. One summer day, Bernie rode along with him. They were invited into the home of an almost-blind lady who offered them a snack. She had been canning white peaches and proudly served them each a dish of warm, sliced peaches. Bernie looked in his little dish and saw worms floating in the peach juice. The lady had been unable to see them as she cooked. He looked in alarm at his father, asking with his eyes what he should do. His father picked up his spoon and said gently, "Let's eat our peaches, son."

Writer Mark Gerzon suggests that "growing whole" is a much better way to describe aging than "growing old." He points out that the human spirit, not the body, is central. With age, many spirits grow authentic and whole. Grandparents teach values. A man in Pennsylvania said his kids told him that when they were tempted to do wrong, they thought about what their grandparents would think and made the right decisions. A friend told me that every day, when her father dropped her off at school, he used to say, "Remember who you are and what you stand for." Now he drops off his granddaughter and says the same thing. A client told me that her oldest son had much more time with his grandparents than did her youngest son. She believes that because he did, her eldest is a more idealistic person.

I absorbed many of my maternal grandmother's values. When I visited her, we attended church. However, I learned most of the lessons while shelling peas or watering the garden. I can still hear her sayings: "Choose your books as carefully as you choose your friends." "Make good use of your time and your talents." "Don't judge another until you have walked a mile in her shoes."

Grandparents differ from one another in age, in health, in physical proximity to their grandchildren, and in character. The closeness of the grandparental relationship varies tremendously. Some grandparents don't like the noise and activity level of children. Others are too ill or brain damaged to be involved with them. I think of a friend's grandma Connie, who was too depressed and self-absorbed to notice her wonderful grandchildren.

Sadly, some clients tell me their parents are just not interested in their kids. My client Ali said that her parents-in-law love their son, Ali's husband, but pay almost no attention to her or her daughter, Paige. She said, "It breaks my heart to see Paige try to get their attention. She can do cartwheels around the kitchen table, and they won't stop talking to their son about the past."

Some grandparents prefer gated villages that keep children away. Some adults complain that their parents will talk about shopping, golf, their friends, or their TV shows—everything but their grandchildren. Other grandparents like to be far from family, "mamboing into the sunset," as one client put it.

My client Patsy's grandmother was an angry, suspicious woman. When Patsy visited out of duty, all she heard were accusations. Her grandmother would shout, "Why didn't you come sooner? Why didn't you bring me anything?" And finally, the last time Patsy visited, she shouted, "Leave me alone."

My client Morris had a good relationship with his mother, who lived in a cottage right behind his house. She was a good grandmother, but she constantly criticized Candy, Morris's wife. Candy had tried for years to please her mother-in-law, but recently she'd given up. She no longer wanted Morris's mother in the house or at family meals. This strife caused trouble between Morris and Candy, and between Candy and their daughters. Morris came into therapy to discuss how to make the women in his family happy, a task he described as "mission impossible."

On the other hand, I know many grandparents who are raising their grandchildren. Dixie has cared for her two grandsons ever since their parents went off to find themselves in South America and never returned. Belle, who, at sixty, works as a clerk in a convenience store, is parenting her nine-year-old granddaughter, whose mother is a drug addict. She said, "I don't get to be a grandma-grandma, I have to be a parent-grandma. There are a lot of us out there."

Laureen moved in with her daughter and son-in-law when their fourth child was born. Laureen was a widow whose daughter's family became her life. While both parents worked, she cared for the children. When Laureen's grandchildren were in their teens, her daughter died in a plane crash. Her son-in-law, never a very available father, dealt with his grief by working harder. Laureen became the nurturing person for the children, and the one who raised them.

## THE WALTERS FAMILY
*"We made him throw away his earrings,*
*but those tattoos are indelible."*

NELL CALLED TO MAKE AN APPOINTMENT for her husband, Charles, herself, and her grandson, Louis. She explained that Louis had been sent to them for the summer. He lived with his mother in Los Angeles and had just been arrested for shoplifting. Louis's older brother, Curtis, was in jail for selling drugs, and Nell's daughter was terrified that Louis also would end up in jail or dead on the streets of their dangerous neighborhood. Nell and her husband wanted family counseling to help them through the summer and to help Louis straighten out before it was too late.

We met the next week—Nell, a middle-aged homemaker wearing a T-shirt that said "Born Tired"; Charles, a railroad employee just off the night shift in his work clothes and heavy boots, and Louis, a skinny kid in black pants and a white T-shirt, whose arms were covered with tattoos. Nell said, "We made him throw away his earrings, but those tattoos are indelible."

As usual I began by asking why the family was in therapy. Charles put his arm on Louis's shoulders and said, "We're here because we care about our grandson. We want to get him through the summer without any trouble." Nell said, "We know Louis is a good boy, but he has been in a bad environment. He's picked up some habits we plan on helping him break."

"Like what habits?" Louis growled.

"Smoking cigarettes and mouthing off," said Nell plainly. "Those are not good habits."

I looked at Louis, but he looked down at his hands and didn't say anything. I asked him why he was here, and without looking up, he mumbled, "They made me come." I asked, "Have you ever seen a therapist before?" He answered, "With my brother, at the prison. It didn't do no good."

Nell said, "Louis, we're coming before you are in big trouble. This is more like a vaccination."

"We love Curtis, but he has a criminal's mind. He lies even when it isn't necessary. He steals things he doesn't need. He doesn't really care if he hurts his family or anyone else," Charles explained. "Louis is different. He's a little mixed up, but basically he's a good boy."

"Louis has got a tough skin," Nell added. "Like the skin on pudding just after it cools, but underneath he is a softie."

Louis squirmed as his grandparents discussed his basic good character, but I suspected they were right about him. For his neighborhood and his lack of supervision, he'd gotten in very little trouble. Underneath his tough-guy veneer was a watchful kid who was listening to his grandparents' every word. I sensed he was eager for protection and supervision, for hugs and structure, even eager to have someone teach him to play checkers and say "Please" and "Thank you." Still, things wouldn't necessarily be easy. Louis was fifteen, used to free time and tough streets. His grandparents hadn't been around children in twenty-some years, and the world had changed a great deal since they'd raised their daughter.

We talked about rules. Nell and Charles announced a media policy—only PG movies, no gangsta rap, and one hour of TV a day. Kids could come to their house, but Louis couldn't leave the yard with anybody they didn't know. Nell would take him to the pool every day and sign him up for swim team. "Swimming is for babies," Louis said.

"Do you think Charles was a baby?" Nell asked. "He was on a swim team, and so was your mother."

"You're just nervous," Charles said. "I'll help you with your strokes."

Louis would go to church every Sunday with them and eat all meals at the table. Nell was big on family dinners. She winked at Louis. "You like my dinners, admit it." He cracked a smile.

Nell said, "Louis doesn't know how to do many things. Charles had to teach him to take a bath. He didn't know to wash his neck. He needs help with reading and math. Basic stuff. Should we make him study?"

"Don't even think about it," Louis growled. "There ain't no way I'm gonna study in the summer."

"If you do your work, we'll go fishing," Charles said. "Remember, Louis, that time I took you and your brother to the river?"

For the first time all session, Louis looked up. "Yeah," he said, "I'd go fishing."

I said, "Let's not worry about schoolwork just yet. It's summer. There are plenty of other things to teach Louis. See how things go."

Nell asked, "Can we come back next week?"

## SESSION FIVE (THE END OF SUMMER)

I hadn't seen the Walters family in more than a month. After a few sessions in June, I'd suggested they take a vacation from therapy. Louis was busy with swim team and new friends. He'd quit smoking, and things were going well, although the family never did get to homework. The cure for Louis was simple and explainable. Louis was with people who loved him, who had high expectations about his good behavior and the time to teach him what he needed to know to meet those expectations. He'd grown like a watermelon vine in July.

Nell had scheduled today's session to talk about fall. Their daughter was driving out to get Louis in a week, and suddenly none of them wanted him to go. The three of them had a rhythm and routine. They had rituals and jokes. Louis had his oatmeal every morning and his bedtime prayers with both grandparents every night. He had a place for his stuff and knew all the neighbors' names.

Nell and Charles looked almost the same as when we first met. Charles had on his work clothes, and Nell had acquired a new T-shirt that advertised Worlds of Fun amusement park. They had taken Louis there the past weekend to celebrate their good summer. Louis was a different kid, bouncier and more open. He looked me in the eyes and spoke up when he talked. If his voice volume reflected his gains in confidence, I would estimate he was 100 percent more confident.

We had my favorite kind of talk—victory talk. Louis had been on the swim team all summer. He hadn't won many ribbons, but he had improved his times and made some friends. Louis and Charles had fished every weekend, and Louis had caught plenty of fish. He and Charles had running jokes about some of the lures they used. Louis's favorite lure was the "purple egg sucking bunny leech."

Charles said proudly, "He knows all about lures, and he knows how to clean and cook fish, too." Nell added, "He even likes to eat them," and they all laughed. "When Louis was first here," Nell explained, "he'd hardly eat anything but soda pop, chips, and Snickers bars. He hardly even knew what vegetables were. He'd never tasted celery."

We talked about the garden. This had been a bumper year for tomatoes, and Louis had stayed busy picking and canning with his grandmother. She helped him set up a little stand, and he sold vegetables from their street corner. Charles joked, "It doesn't pay as well as selling drugs, but it doesn't get you put in jail."

The issue today was school and Los Angeles. I asked Louis what he wanted to do. He said, "I like it here, but Mom needs me."

"It's been hard on our daughter to have him away. She's happy about his summer, but she misses her boy," Charles said. "We talked some about her moving here, but she doesn't want to leave Curtis. Right now she sees him twice a week at jail, and he needs those visits."

"The schools are bad in Louis's area," said Nell. "I worry that he'll never go to college if he stays in Los Angeles."

"It would be hard, but we could pay for private school," Charles said.

"Those are for snobby rich kids." Louis frowned. "No way."

We talked about money, about schools, and about family loyalty—how hard it is to make decisions that hurt one family member and help another. I thought Louis was strong enough to make it here or Los Angeles, but I wasn't sure. No one was sure. I could understand his mother's desire for connection, but she hadn't seen the changes. What would she think of the new Louis? I could respect her loyalty to Curtis, but should Louis have to pay for that loyalty? Should the squeaky wheel be the only one that gets oiled?

We didn't resolve anything that session. We agreed to meet for more talk the next week, when the daughter was in town. As the family left, I said to them all, "Whatever you decide about fall, this was a good summer. You all can be proud of yourselves. Charles and Nell, you gave Louis a great gift: your time and knowledge. Louis, you did a lot more than stay out of trouble. You lost your bad habits and gained good ones."

Charles rubbed his head. "He's a hell of a fisherman. I hope he stays with us, but I hear they have an ocean out by Los Angeles with some fish in it."

THE LONGER I WORK with families, the more I respect and appreciate those families who decide to make the sacrifices necessary to live near one another. Physical distance makes a big difference in the quality of the relationships. Recently I met an Italian taxi driver who grew up near his grandfather, who knew everything about the Phillies. He was constantly scouting for them, and he called the team office if he saw a good player. My taxi driver and his grandfather read the sports pages and went to all the games together. They constructed a relationship around baseball. In contrast, the taxi driver sees his grandson only once a year. The boy lives in Florida, and my driver still lives in Philadelphia. The boy likes baseball, but they've seen only two games together.

My cousin Steve had a very close relationship with our grandmother Glessie. All through his school years, he went to her home for lunch and after school. He told me that when he was a teenager, he couldn't trick her. Steve tried to smoke, but he swore that Glessie could smell cigarettes from anywhere in her house. He laughed and said she could even smell it on TV. If a man lit a cigar on TV, Glessie'd run into the room and demand to know who was smoking.

Annie, a divorced friend of mine, has parents nearby who help her with the kids. Annie leaves for work at six in the morning. Her kids walk a block to their grandparents' for breakfast on school days. Late afternoons, Annie's dad picks the kids up at school and drives them to their piano lessons and basketball practices. Tuesdays, her mom fixes dinner in her crockpot for Annie's family.

Intermediate distances are manageable. Sharon takes her son and daughter to her parents' farm four hours' drive away on the Loup River in the Sandhills. The children gather eggs, play in the river, and help with animals. All their relatives are around. In town everyone knows their grandparents, and they praise and tease the grandchildren. Sharon's son cries when he has to return to Lincoln.

The farther the physical distance, though, the harder it is to keep families connected. There are ways to surmount distance problems; it needn't be terrible, but staying connected requires conscious work. Phone calls and letters help. E-mail helps, and many of the old learn about computers so that they can stay in touch with grandchildren. However, without proximity, the precious dailiness of relationship is harder to maintain.

I have one friend who tapes herself reading stories and sends a new tape to her faraway grandson every week. Another couple I know bought a cabin on a lake so that their children would have a great summer home to visit. Another friend's parents take a big trip with each of their grandchildren when the grandchild turns ten.

One of the ironies of our times is that because adults are living longer, more people have grandparents. However, these grandparents are farther away and play a less significant role in the lives of kids. My friend Jim wrote me about how important his parents are to his children. He pointed out that one implication of having children late in life is that children have less time with their grandparents. Because he and his wife had kids early, their children had known all of their grandparents and great-grandparents. If they had waited even ten years, their children would have lost thirty years of grandparenting time. He felt that their children were "rich in grandparents."

## GLORIA *(age 75)*
*"We didn't have the gangs, the guns,*
*and the drugs. Neighbors looked out*
*for each other, and families were closer.*
*Most children knew right from wrong."*

I VISITED GLORIA at the home she shares with her daughter, Thea, and grandson, Ricky. She is young-looking, with pretty gold teeth. She moves gracefully and probably could have been an athlete or dancer if she'd had the chance when she was young. We drank tea in the living room, which had a picture of a Mount Rushmore with heroic African Americans instead of presidents. A hutch in the corner was filled with her grandson's sports trophies, and a white Bible sat on the coffee table.

Ten years before, Gloria's husband had died of lung cancer, and two years before, Thea divorced her husband. Gloria invited Thea to move in. They have more money this way, and Gloria can watch Ricky after school and drive him to his practices if Thea is working. If Thea has to work on Sundays, Gloria takes Ricky to church. She makes sure he says his prayers at night. Gloria laughed. "They don't mind my cooking, either."

Gloria was born in St. Louis in a two-family flat. Her grandmother lived on the ground level, and her family lived upstairs. She was born at home, the second oldest of seven kids. She described her family as close. Her father worked at a foundry, and her mother took in "wealthy Caucasian men's" washing. She was proud of her family. They always had the radio on, but they weren't allowed to listen to "Amos and Andy," which her parents considered a disgrace. Her dad loved the news, and Saturday morning, Gloria listened to the Metropolitan Opera. Her dad had worked to register black voters—very dangerous in that time and place. Gloria said, "I get angry when people don't vote. They don't know their history."

Gloria was a good student who got a scholarship to a state university. She was the only black person in her Spanish class, and she had a racist teacher who wouldn't assign her a conversation partner. White guys harassed her. She considered dropping out of school, but a group of black students met in the student union and supported one another. These students didn't protest anything because they were fearful of retaliation in that pre–Civil Rights era. She met Richard in this group. He was a business major already supporting his mother and two sisters.

Gloria and Richard married and had two kids. Their son is a doctor on the East Coast, and Thea, her baby, is a nurse. "Richard made a decent living," Gloria said. "But he was a good father, too." One time a young guy asked Richard what was the most important thing about business, and he answered, "Family."

Just then the school bus stopped in front of the house, and Ricky jumped down. He was a husky kid in a middle-school letter jacket and expensive basketball shoes. When he came in, he smiled shyly at me and hugged his grandmother. Gloria tousled his hair and said, "How you doing, baby?"

"Remember, I've got practice at four-thirty."

Gloria said, "I know, I know. You get your homework done and I'll take you. Now, what have you got to show me?"

She looked over his school papers carefully, praising the good ones and worrying over a C in geography. "Now, I told you to study that map before the test. What do you have to work on today?"

Somewhat reluctantly, Ricky pulled out a page of math problems and his geography book. "We're supposed to read the next chapter."

Gloria said, "I want you to look up all your wrong answers and correct them for me."

Ricky said, "The teacher didn't say we had to."

Gloria announced, "I say you have to. Do you think we just care about your grades around here? We want you to learn this stuff."

Ricky sighed, and Gloria sent him off. "Get yourself some of those lemon bars and milk, and then get to work."

While Ricky was in the kitchen, Gloria told me about her own schooling. Their house was a long way from the streetcar line and the black children's school, and as she and her siblings walked to school, bullies beat them up. The schoolhouse was built by the parents, a small unheated place that met for six months a year, while the white children's school met for nine. They got the white kids' books after they were worn out.

Gloria said, "My family valued education. It was the only way up. Ricky is going to be a good student, no matter what. Schoolwork comes first around here."

I asked if she thought it was easier for black kids now. "We didn't have the gangs, the guns, and the drugs," she admitted. "Neighbors looked out for each other, and families were closer. Most children knew right from wrong. However, our daddies could be killed for any little reason. Ricky has more luxuries than we had. Those shoes he has on cost more than my daddy made in a month."

She paused and sipped her tea. "The laws are better now, but attitudes are the same. Whites still feel superior to blacks. Ricky is still going to have to work twice as hard as a white child to make it."

Ricky came in with a math question, and Gloria helped him figure it out. She said, "I'm lucky I can help him with his homework. Some of my friends weren't able to get the schooling I did." She patted his shoulder. "His grandfather would be proud of him."

Gloria looked at the clock. "I hate to hurry you, but I'd better go supervise my boy. He's got some serious work to do before basketball practice."

RICKY IS LUCKY to have Gloria, but when children are not so lucky, there are alternatives. It's never too late to find a grandparent. The Oneida Indians have a simple adoption plan. If a relative dies, one adopts a new person to fill that role. As I interviewed people for this book, I found some new grandparents for myself. Through his church, my nephew met a grandfather, who now takes him to wood-carving lessons and bluegrass festivals.

Children may connect with the chess player next door, or the man who does carpentry work in his garage. I know one woman who met a grandmother by literally crashing into her during rush-hour traffic. As the two women exchanged insurance information and addresses, they realized they lived near each other. The older woman sized up the situation: a young, rushed, working mother with three kids in the car. She asked, "Do you have family in our town?" When the young mother said no, the older lady said, "Let's get acquainted. Bring the children by tomorrow."

Grandparents also can be inherited through marriage. I was fortunate to inherit my husband's maternal grandmother, who for twenty years until she died was my only grandparent. They can be hired sometimes, as my parents hired our housekeeper, Carrie. They can be found in churches and schools.

## Foster Grandparents

THE FOSTER GRANDPARENT program illustrates the kinds of things the old bring to the young. I observed this program at an inner-city school on a rainy morning in March. The coordinator introduced me to the Murrows, foster grandparents who came twice a week to work with two different sets of third-graders. The Murrows were in their seventies, gray-haired, and casually dressed in slacks and sweatshirts. Mr. Murrow was a little nervous about being observed. "I'm a retired bus driver, not a professor," he said. "I hope you'll think I do okay."

Mrs. Murrow told the coordinator that they would come the next day to work with "their girls" but then they were going to the Ozarks for a dog-wood festival. She asked permission to send the kids postcards, and also to give them their Easter candy early.

As we walked down to the classroom, Mrs. Murrow told me, "We get the ones who have difficult home situations and need a little extra TLC at school. These kids can be a handful, but they are fun."

When we got to the classroom, we were immediately surrounded by children who were calling out, "Grandpa, look at this," or, "Grandma, read me a story." Mrs. Murrow explained that to make everyone more relaxed, the children were taught to call them Grandpa and Grandma.

Dominique, Mrs. Murrow's Tuesday girl, grabbed on to her grandma's leg and wouldn't let go. She wore flowered stretch pants and a teddy bear T-shirt with a hole in its shoulder. She asked, "Are you coming back for me?" Mrs. Murrow hugged her and said, "Today's Monday, but I wish I could come every day for you."

The teacher switched the lights on and off as a signal for the kids to return to their seats, and reluctantly the children moved away. Mrs. Murrow walked Dominique to her desk and patted her on the shoulder.

We walked to the media center with Connor, a small boy with uncombed hair and a bruise on his cheek, and Dominique's brother Devon, a tall, dark-haired boy with bright eyes. Mr. Murrow would help Connor with reading while Mrs. Murrow worked with Devon on his owl report.

First, though, Mrs. Murrow introduced me to the boys, both of whom mumbled hello and looked at their shoes. She said kindly, "Here's what to do when you are introduced. You look the person in the eye, shake their hand, and say, 'It's nice to meet you.'" The boys nodded, and she continued. "Practice with this nice lady." They looked me in the eye, shook hands in turn, and said, "Nice to meet you." Mrs. Murrow praised their good manners.

Connor and Mr. Murrow sat down at a child-sized table, and Connor opened up a book on volcanoes. They read together slowly. With each syllable, Connor pounded his pencil against his cheek.

Mrs. Murrow helped Devon get organized for his report. She said, "Let's think this through. What will people want to know about owls?" Devon wrote, "Owls have short beaks. They eat rats and mice." Mrs. Murrow solemnly said, "Good points." He wrote with a stubby pencil on a Big Chief tablet, and his face almost touched the paper. "You're on the right track," Mrs. Murrow said. "Keep going."

Connor and Mr. Murrow read about volcanoes from the past. Once Mr. Murrow interrupted to exclaim, "Isn't it sad that the people who didn't make it to the boats were buried?" Devon asked how to print a little "b." Meanwhile, Connor strayed a little. He asked about Mr. Murrow's liver spots, and Mr. Murrow answered, "You get these for your sixtieth birthday present."

Once Mr. Murrow admonished, "Keep your eyes open so you can see." When Connor said, "I want to draw a monster," Mr. Murrow said, "Wait till we finish this page." He had his arm around Connor and watched patiently while he drew, commenting on each new detail. He laughed when Connor drew liver spots on the monster, and Connor smiled sheepishly.

Devon's report proceeded. "Now, how did you know that?" Mrs. Murrow often asked in admiration. When Devon drifted into a paragraph on dinosaurs, she gently reminded him that he was writing about owls. Connor finished his picture and handed it to Mr. Murrow. He said he'd take it home and put it in his collection of papers from Connor. They read from a book on zoos. Mr. Murrow asked if Connor had ever been to a zoo, and he shook his head no. Mrs. Murrow informed both boys about proper zoo etiquette. She explained how you mustn't feed or tease the animals or try to touch them. When Mr. Murrow said perhaps they could take a field trip to the zoo the last day of school, Connor inhaled sharply at the thought. Devon's bright eyes widened, and he nodded in agreement with the plan.

Connor read some more, and Mr. Murrow said, "You're getting good at sounding out words." Mrs. Murrow helped Devon put his report on the computer. When the bell rang, Mrs. Murrow explained to both boys about their trip to Missouri. She had them write down their addresses and promised they each would get a postcard that showed the dogwoods in bloom. Devon asked if dogwood flowers looked like dogs. "Ummm," she said, "good question. You decide when you get the postcard."

Mr. Murrow told the boys to reach into the grocery sack and pull out their Easter baskets. Mrs. Murrow warned them to put the baskets in their lockers so that they wouldn't hurt other kids' feelings. She told Devon to make sure that his sister knew she would get one the next day. The baskets were about the size of a small shoebox and decorated with shiny green paper and bunny stickers. Both boys held their baskets gingerly, as if they were precious objects. Connor asked, "Is this all just for me?"

The Murrows had their arms on the boys' shoulders when they walked them toward their rooms. They stopped at their lockers first, and then walked them to the door of their classroom. Mr. Murrow said, "Watch for our postcards from Missouri." Mrs. Murrow asked, "Do you know where Missouri is? We'd better come in and show you on the map."

# CHAPTER 10

# Building a Village

*You don't give back to the same people who give to you.*
*Not at all. You give to different people and they in turn*
*will give to someone entirely different. Not you. That's*
*the sloppy economy of gift and love.*

—LORRIE MOORE,
*Who Will Run the Frog Hospital?*

*Time is everything and nothing.*
*We are all connected and we are all alone.*

—BILL KLOEFKORN

AS I SAID EARLIER, THE LAKOTA BELIEVE THAT IF THE OLD DO
not stay connected to the young, the culture will disintegrate. We are seeing
signs of this disintegration in our culture. Children watch television instead
of hearing stories. They are frightened and unruly, numb from hurry and
overstimulation. Teenagers run in unsupervised gangs. Parents feel isolated and overwhelmed, and elders go days without speaking to anyone. No
generation's needs are truly met. Segregated societies are intellectually
stagnant and emotionally poisoned. Only when all ages are welcome into
the great hoop of life can a culture be a healthy one.

We all are more alike than we are different. We all want the Five R's—respect, results, relaxation, realization, and relationships. Our challenge is to create a culture that allows our elders to have these things. We need to help the old heal from their many traumas and grow their souls. We need to understand time-zone issues, to translate across language systems, and to know that at a deep-structure level, we all are one.

Our elders have special needs and special gifts. If we will slow down and listen, we can learn from the old. They can tell us stories about communal living and remind us what human communities can offer. Freud said that the goal of psychotherapy is the return of the repressed. Ironically, what we have repressed most in this last half of our benighted century is our deep need to be part of a community, to belong to a group of people who know one another well.

As I said earlier, without community there is no morality. We behave well around people who matter. Our elders can help us reestablish human connections to our neighbors. They have the collective wisdom we need to rebuild our villages.

## Cinco de Mayo

ON MAY 5, I observed kids from an after-school program visiting their "partners" at Shady Lane. It was a gorgeous day. April rains had left the grass green and lush. Crab apple and pear trees and lilacs and magnolias bloomed. I walked into the lobby of the rest home, past an aviary with finches, canaries, and lovebirds. Some residents were gathered around a woman and her cocker spaniel from the "Pets Are Saints" program. Nan, the activities director, led me back to a sunny room filled with books, music, and art supplies.

A group of elders waited there for the children to arrive. Max, an old farmer so thin he looked like an insect, sat by the door watching for Mandy. Just that morning, Max had fallen and hurt his back, and Nan had given him a shoulder massage. She called for a medical evaluation, saying over the phone, "Max never complains, but he's very tense. I don't like how he's moving."

I was introduced to Charlotte, a 100-year-old former schoolteacher; to Lillian, a round woman in purple velour who used to be head cook at a fraternity; and to Susie, who had wild white hair, and earrings shaped like bingo cards. Nan said of Susie, "When she came here, she wouldn't participate in any activities, but when she met the children, she got involved." Finally there was Doogie, who had worked as a stock person at a grocery store for twenty-five years. His eyes never left the window as he watched for Ashley, now a fifth-grader but his friend since she was in kindergarten.

Because of the Cinco de Mayo celebration at their school, the kids were a little delayed. While we waited, Nan told me that when the kids first came, they were nervous but that she explained to them that most of the residents were somebody's grandparents. She asked each child to give his or her coat to a resident to watch. That got them started with a physical connection and a person to trust.

Some bonding just happened. Nan pointed to Lillian and laughed. "She and her partner, Tania, are two peas in a pod." Lillian said, "We get along just fine. We understand each other."

Nan said that the biggest problems for her programs were logistical. The average age of the residents was eighty-five, and they were often ill or at doctors' appointments. A resident might miss a few weeks and return eager to see her partner, only to hear that the child had a dental appointment. "Sometimes," Nan said, "there are tears when the kids don't show."

Strong relationships were sometimes disrupted. Brandon's mother had two jobs and a boyfriend with a drinking problem. Brandon was a chubby kid with a repaired cleft palate. As Nan put it, "He's needy and squirrelly and the other kids steer clear of him." But for the past three years he had bonded with Charlotte. He called her Sunday nights before he went to bed, and he visited her over the holidays. Nan said, "Charlotte has really nurtured this boy." However, at the end of the school year, Brandon's mother and her boyfriend were moving to Oklahoma. Brandon would have three more visits with Charlotte and then say good-bye forever.

We heard the kids before we saw them, laughing and talking in the hall. They entered the room and headed straight for their partners. Tania, a round African-American girl with ankle bracelets and multicolored sandals, ran over to hug Lillian. Ashley, a tall quiet girl with swinging blond hair and a dimple in her chin, smiled at Doogie. Brandon approached Charlotte, and she gave him a hug. "My boy is here at last." He pressed against her wheelchair, looking very relieved to see her. Chad, in khaki shorts and a "Get Pumped" T-shirt, told Max that Mandy couldn't come today, then said hi to his partner, Susie. Nan said, "We're going out for miniature golf. Max, come with us and enjoy the other children."

These children understood how the walkers and wheelchairs worked, and they knew to move slowly and help their partners over rough patches of carpet. Chad handed Susie her cane, and Brandon wheeled Charlotte outside. Nan helped Max, who looked disconsolate and in pain.

Outside, all the kids except Brandon set up the miniature golf game under a big sycamore. They looked happy to be useful and doing things for adults that those adults couldn't do for themselves. Brandon rolled Charlotte into the sun and put a coverlet over her knees. "Go play with the others," she suggested. "I think I'll stay with you," he responded.

Nan announced the rules: "The lawn is uneven, so hold on to your partner when you're off the cement. Sit down if you get tired or dizzy. You don't need to keep score. The main thing is have fun."

Ashley and Doogie went first. Soon Ashley yelled out, "Doogie made a hole in one." She shot next, and Doogie grinned at her good aim. Lillian took Tania's hand, and they walked onto the grass. As Tania told her about science class, Lillian said, "Oh, my heavens on earth, that's incredible." Tania said, "I don't know how to play golf," and Lillian said, "I don't either. Who cares?" They smacked away at their balls.

Brandon told Charlotte that he'd been having stomachaches. His guinea pig wasn't doing well. He'd hoped she was pregnant because she was so fat, but now his mom thought his guinea pig might have a tumor. Charlotte listened, patted his arm, and clucked sympathetically when he paused. When Brandon finished his story, Charlotte asked, "Have you called a vet?"

Susie and Chad were the last pair out. Chad held Susie's cane when she putted. I noticed they both had wild hair, only Chad's was brown and punk-styled. I heard him say gently, "Come on, Susie, you can do it. That's a good one." Lillian showed Tania her nails and explained she'd just had a manicure and pedicure. She examined Tania's nails and said they had potential. Susie told Chad they made a good team. There were cheers when anyone had a hole in one. Many people watched the game from inside the building.

An orderly came out for Max, who sat with Charlotte and Brandon. Max said, "I want to see how these kids do," but he was persuaded to go in for an X ray. Max moved like the last grasshopper after the first frost, slowly and with great effort.

The game continued in a nonlinear manner. The elders held on to their partners; the kids moved slowly. Everyone praised good shots lavishly and laughed at bloopers. Once Lillian almost fell down, and Tania and Nan rushed to hold her up. Doogie beamed proudly when Ashley announced, "Doogie has made three holes in one." Lillian asked Tania if she had naturally curly hair, and when she shook her head yes, Lillian said, "The Lord has been good to you."

Charlotte asked Brandon to wheel her out of the breeze. She told him about when she was little and her family moved from the farm into town. She said, "I was afraid those town kids would think I was a country bumpkin."

Ashley found a foot-tall dandelion, and Lillian said admiringly, "That could go in the *Guinness Book of World Records*." Lillian called the group's attention to an announcement from Tania, who said proudly that her class had been selected by NASA as a signature class. They all would sign their names on a piece of paper that would go into outer space with John Glenn.

The residents oohed and ahhed at this news. Ashley and Doogie sat down on a bench to rest.

I visited with Nan, Charlotte and Brandon. Charlotte's granddaughter was a hostess for a cable TV home show, and Charlotte asked Brandon if he'd watched this week. Brandon said her granddaughter had done a good job. Nan told me that Susie's son was a regular on a soap opera and that Max's cousin's daughter was married to a man who raced in the Indy 500. She said, "We're all family here, and we're proud of our stars."

Doogie and Ashley played on, but Lillian and Tania were holding hands and talking under the tree. Lillian was telling her a recipe for chili for one hundred. Susie asked Chad what "get pumped" meant, and he said, "You know, it's like 'Get beefed.'" Susie persevered, "What does that mean? Eat beef?" Ashley and Doogie were examining a gopher hole by the sidewalk. I was struck by how kind the children were to their partners, how attentive and careful they were of their bodies and their feelings.

Nan brought out raspberry lemonade in Styrofoam cups. Brandon got cups for himself and for Charlotte, who thanked him by saying, "You are a mighty fine boy." Doogie watched proudly as Ashley chatted with the others. Lillian said, "We want a cooking project next time." Susie returned to the chairs a little winded, leaning heavily on her cane, and Chad helped her sit down. Nan said to Susie, "You'll sleep like a log tonight." As Tania and Ashley handed out cookies, Tania said enticingly, "Don't you want to spoil your supper?" Charlotte took a cookie but handed it to Brandon. "You eat it for me, sweetie."

Nan told me that she came to work at Shady Lane ten years before during a family crisis. "I was one of the walking wounded. This place patched me up." She said that many of the staff would say the same thing. "They get what they need working here. The old keep them calm and sane." I reflected on the irony that the old, with all their loss and trauma, with so many injuries of their own, end up being the great healers in our culture. Nan nodded. "The old and the young. They keep the rest of us going."

She told me about a university program that brought foreign students in, ostensibly to practice their English. She said, "Really, though, these students come from cultures where the old are important. They miss their grandparents, and they talk for hours to their mentors. They hold their hands and bring them little presents. She said the same of foreign workers at the home. "They don't say much, but I can tell they are horrified by how Americans treat their parents and grandparents."

I sat in the late-afternoon sun and watched this group. For the first time, watching this nonlinear golf game where no one kept score, I understood something important about the old. They are about process, not product. As opposed to the rest of us, who have been socialized to keep our eyes on the prize, for the old the prize is the moment. They know that nothing really lasts, not lows or highs, successes or failures. All they have in the end are memories of good moments.

End points held no allure for this group. For the residents, the end point is death, and most were in no hurry to get there. They liked to linger where they were. To fall in love with the process is really the great wisdom of this life stage. The secret of life is to appreciate, or, as Ram Dass said, to "be here now." It is to "hold on to your partner; sit down when you are tired or dizzy. You don't need to keep score; the main thing is to have fun."

The bus driver came back, and the children said good-bye. Nan announced, "Next week we'll make homemade ice cream. Lillian and Tania will be in charge." Lillian and Tania embraced, and Lillian said, "Write out your name real pretty. Who knows what kind of outer-space creatures will see it?" Susie told Chad, "Get beefed this week." Doogie smiled broadly at Ashley and said, "Don't do anything I wouldn't do." All the kids except Brandon headed for the bus. Brandon stayed behind, hugging Charlotte and not letting go. "There, there," she said. "You call my former student this week. He's a good vet. Tell him to send me the bill. Things will work out." Brandon stayed until Nan gently pried him away. Charlotte patted his arm. "You are my boy. Don't you forget it."

\* \* \*

OVER AND OVER I've met elders who have helped children and adults. I think of Wilhelmina and my client Erin, who had been arrested for possession of marijuana and sentenced to mandatory community service. Her first assignment was to help weatherize Wilhelmina's house. While Erin worked on Wilhelmina's place, the two of them got acquainted. Wilhelmina didn't do anything particularly special, she just had time. Unlike Erin's mother, Wilhelmina wasn't overburdened with crises of her own. She asked about school and listened to Erin's problems with friends and teachers. She taught her the names of the birds in her backyard and sent some asparagus and rhubarb home with her. When Erin moved on to another house, Wilhelmina encouraged her to keep coming by. Two years later, Erin is still dropping in and she hasn't had any more legal troubles.

As my friend Carl said, "Old folks will mellow us out and teach us what we need to know." Robert Bly writes eloquently about how much young men need older men—to show them how to be men, to listen, and to talk. In a nation of fatherless boys, older men can become their "good fathers," who teach them how to knot a tie, fish, work on a car, or throw a ball. Old gardeners teach young people to grow things, and old cooks share their recipes. Older musicians, such as Jane Jarvis, Benny Waters, or Claude Williams, teach the young the old songs.

## Rose's Party

THE LIGHTNING BUGS, a trio that sings Mills Brothers music, performed at a party in honor of Rose and Bud Chapman. It was a Saturday night in July, and the host was Ben, a musician with the Self-Righteous Brothers. He was young and handsome, with an energetic wife and a baby daughter, Marina.

When we arrived, the place was packed with young musicians and children. Everyone was eating pizza and appetizers and drinking beer or lemonade. A sign over the mantel read, "To Bud and Rose, Two Charming People Living Life to the Fullest." Rose's old trap set and bass fiddle were on display in the corner. Ben had gone over to their house to answer an ad he saw in the newspaper for these instruments, and, as he put it, "Rose and Bud charmed me so much that I wanted to throw them a party."

Rose was born in 1907 in a clay adobe home, the thirteenth of fourteen children. Her musical career began in 1928 when her music teacher announced she was a natural and invited her to play in his band. She dressed up in a tuxedo and played as a man. Over the years she played with the Golden Slipper Orchestra, The Ingenues, Bob Rock and His Musical Pebbles, and Bonnie Krejci and the Melody Maids. After she married Bud, she asked him to come along and help load equipment. She formed her own all-girl band, which traveled around the country in a thirty-passenger bus. The promo pictures were a history lesson in fashion over the century. Rose appeared in a white cowgirl suit with a hat that had her name written on the brim. She played bass in a strapless glittery white dress with a full skirt, and in a bright red sundress with staves and musical notes embroidered in silver on the hem and bodice.

Rose and Bud sat on the couch in the place of honor. The Lightning Bugs played "In a Mellow Tone," "Cab Driver," and "Across the Alley from the Alamo." They played "Tennessee Waltz," a song they learned because older people requested it so often.

Marina, in black-and-white overalls, squealed for joy with the music. Rose clapped along to "Jambalaya" and requested "Sentimental Journey." Ben played along on Rose's old ukulele. Periodically someone would interject a story about Rose. While Ben's mother-in-law took pictures, the Bugs played a polka medley. The room buzzed with polka fans of every age. Rose lit up, and Ben said, "I'll bet you've played a million polkas." She nodded in agreement. Bud tapped his toes.

The Bugs ended their show with "Yellow Bird" and everyone had cake in Rose's honor. Rose had stopped playing professionally at age eighty-two and she missed it. She said, "Playing music always gave me a push." As we left she smiled broadly and said, "Oh, it was a beautiful party, a marvelous party." She looked at Ben and his friends. "We sure hit the right boys."

* * *

ONE OF OUR MOST BEAUTIFUL STORIES is the Christmas story. It says, in the cold and dark of winter, a child is born. With this child comes light, warmth, and great riches. Babies have an amazing power to comfort and heal. Once I was in the Manor Rest Home when a visitor showed up with a baby. She was immediately surrounded by residents. Even people who had seemed comatose woke up to watch the baby. People who hadn't gotten out of bed in a week suddenly were ringing for a wheelchair. A group of residents with infectious illnesses pressed their faces against a window just to see the baby.

One time after I had worked for many hours, speaking and afterward signing books, I was approached by a mother and a newborn baby. She had noticed how tired I looked and thought I might like to hold her daughter. As I took her beautiful daughter into my arms, I felt health and energy surge through me. I felt refreshed—the way I feel after a swim or a sunset.

With children, the old can repeople their lives and fill the empty places in their hearts. They can get practical help and connections to new points of view. We all benefit from having kids around. I heard an NPR story about a woman who took her infant to work with her. She was with the forest service in an area where day care for babies was unavailable. The woman said the arrangement was good for her and the baby, but also for the office as a whole. She said that when her group was in a tense meeting, the baby would usually burp, poop, or make google eyes and everyone would laugh, breaking the tension in the room and putting everything back in perspective. She said that since her baby had been coming to work, office morale had been higher. Her boss agreed.

Many different groups are catching on to the importance of intergenerational bonding. They are realizing the synergy that comes from combining different ages. Churches, increasingly, are forming "families" that cut across generational lines. It's a much better way of organizing people into groups than is age. One church in Kansas has potluck dinners every week with formed families of all ages. A Suzuki piano teacher I know recently started an intergenerational music theory group, and she told me that the members love it. A new energy erupts when she puts ten-year-olds with fifty-year-olds and fourteen-year-olds. They laugh and talk. She can hardly get them out the door.

Children often need some orientation to the old. For example, teenagers may need to be told that loud music makes hearing speech hard for people with hearing aids. They converse better in quiet environments. With a little exposure and education, children rapidly become relaxed. I think of how much my daughter liked playing her violin at the Manor. And when my mother spent her last sad year in the hospital, Sara would play her violin there on Saturday nights. Old patients would ask to be wheeled down to my mother's room so they could hear "the little girl play the pretty music."

A teacher told me a story about "Bloody Mary," an old lady who was much tormented by local children. Night after night, her house was egged and her trees covered with toilet paper. Alone and frightened, she shot a boy who was breaking into her home as a prank. Although she was found to have acted in self-defense, her home was burned down by outraged people. Even though Bloody Mary died in the early 1990s, local children still regarded her place as haunted. They made up horrible stories about her to frighten one another.

This teacher had her students do research on Mary. They spent a semester interviewing people who really knew her and reading her letters and the articles from the paper. By the end of the semester, many of the children felt close to this sad woman. They built a small memorial garden in her honor.

## Golden View

ON A MAY MORNING I drove to a small town to visit Golden View. The drive was relaxing, past abandoned farmsteads with sagging barns and irises still blooming around the foundations, past green fields of wheat and neat white farmhouses. I passed a freshly mowed meadow and breathed deeply. Meadowlarks sang from the fenceposts. Just beyond a cemetery, Golden View lay on a ridge with a big blue morning sky be-hind it.

Golden View had a residential-care unit, a nursing home, and a day-care center with twelve babies and forty children altogether. Janet, the recreation director, took me to the day-care center first. Four toddlers in dresses as bright as spring flowers were being loaded into their stroller for outdoor play. Janet explained that the children would be in a courtyard surrounded by their elders.

Janet said that Golden View was a community. Babies were in the day-care center, then they came for after-school and summer programs when they were in elementary school, and worked as volunteers here in their teens. As young adults, many returned to work at Golden View. Some of the day-care children's parents worked here, and they dropped by often to play with their kids.

The children grew up with old people and were not afraid of them. They were educated to be polite and empathic. When the children reached school age, Janet put cotton in their ears so they would know how things sounded without good hearing. She also had them walk around blindfolded so they got a sense for the importance of eyes. Janet laughed and said certain things were easy. Children liked to run the electric wheelchairs and watch people put in their dentures and hearing aids. The old liked to give treats to the children and to hold them on their laps.

Janet pointed to Regan, one of the flower girls in the stroller, and said, "Her great-grandmother is a resident. You'll see them together soon." A parade of toddlers had formed, and they were marched, singing, into the courtyard. We wheeled the strollerful of flower girls behind them.

Outside, a row of silver-haired ladies and one old man in overalls waited in the sun for the children. Janet and I unbuckled the toddlers from the stroller, and Regan ran to her waving great-grandmother. A worker handed Aletha a whimpering baby. Aletha said, "You don't know me very well. Let's play patty-cake."

The children meandered around the sunny courtyard while the residents watched and laughed. One lady was dozing but awakened when a boy in a cowboy hat rode his bronco right into her leg. Some kids tossed and caught beach balls with the residents. One two-year-old boy, Derek, walked along the line of wheelchairs, solemnly shaking everyone's hand.

The staff helped the children onto and off laps and made sure the residents were warm. A nurse's aide came out from the nursing home. She hugged her grandmother and picked up her son to nurse. The cowboy was now a car, walking backward and sucking his thumb. Aletha joked, "He's going in reverse."

A staff member changed Derek's diaper on the grass. While Regan tried to eat a petunia, Miranda, a one-year-old in a white playsuit, crawled on Miriam's lap. The flower girls chased a butterfly, and a baby sucked her toes under a sycamore tree. The older man, who wasn't very alert, saw my big black purse on the ground and shouted, "That dog looks dead to me."

One lady, covered with a handmade quilt, held a baby and cooed, "I'm not gonna give you back. You can sleep on my pillow." Her neighbor said, "The parents will be sad." She responded, "They can make another one." Everyone laughed, and the baby burbled contentedly.

The residents noticed who had new shoes and hairstyles. They noted small changes in the children, such as who was walking or speaking better, and who had a new tooth. The children roamed freely and happily, aware they were being watched by many pairs of eyes. Every now and then, they would stop and look at an adult, who would blow them a kiss or say a kind word of encouragement. They would beam and carry on. Regan wandered away from her great-grandmother but came back for a hug every few minutes. The mother returned to work, and Miranda asked Miriam to tell her a story.

Time moved slowly. The old man gave the cowboy a high five. The flower girls rolled beach balls at one another. Aletha said, "We're impressed with our children. We've helped them grow up. They are much better behaved than most young children."

I left at lunch time and retraced my route past the little farms into the city. I smelled the fresh hay and heard a meadowlark sing. In Lincoln, the sky was still blue but smaller and obscured by buildings and city haze. I drove past malls and liquor stores, Quick Stops and condos. Already I missed the quiet, slow pace of the place I'd spent my morning.

Golden View is an example of a creative solution to the problem of connecting generations and building community in the 1990s. As a culture, we have difficult problems to solve. And as modern medicine allows more of us to live into old-old age, these problems will multiply. We cannot possibly solve these problems if we are xenophobic. We must work together as a people to build the kinds of rituals, communities, institutions, and language that allow us to love and care for one another, to cross the time zones and be one country.

As I suggested earlier, we need new words, like *interdependency* or *mutuality*, which take the sting out of the old-old stage of growth. Good mental health for all of us is not a matter of being independent or dependent, but rather of accepting the stage we are in with grace and dignity.

Words of address make community. *Elder* is a much better word than *elderly*, but we have even better words, words more sacred to most Americans—*grandmother* and *grandfather*.

As a culture we need to examine our language and our deep-seated biases against the old. In short, we need a more user-friendly culture for our elders. We need to change everything from the lighting in restaurants to the print size of books, from how we build housing developments to how we structure Sunday school classes. A user-friendly culture requires us to reorganize the medical system to once again give the old relationships with their doctors, and to create better public transportation and better media.

## Jazz in June

JAZZ IN JUNE is another program that allows people of all generations to connect. Every Tuesday night in June, our city has a jazz concert on the university campus. Hundreds of people walk through the sculpture gardens, past the Henry Moore statues, goldfish pools, and flowers to the open space by our modern art gallery. Families spread blankets and open hampers of picnic foods. Vendors sell T-shirts, CDs, and cookies.

People of all ages sit on blankets or lawn chairs. Urban jazz aficionados share turf with guys in seed caps. Children of all sizes and colors run and dance among the adults. An old gentleman in a wool suit walks his cocker spaniel to a sunny spot. A young woman with a spiked haircut and a blue tattoo walks her ferret on a leash. A man in black boots and a turquoise cowboy suit furtively smokes a cigar under a crab apple tree. While two women in straw hats and summer dresses share cheese cubes and wine, an in-line skater with green hair chats with my bald-headed neighbor, Ron. Baby carriers and wheelchairs line up by the water. Teenagers Rollerblade past middle-aged women knitting. A skateboarder almost collides with a birdwatcher.

While Ed Love leads his group in "Strike Up the Band," a gray-haired grandmother in sweats plays cards with her two granddaughters, one with braids, the other with a long ponytail. They are at that lovely prepuberty stage, full of zest and sparkle. Radio-show host Scott Young talks on a cellular phone while Frisbees whiz around him.

The star of the night is a toddler in a yellow sunsuit with blond curls and brown eyes. She is following a white kitty, tippy-toed and unsteady, but calling out with delight. Later she boogies to the music and, still later, she runs over to the old gentleman in the wool suit and plops onto his lap. Her parents spend most of the night retrieving her.

The band plays a Charlie Mingus number called "Remember Rockefeller at Attica." One grandmother brings her two grandchildren near the stage. The girl is chubby, with dimples everywhere, and wears her hair in cornrows; the boy wears blue and is very lively. Grandmother hands them jars of bubble-making soap, and they blow bubbles and chase them through the crowd.

The bubbles float over the relaxed, happy people. They are outdoors hearing good music, surrounded by beauty and by their neighbors, a perfect nineties community. Bubbles float over the knitters and the card players, over the white kitten, the old gentleman, and the wheelchairs. Bubbles float over the women with the straw hats and the girl with the ferret. A big bubble hits the toddler in the sunsuit right in the face, but she doesn't cry. She is grooving to the music and the crowd.

*I am one more leaf on the great human tree.*

—PABLO NERUDA

My life is richer because of these last years with my elders. Writing this book, I learned the critical difference between young-old and old-old age. I saw the effects of stress and loss, and I learned the importance of connections and control. I witnessed the incredible calculus of old age—that as more is taken, there is more love for what remains. The great lesson to be learned in this last developmental stage is acceptance. That lesson well learned brings serenity. In the end, everything is about love.

In the houses of all five of my aunts, I listened to family stories, looked at pictures, and ate their home-cooked meals. In their faces and gestures I saw the faces and gestures of my children. As I talked to them, I better understood my own parents and I learned about myself. I understood more of our country's history and I received lessons in how to age.

The people I interviewed taught me what I most needed to know. My friend Sally gave me hope for my own old age, and Effie showed me the therapeutic value of poetry. Alma showed me the joy that can come from a life lived in the service of others. She helped me see clearly the limits of a psychology based on individual achievement at the cost of relationships. George taught me about the strength and compassion of a person well planted in both the pre- and post-Freudian cultures. With his life, he demonstrated an admirable synthesis of old and new ideas about mental health.

My clients taught me that my generation does have knowledge that we can give our elders. I have taken great pleasure in helping my older clients work through some of their sorrows. However, most of the lessons were from them to me. Gladys taught me about courage under pressure. Charles and Nell showed me how to rescue a child on the edge of disaster.

Before the pioneers came, the Native Americans of the Great Plains survived the harsh winters by having grandparents and grandchildren sleep beside each other. That kept both generations from freezing to death. That is a good metaphor for what the generations do for each other. We keep each other from freezing. The old need our heat, and we need their light.

To learn from the old we must love them, and not just in the abstract but in the flesh, beside us in our homes, businesses, churches, and schools. We want the generations mixed together so that the young can give the old joy and the old can give the young wisdom. As we get older, we sense more the importance of connecting old to young, family member to family member, neighbor to neighbor, and even the living to the dead. In connection is truth, beauty, and ultimately salvation. Connection is what makes life bearable for us humans.

# Surullinen Tango

I AWOKE THINKING OF MY FATHER, FRANK BRAY, WHO WOULD HAVE been eighty years old today. It had been thirty years since he'd had his first stroke, twenty-one years since he'd died. I thought about how sad his life was, how short and filled with his father's insanity, his childhood poverty, his family's shame and chaos, the war, his dislocation from his beloved Ozarks, and, at the end of his life, those crippled, half-blind, brain-damaged years. He lived a lonely, restless life and never found a real home.

My morning was busy. I drank coffee with my husband, went running, and baked a pie with Aunt Agnes's home-canned mincemeat. I fixed lunch for my son and his girlfriend, who came by in the early afternoon. Zeke had taken Jamie to Wilderness Park and proposed to her in a wild, extravagant Frank Bray kind of way, and she had accepted. We hugged one another, and I took their picture. I cried for them, for the bigness of it all, and for my father, who on his eightieth birthday wouldn't know that his first grandson had proposed.

Later my daughter Sara and I walked in the snow. I told her of a conversation I'd had thirty-five years before with my father's mother. When I learned my cousin Karleen was getting married, I was worried about my lack of success with men. I wondered if anyone would ever love me, if I'd ever be a bride. Glessie, a large woman who'd had many husbands, said, "You must play the cards you are dealt. Almost no one gets a perfect hand. You have more than enough cards to be loved." She turned out to be right. I was never as pretty as my close friends, but eventually I figured out how to get boyfriends—I talked them into loving me.

Sara and I discussed her upcoming semester. She would be gone four months, living in the mountains of northern Thailand and visiting a refugee camp. I felt proud of her courage and spirit of adventure, but I was also frightened for her and aware of my approaching emptiness. I felt about her trip the way my aunt had felt when my dad left for the war sixty years ago. Aunt Grace told me, "When Frank left, we all cried at the station. Nobody in our family had ever gone that far away before."

Later, Jim, Sara, and I went to a friend's place to a house concert with Dan Newton. We drove across town in the snow, joking and talking of Zeke's wedding. When we arrived, it was good—laughter, music, and plenty of gumbo, cornbread, and pies. There was a fire in the woodstove and rosy light from shaded lamps. Dan had driven down from Minneapolis with his wife and young son. His father was there. The last time I'd seen Mr. Newton, his wife had just died of cancer, and when Dan played music, he'd had to leave the room. But tonight he was smiling and holding his grandson on his lap.

Dan is one of the finest accordion players in the country, a musicologist and composer. He wore jeans, a faded black shirt, and work boots. Dan can play anything, but tonight he played old European music—musettes, tangos, and waltzes from Paris in the 1920s and 1930s, from Europe, after one war and before another. He played *La Vrairie Valse Musette, Samba Oleek,* and the Surullinen Tango. It was emotional music, very visual and evocative. I could shut my eyes and see the rosewood floors and the chandeliers in an old ballroom. I could see a woman in silk dancing with a man in a tuxedo and spats. I kept my eyes closed. The sounds of the fire and my friends, the smells of the gumbo faded, and I was with the music.

I watched this first couple, then I saw more couples twirl into the light. I saw European Jews with slim bodies and dark hair, dancing with precision and joy. I saw wounded soldiers from the war, now healed as they danced. I saw Aunt Betty, a young farm wife, pull her reluctant lumberjack husband onto the floor. Aunt Margaret, in a white dress, moved gracefully into the arms of her welcoming husband. Aunt Agnes and Uncle Clair, black-haired and healthy, danced into a circle of light.

Aunt Henrietta, an adored Ozark girl in her best dress and flowered hat, waltzed with her handsome lover, Max. Uncle Otis carried my beautiful dark-eyed fourteen-year-old aunt Grace into the same light that touched the others.

My father, whose blindness and limp had vanished, strode onto the floor. He was sturdy and smiling. He danced gracefully, and his black, wavy hair caught the light of the chandelier. I pictured my grandmother Glessie, all three hundred pounds of her, dancing exuberantly with him. And there was her husband Mark, my crazy grandfather. His face was calm now, and his broken bones were healed. He embraced my father and asked Glessie to dance. They wheeled Granny Lee among the dancers. She stood up, whole again, and swayed to the music.

My mother swept onto the floor, young and slim in her WAVES uniform, her heels clacking as she spun around with my father. Her parents danced behind her, my grandfather in overalls and a felt hat, my grandmother Margaret Agnes in her housedress and apron. They moved a little awkwardly, as they had never danced before. Then Zeke, Sara, and Jamie were there. They took my parents' hands, and my grandparents' hands, and formed a circle that included the living and dead, Jim, me, my beloved aunts and uncles, and every dancer on the floor. We circled the ballroom. The light formed stars in our hair. Our feet knew what to do, and our limbs swung freely. The tango played on and on.

# Permissions

**Mary Pipher, Ph.D.**, is an internationally noted psychologist and author. She lectures extensively and has become, through her books, a household name. *Reviving Ophelia* has been a *New York Times* bestseller for nearly three years. *The Shelter of Each Other* has been a *New York Times* bestseller in hardcover and paperback. Mary Pipher lives in Lincoln, Nebraska.